RICARDO FAYET

Amazon Advertising for Authors

Unlock Your Full Advertising Potential

First edition

ISBN: 978-1-78613-019-8

Editing by Sandra Wendel
Cover art by Raúl Gil

This book was professionally typeset on Reedsy.
Find out more at reedsy.com

Contents

Introduction

Amazon is not only the world's leading online retailer (*The Everything Store* as dubbed by Brad Stone in his book), it is on its way to becoming the world's largest online advertising platform.

In 2021, the US digital ad market was dominated by Google (26.4%) and Facebook (24.1%), with Amazon coming in third at 14.6%.[1] But in the first quarter of 2022, Amazon's ad revenue grew by 18%, while Google's grew by 12%, and Facebook's shrank for the first time ever.

This is the result of several factors: the continuous growth of online retail (spurred by the pandemic), Amazon's investment into its ad platform, and the privacy changes introduced by Apple in 2021, which severely hampered advertisers' ability to refine their targeting on Facebook and Instagram.

Amazon is in a unique position where they don't need to rely on pixels, nor on third-party companies offering data because they own the whole retail funnel as well as their customers' data.

In other words, Amazon is the same place where customers receive the ads, share their data, and purchase products (producing direct traceable revenue for the advertiser). This is what makes the platform so powerful for authors: you get to place your ads in the exact place where readers go to find, and buy, their next books. You reach readers at their point of consideration, or purchase, rather than while they're scrolling through an endless feed of puppies or dancing teenagers.

"If Amazon Advertising is so great, why isn't every author and publisher

---

[1]   Source: 2022 CNBC article "Amazon is bucking the online ad trend and just beat out Google and Meta:" https://www.cnbc.com/2022/08/03/amazon-online-advertising-meta-twitter-snap-and-pinterest.html

advertising their books on there?"

Because it's not an easy platform to advertise on. Setting up your first campaigns is relatively straightforward, but getting them to deliver impressions and clicks, let alone produce some sales, requires both knowledge and analytical skills. I have seen countless authors start and give up after just a few weeks, concluding that Amazon Advertising was just "not for them."

This is a feeling I can certainly understand. Unlike Facebook or BookBub advertising, which requires a fair bit of creativity (to design the image and come up with ad copy, for example), Amazon Advertising is a purely analytical ad platform. It won't tickle your creative juices, and you might have to spend a fair bit of time on spreadsheets instead, which I imagine sounds boring to a creative person, doesn't it?

Well, my first objective in this book is to get you excited about Amazon Advertising and decode every single aspect of the platform for you. I've personally worked on the Amazon Ads of dozens of different authors in the past few years, in genres varying from epic fantasy, science fiction, and cozy mystery, to self-help, business, and spirituality. I've created and optimized thousands of campaigns, and managed hundreds of thousands in advertising spend, helping double the income of several of the authors I worked with.

In this book, I'll share everything I've learned over the years, from the core principles of Amazon Advertising's platform, to the nitty gritty of optimizing bids and placements.

Can't I just hire someone to run the ads for me?

Before you ask: no, I don't offer Amazon Ads management to private clients anymore. I progressively stopped doing so in order to have the time to write this book, and now prefer dedicating 100 percent of my focus and working time to Reedsy.

That said, I have personally vetted—and sometimes even trained—several advertising experts who specialize in working with authors. You'll find them all in the Marketing section of the Reedsy Marketplace under "Choose a service: Advertising":

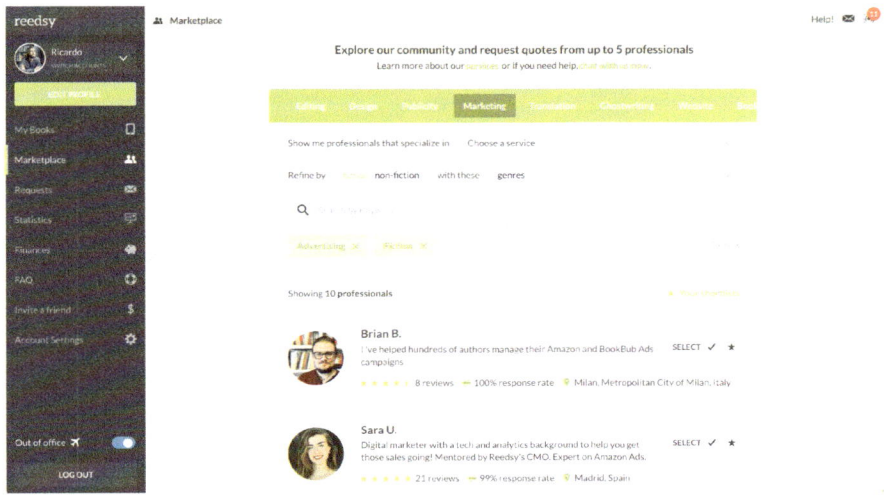

You can find advertising experts on the Reedsy Marketplace.

I do believe that outsourcing Amazon Ads is a decision that should not be made lightly. You'll not only need your ads to be profitable, you'll need them to be profitable enough to cover the ads management fee of the expert.

In general, I advise authors to leverage existing resources (read this book) to learn how to run Amazon Ads on their own—and only consider hiring a professional in these instances:

1. You've already been running Amazon Ads on your own for at least a few months, and
2. They have proven to work well for your books and have managed to turn a profit, and
3. You don't enjoy managing them yourself or want a proper expert to take them to the next level.

If that's the case, then head on to Reedsy to get some quotes, or feel free to reach out to me directly at ricardo@reedsy.com to get some personalized recommendations.

Who is this book for?

I believe that Amazon Ads can work for any book (or series) that is commercially viable. What do I mean by that? A book that has been written with a clear target market in mind, or fits nicely into a commercial niche; a book with an eye-catching, genre-appropriate cover, as well as an enticing book description; and a book with a good number of positive reviews.

If your book doesn't meet these criteria, it just isn't ready to be advertised. Any money you spend on Amazon, Facebook, or BookBub ads will be wasted, as it won't translate into sales. Instead, you'll want to put that money toward an experienced editor or a professional cover designer (or both).

If you already have a commercially viable book—or, even better, a series—congratulations: you're ready to make the most of Amazon Advertising.

Over the next few chapters, you'll learn some of my most advanced Amazon Ads tactics. Some of these may look complicated at first, but don't worry, I'll break down everything and offer concrete, actionable examples that you can immediately apply to your own account.

If you're serious about making money off your book via Amazon Ads and willing to put in the work to make the most out of it, then you have the right book in your hands. That said, if you're entirely new to the world of advertising, I recommend that you first start with book one in our Reedsy Guides to Marketing: *How to Market a Book: Overperform in a Crowded Market.*[2] This book—available to download for free on all retailers—can serve as a helpful introduction to the basics of book marketing. It contains several chapters on advertising, which will help you better understand the different advertising platforms, as well as how and when to make the best use of Amazon Ads.

---

[2] *How to Market a Book: Overperform in a Crowded Market,* by Ricardo Fayet: https://blog.reedsy.com/books/how-to-market-a-book/

What you'll learn

If you've never played with Amazon Ads in the past, and know absolutely nothing about the advertising dashboard, you'll want to start with the two short preliminary chapters immediately following this Introduction. I go over the basic architecture of an Amazon Advertising campaign, as well as the different metrics and statistics available in the advertising dashboard.

If you've already played around with Amazon Ads, you'll likely be familiar with these elements, so you can move straight into Part I.

Part I is probably the most abstract, and yet most important, part of this book. It outlines four foundational principles (I call them pillars) of Amazon Advertising, which will provide the groundwork for the following parts:

- Part II focuses on setting up your first advertising campaigns.
- Part III delves into finding and testing a maximum number of targeting options.
- Part IV solves the classic issue of ad deliverability—that is, when your campaigns barely earn any impressions and clicks.
- Part V teaches you how to optimize your campaigns to make a profit.
- Part VI shows you how to scale your advertising activity and take your profitable ads to the next level.

Finally, you'll find a Glossary and a Bonus Resources section at the end of the book. In the former, I'll define every term of marketing, advertising, or Amazon jargon that I use in the book, so that you can quickly check on their meaning. In the latter, I'll share some magical spreadsheets to automate most of your advertising work.

To make the most of your reading experience, I recommend that you implement the various teachings as you go along. That way, you can immediately put the advice into practice. For example, Part II of this book is all about setting up your first campaigns, so you'll want to actually do that before you move on to reading Part III.

While I'll regularly include screenshots of the Amazon Advertising interface, as well as practical examples, it can also be a good idea to read this book while having your advertising dashboard open, so that you can implement tactics directly on the go.

Although the screen captures are current as of this writing, Amazon will change the navigation and look from time to time. I will strive to keep this book updated to reflect any important changes, so make sure you have the latest version of it.

Let's get started!

Preliminary Chapter 1: Amazon Advertising architecture

Amazon is an ideal platform to start advertising your book because, in contrast to Facebook or BookBub advertising, it requires little creative work from the author. You don't have to come up with an ad image and don't even need to worry that much about writing advertising copy.

So what do you need to worry about? This chapter goes over the important elements of an Amazon Sponsored Products campaign (the most common type of campaign you'll use). From targeting to bids and budget, I'll give you a quick overview of what to pay attention to when setting up and optimizing your campaign.

> Note: This chapter (and the next) are intended for readers who have little to no previous experience with Amazon Advertising. If that's not your case, feel free to skip straight to Part I.

Geography

The first thing to note with Amazon Ads is that, most of the time, you will need different advertising accounts to advertise in different Amazon country stores. For example, to run ads on the Amazon.co.uk store, you will need a specific Amazon Advertising UK account.

You can create such accounts from the Marketing Resources section of your KDP dashboard.

Advertised products

When setting up an advertising campaign, decide which products you want to advertise. Since your KDP (or Amazon Author Central) and Amazon Advertising accounts are linked, you will only be able to advertise titles that you have authored or published yourself.

Amazon sees different formats of a same title as different products, allowing you to select the specific format(s) the campaign should advertise.

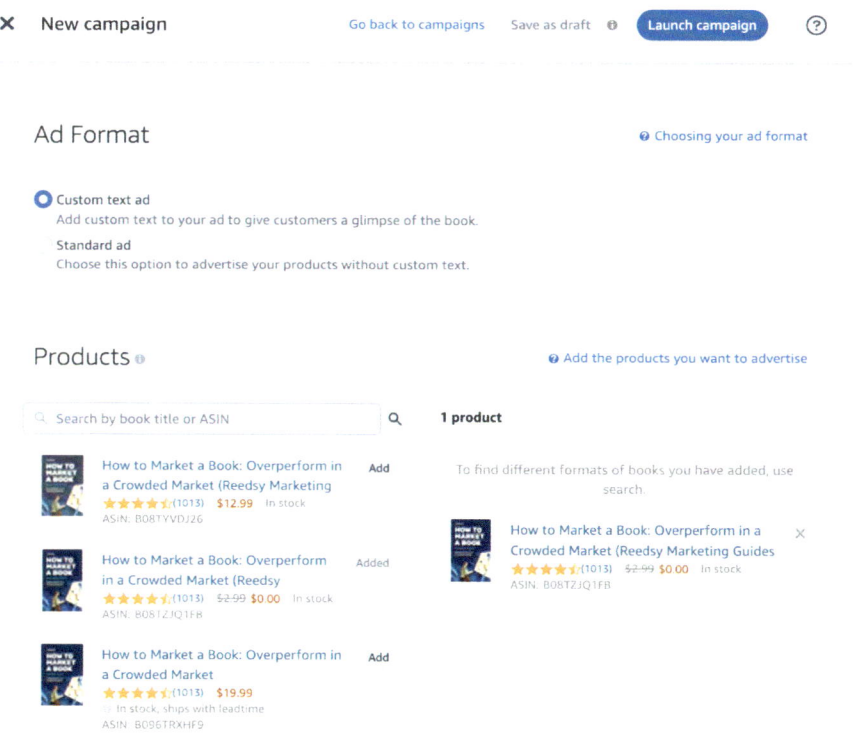

In this example, the campaign would only advertise the ebook version of *How to Market a Book: Overperform in a Crowded Market*—and not the paperback or hardback formats.

As you'll see later, deciding which formats and titles to include in the advertised products of a campaign can have massive consequences on its results.

Targeting

Targeting is probably the most important element of your Amazon Advertising campaigns. It decides what search results or title pages Amazon will place your ads on, as well as your likelihood to beat other advertisers for those placements.

There are infinite targeting options, but they can be classed in three categories:

- Automatic targeting: you let Amazon do the targeting for you.
- Manual keyword targeting: you provide keywords to guide Amazon's targeting.
- Manual product targeting: you provide individual titles (ASINs), or Store categories, to guide the targeting.

Throughout this book, I'll refer to keywords, ASINs, and categories as targets and show you how to incorporate them into your advertising strategy. ASIN is an identifying product number Amazon assigns to your ebook. You can find it on your Amazon description page for your book.

Negative targeting

Negative targeting is the opposite of targeting: instead of telling Amazon what to go after, you tell them what *not* to go after. In this way, your ads don't inadvertently end up in front of the wrong readers' eyes.

Depending on your targeting type, you may add either negative keywords or negative products (ASINs) to a campaign. The first will prevent your ads from appearing on search results *as well as product pages* containing your keyword, while the latter will only prevent your ads from showing up on those products' Amazon pages.

- Automatic targeting: you may add negative keywords.
- Manual keyword targeting: you may add negative keywords.
- Manual product targeting: you may add negative products (ASINs).

If that sounds confusing, don't worry, we'll do a deep dive into negative targeting in Chapter 7.

Bidding

Amazon Advertising uses an auction system to award placements to advertisers. As a result, you need to set a bid for each of your targets (or group of targets, in the case of automatic targeting campaigns).

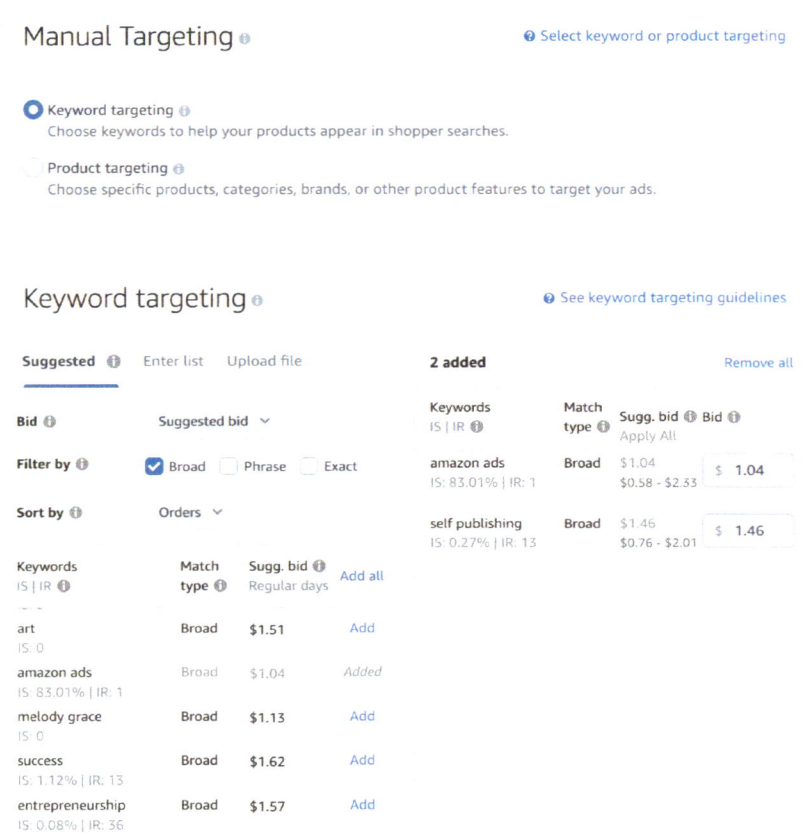

For example, this campaign would be targeting two keywords: *amazon ads* and *self publishing*, with bids of

- $1.04 for *amazon ads* and
- $1.46 for *self publishing*.

As you can see, Amazon auto-suggests new targets for you to add to a campaign, as well as associated recommended bids. Whether you want to follow those recommendations, though, is another story. More on that in the coming chapters.

Creative

The Creative section is only available in Custom text ad campaigns. It can be used to add 150 characters or Custom text to your ad.

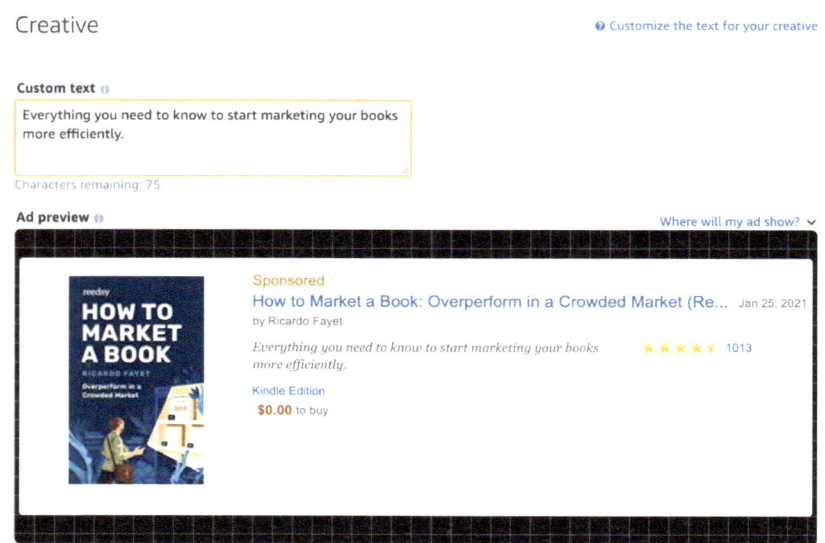

If you don't select Custom text ad, but instead go for a Standard ad campaign, you will not be able to add custom text to your ads. There are, however, other advantages to using Standard ad campaigns — we'll discuss them in Chapter 6.

Budget

Last, and least, comes the budget. Least, because budget is seldom an indication of how much your campaign will actually spend per day: Amazon Advertising is notoriously bad at spending their advertisers' money.

While you can theoretically start with a budget as low as $1 per day, you'll usually want to use much higher budgets to encourage Amazon to deliver impressions and for your ads to start gathering some vital data.

Now that you're familiar with the different elements of Amazon Advertising, let's move on to the Amazon Advertising dashboard.

Preliminary Chapter 2: The advertising dashboard

This is the dashboard that you'll be looking at so often that you'll inevitably develop a love-hate relationship with it. To maximize the love, and minimize the hate, it's important you understand what you're looking at and learn to immediately find the valuable information among the heaps of metrics and percentages.

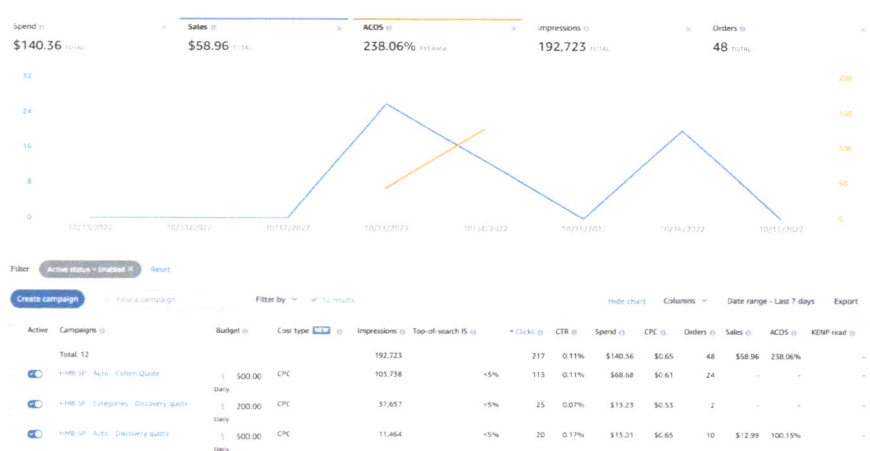

Example of my Amazon Advertising dashboard

The top section—with the graphs—offers an overview of your advertising performance over your selected time period. You can select up to two metrics to include in the graph (blue and orange), and up to five metrics to display at the top.

This top section will show the aggregate results of all the campaigns in the table below it. It's worth noting that if you filter that table, the top metrics and the graphs will change accordingly. For example, if I filter my campaigns by "Orders > 0" to only include those campaigns that have generated at least one order in the past seven days, I get different aggregate stats at the top for Spend, Sales, ACOS, Impressions, and Orders.

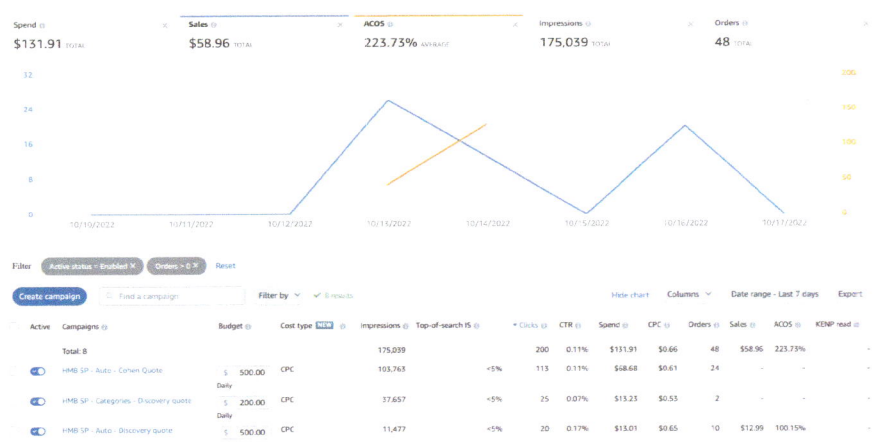

Filtering the campaigns changes the aggregate stats you can view.

Amazon Advertising metrics

As you may have guessed, the table below the graphs section lists the performance of all your campaigns. If this is your first time opening the Amazon Advertising dashboard, the first thing you'll want to do is to customize the columns to include all relevant metrics for your books.

If you don't know what those are, here's a breakdown of each single one that is currently available on authors' Amazon Advertising dashboards.

- **Budget**: The daily budget of the campaign, set by the author. This should not be confused with the Spend.
- **Spend:** The actual amount of money spent by the campaign over the given time period. While a campaign will never spend over your daily budget, it is not uncommon for Amazon Advertising campaigns to only spend a tiny fraction of your budget.
- **Impressions**: The impressions generated by the campaign's ads—that is, the number of times one of your ads is seen by an Amazon customer. It's worth noting that if the same reader views an ad multiple times, Amazon will record multiple impressions. However, Amazon will only record impressions for ad placements that have actually been "seen." For example, if your ad is placed on page two of a scrollable carousel, and the reader doesn't scroll to that page, Amazon will not count it as an impression.
- **Top-of-search Impression Share (IS)**: To understand this metric, we first need to understand what a Top-of-search impression is. While your Amazon Ads are eligible to show on a variety of places, the most valuable placements are the ones at the top of search result pages (more on that in Chapter 22). The Top-of-search Impression Share is the percentage of top-of-search impressions that the campaign received of all the top-of-search impressions it was eligible to receive. In practice, you'll rarely look at it on a campaign level, but rather on a keyword level.
- **Clicks**: The number of clicks generated by your campaign over the time period. These include clicks on any clickable element of your ad (including your author name or review rating), as well as multiple clicks from the same user.
- **Click-through-rate (CTR):** The percentage ratio from impressions to clicks. This is a vital indicator of how appealing and well-targeted your ads are. Part IV of this book focuses solely on how to improve your CTR.
- **Cost per click (CPC)**: The ratio of spend divided by clicks, or the average amount of money spent per click over the time period.
- **Orders:** The total number of orders generated by the campaign over the time period. Any sale, or free download, of any of your advertised

products, generated as a result of the campaign, will count as an order. If a user buys multiple copies, these will count as multiple orders.

- **Sales:** The total dollar value of the Orders generated by the campaign over the time period. For example, two orders of a $3.99 ebook will yield a Sales value of $7.98.
- **Advertising Cost of Sale (ACOS):** The percentage ratio of Spend divided by Sales. As it compares Sales to Spend, the ACOS can serve as an estimation of how profitable a campaign is. However, as we'll see in Part V of this book, it is inherently flawed and rarely reliable as a metric.
- **Kindle Edition Normalized Pages (KENP) read:** This metric will only apply to ebooks enrolled in KDP Select, and thus earning royalties for pages read by readers subscribed to the Kindle Unlimited program. It represents the total number of pages read in Kindle Unlimited as a result of the campaign.
- **Estimated KENP royalties**: Directly correlated to the KENP read, this metric represents the total amount of Kindle Unlimited–related royalties earned as a result of the campaign. Amazon calculates it by multiplying the KENP read by the current Kindle Unlimited payout per page rate.[3]

Depending on your products, and your advertising goals, you may not want to display all these metrics as columns in your Amazon Advertising dashboard. For example, if you're advertising books that are not in KDP Select, you can exclude the KENP read and Estimated KENP royalties columns. Or, if you're advertising a free ebook, you can remove the Sales column.

---

[3] Historical list of Kindle Unlimited payouts per page, by Written Word Media: https://www. writtenwordmedia.com/kdp-global-fund-payouts/

Inside a campaign

Now, what happens if you click on one of these campaigns? You enter into it and can navigate its different elements from the sidebar.

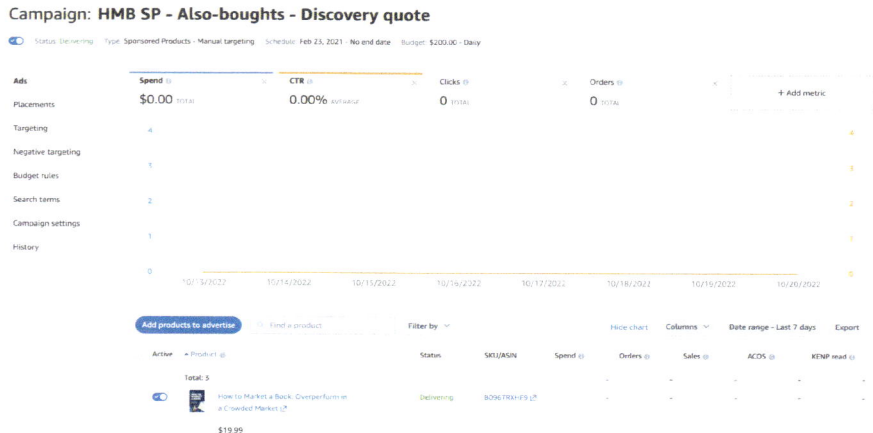

The sidebar navigation for Amazon Ads campaigns.

Let's go through these sidebar sections to understand what each one is about.

> Note: depending on how you set up your campaign, you might have a slightly different structure, with an intermediary ad group level. We'll have an in-depth look at the difference in Chapter 6, but ultimately, the sidebar sections remain similar across both structures.

· **Ads:** This section lists all the products currently and historically advertised in the campaign. The graph and table view is identical to the one on the broader account level, allowing you to visualize the results of each advertised product. From here, you can add new products to the campaign as well as pause or archive existing ones.

- **Placements:** This section breaks down the different placements where your ads have appeared and shows their individual results. It allows you to increase your bids for a specific segment by a percentage of your choice. More about placement optimization later.
- **Targeting**: By far the most important section, targeting lists all the keywords, products, or categories targeted in the campaign. Here, you can visualize the results of each target, modify their bids, pause, or archive them, and even add new targets to the campaign.
- **Negative targeting:** Same as the targeting section, but for negative targets.
- **Budget rules**: Allows you to create and edit rules to automatically increase your budget based on schedule or performance. As you'll see in this book, budget is one of the most inconsequential parts of Amazon Advertising, so budget rules are, in my opinion, fairly useless. So much so that I won't mention them again in this book.
- **Search terms:** Another important section of the campaign, it shows you the exact searches and product pages that your ads have appeared on, as well as their results. It is particularly helpful to find new targeting ideas and spot any nonperforming or irrelevant terms to add to your negative targets.
- **Campaign settings**: Here, you can adjust your campaign's budget, set an end date, and modify your campaign bidding strategy (more about that in Chapter 19).
- **History**: Allows you to visualize all historical changes made to your campaign. This is another section I almost never look at.

Now that you're familiar with all the elements of the Amazon Advertising dashboard, it's time to explore how the platform actually works, starting with its foundational purpose: making money.

I

Pillars of Amazon Advertising

Before we venture into the ins and outs of Amazon Advertising, we must first identify its core principles—or foundational pillars. While the surface (the interface, the targeting options, the reporting dashboard, and so on) often change, these core principles rarely do. As such, understanding them is the key to navigating the inner workings of the platform and harnessing new opportunities before other authors do.

1

Pay per click advertising

One of the main elements that differentiates Amazon Advertising from other advertising platforms popular among authors is that Amazon is a *pay per click* advertising platform. Crucially, this means that authors advertising their books on Amazon are only charged when readers click on their ads.

This is in stark contrast to Facebook or BookBub CPM ads, which operate on a cost per thousand impressions—or Cost per Mille (CPM)—basis, and therefore charge authors for displaying their ads in the first place, no matter whether people then click on them or not.

In the unlikely event that your ad was shown by Amazon a million times without anyone ever clicking on it, all that brand exposure would be for free. Now, that wouldn't necessarily be good news for you (we'll explore why in this book), but it serves to exemplify the fact that Amazon Advertising offers a certain margin for error.

If your cover isn't right, if you're not targeting the right audience, if you're using ineffective advertising copy—or for any other reason that can lead to readers not clicking on your ad—you won't be monetarily penalized for it, because Amazon Advertising doesn't charge for impressions, it only charges for clicks.

On the other hand, this makes Amazon Advertising directly, financially liable for the relevancy of the ads served to readers. If they choose to serve irrelevant or ineffective ads, that readers don't click on, Amazon won't make any money. This is the main reason why many authors struggle so much to get their ads to serve in the first place—and to scale afterward. More often than not, it's just as hard to get Amazon Advertising to spend your money as it is to get a positive return on your investment in the platform.

Why?

First, there's a lot of competition (I'll get to that in the next chapter), but even more importantly, Amazon is quick to hamper the deliverability of campaigns that don't perform well. And what does performing well mean in Amazon Advertising terms? One thing: attracting clicks.

If we go back to our extreme example about getting a million impressions on your ad with no clicks, this is effectively impossible, because Amazon would stop showing your ad much sooner than that (probably after a few thousand impressions and no clicks).

Amazon has zero interest in showing ads that readers don't click on: not only is this a missed revenue opportunity for Amazon (they could have shown an ad that got a click instead), it also makes for a terrible user experience on the reader side. Imagine browsing Amazon as a reader and only seeing ads for books that you're *not* interested in.

The click-through-rate

Paradoxically, the fact you don't pay for impressions on Amazon means that you need to watch your click-through-rate (the ratio from impressions to clicks, hereafter abbreviated CTR) all the more closely. Otherwise, you might not lose a lot of money, but you won't be able to get Amazon to serve your ads, so you'll be wasting your time looking at a dashboard that barely changes from one week to the next.

Multiple factors can impact the click-through-rate of your campaigns, and they can generally be separated into two categories:

- Targeting-related factors: the keywords or products you use for targeting, your bids, and your placement optimization, for example. If you target the wrong people, or bid too low for your ads to show up on

prominent placements, your CTR will naturally suffer.
- Ad-related factors: basically, every single element that is displayed on your ad.

I've found that authors often obsess over the targeting-related factors, tweaking their bids, pausing targets with a low CTR, and so on. And for good reason: that is an important part of the campaign optimization process, to which the whole Part III of this book is dedicated.

What authors often overlook, however, is that the ad-related factors are just as important, if not more. So let's take a look at them, by order of importance.

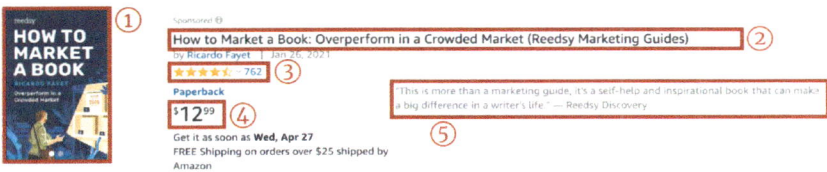

Example of a Sponsored Product ad in search results

1. **The cover**: This is by far the most important element of your Amazon ad. It needs to not only grab the eye of the reader, pique their curiosity, but also instantly show them that this book is exactly what they are after. I will not go over the importance of having your cover designed by a professional cover artist with experience in your genre—I stressed this enough already in my first book. I will say this, though: any money you pour into Amazon Advertising with a nonprofessional cover will be forever wasted.

2. **The title:** This is the first thing readers will *read* if your cover grabs their eye. It needs to either intrigue them, amuse them, or give more information about the genre or topic of the book. Remember the old "show don't tell" adage? Well, while your cover serves to show your

readers what your book is about, your title can be used to flat out tell them (especially in nonfiction, case in point in the example above).

3. **The reviews**: This is the only element of social validation on your ad. Generally, the star rating will always be between 4 and 5, so what will really matter to readers here is the number of ratings. The higher it is, the more successful your book will be perceived, and the more likely readers will be to take a chance on it.

4. **The price:** The price can be just as important a factor as the other elements, especially if it's significantly different from other books in your niche. Since Amazon Advertising reaches readers who are actively looking for their next book, it can tolerate higher price points than Facebook or BookBub ads. That said, do keep in mind that most readers you'll reach with your ads will not be familiar with you and your books. Therefore, lower price points will always draw more clicks (and ultimately sales).

5. **The ad copy:** As I discuss later in the book, not all ads feature ad copy. When they do, that copy is minimal (compared to the book title) and, as such, often ignored by readers. It can, however, certainly play a role for those who do read it.

It is absolutely vital—and I cannot overstate this—that you nail all these elements to the best of your ability, *before* you start advertising on Amazon (or anywhere else, really). Often, a change in cover, or in a series title, can have a much bigger impact on your CTR and overall campaign performance than any targeting or bidding change you could make.

The conversion rate

Not managing to get Amazon to spend your money is a common issue, but there's an even worse scenario with a pay per click advertising platform: getting a lot of clicks but no sales. In this scenario, you're not just failing to make money, you're actively losing it.

Which brings us to the second ratio, which needs to be closely monitored:

the ratio from clicks to orders, or conversion rate. The fewer clicks you need in order to generate one sale of your book, the more cost-effective your advertising will be on Amazon.

While your targeting decisions will affect the conversion rate to some extent, the most important conversion factors here have to do with your product page. When a reader clicks on your ad, they are taken to the book's product page—and will therefore make their purchasing decision based on the information on that page.

Factors impacting the click-through-rate		Factors impacting the conversion rate	
Click-through-rate: ratio from impressions to clicks		Conversion rate: ratio from clicks to sales	
Factor #1	Book cover	Factor #1	Product description
Factor #2	Title	Factor #2	Customer and editorial reviews
Factor #3	Reviews (quantity and star rating)	Factor #3	Look Inside
Factor #4	Price	Factor #4	Book cover
Factor #5	Advertising copy	Factor #5	Price
Factor #6	Author name	Factor #6	Multiple format availability

Factors affecting the click-through-rate and conversion rate.

Ranking the elements of the product page based on their potential impact on the conversion rate isn't easy, as some of these were already present on the ad (such as the cover, the title, or the price). The most important element, though, is unequivocal:

1. **The book (product) description:** Amazon Ads display precious little written information about the book (the title, and sometimes, the ad copy). So the first thing a reader will do after clicking on the ad will be to read the book description. You'll find entire books out there on the art of writing an effective book description, or book blurb, so I

won't go too far into the subject here. Instead, I'm recommending two of my favorite books on the topic in the footnotes,[4] and leaving you with one simple piece of advice: check out and carefully study the descriptions of all the best-selling books in your genre. Try to identify some common elements or tropes (maybe they're all written in first person or they hit the same keywords or they use a similar formatting), and take inspiration from the competition for your own description.

2. **The customer reviews:** While the ad features the star rating and number of reviews, readers will likely want to actually read some customer reviews from previous buyers. Here, it's important to pay attention to the top reviews specifically, as these are the first ones readers will see when they scroll down to the reviews section. Having a huge number of reviews with a solid average rating is ideal—but if your top three reviews are all negative, that alone can detract most readers from buying the book. Sadly, what I'm describing is not an uncommon scenario—and it's a particularly nefarious one, as it's hard to revert (short of asking your reader base to upvote the positive reviews, there's little you can do about a troll review showing up at the top of your reviews).

3. **The editorial reviews:** If you click on the star rating next to a book, you're taken straight to the bottom of the description page, where the customer reviews are featured. However, most readers will rather scroll down to get there, and by doing so, they'll come across the Editorial reviews section. If they see accolades there from trusted publications, review sites (For example from Reedsy Discovery), or well-known authors, this might just give the potential buyer the extra push they need to hop over the fence and buy the book.

4. **The Look Inside:** This feature allows readers to "look inside" and read the first few pages of a book—usually up to 10 percent of its total content. If your first chapter doesn't grab them, they're likely to stop

---

4   7 *FIGURE FICTION: How to Use Universal Fantasy to SELL Your Books to ANYONE,* by T Taylor: https://books2read.com/u/49Ler0 | *Book Blurbs Unleashed: Advanced Publishing and Marketing Strategies for Indie Authors,* by Robert J. Ryan: https://books2read.com/u/baoK1x

reading the sample, and definitely won't purchase the book. Inversely, if you manage to hook them and get them to finish the sample, their only way to know what happens next is to buy the book.

5. **The book cover:** Feeling like déjà vu? Don't worry, this is not a mistake: the cover can play an important role both for the click-through-rate *and* the conversion rate. You may wonder, "But if readers have seen the cover on the ad already, and they clicked on it, surely the cover won't make a difference in their purchasing decision once on the page?" That is some sound rhetorical reasoning right there, but here's the trick: cover images on Sponsored Product ads are relatively small (thumbnail size). On the product page, however, they're almost three times bigger! And they can be further expanded by clicking on the image, or using the Look Inside feature. So you can bet readers will take a longer, more precise look at the cover once on the product page—and any details they may see there can sway their decision for better or worse.

6. **The price:** The same thing goes here. While book prices are generally featured on Sponsored Product ads, readers will not always look at them before clicking. They will, however, definitely look at the price before buying. And they will probably compare the prices of the different formats you have available, which brings me to—

7. **Multiple format availability:** Many readers swear by print, others by Kindle, and many others have now flocked to audio. One of the best ways to maximize your changes that readers will actually buy something once they're on your product page is to make sure that their preferred format—be it Kindle edition, paperback, hardback, or audio—is available.

As a rule of thumb, if you're noticing that fewer than one out of twenty clicks convert to an order, you should take a hard look at each of these elements, because it's likely that one of them (at least) is hurting you.

In other words, your minimum conversion rate objective should be 0.05%. Anything lower than that is probably the symptom of a deeper problem with your product page, which you'll want to fix before you continue advertising.

Of course, you should take this rule of thumb objective with a pinch of salt, as normal conversion rates will vary greatly from one genre to another. Niche nonfiction typically sees higher conversion than broad, commercial fiction. The availability of your books in Kindle Unlimited can also affect the conversion to Orders. And finally, price can play a huge role.

For example, my current Amazon Ads promoting the free *How to Market a Book: Overperform in a Crowded Market* convert at 30 percent—but that's not unusual for a free book. In contrast, a full-price (think $3.99 or more), first-in-series romantic comedy will do very well to even beat the 5 percent conversion objective, no matter how optimized the product page may be. If you have a trusted group or network of author friends in your genre, it can be a smart idea to share your Amazon Advertising conversion rates from time to time and see how yours compare.

Once you get neck-deep into setting up your first campaigns, optimizing targets, and tweaking bids, it's easy to forget about these two vital ratios. So make a mental note to regularly check both the click-through-rate and conversion rate of your campaigns.

At the end of the day, Amazon might (and certainly will) change its advertising platform over time, but it probably won't move away from pay per click advertising. They might introduce other bidding optimization strategies, but, ultimately, you'll always be paying for each click, with all the implications that this carries.

2

Three types of campaigns

One of the first questions you should always ask when evaluating an advertising platform is where and how do the ads show up to the buyer? At this time, indie authors accessing Amazon Advertising through their KDP dashboard have access to three types of campaigns:

1. Sponsored Products
2. Sponsored Brands
3. Lockscreen Ads

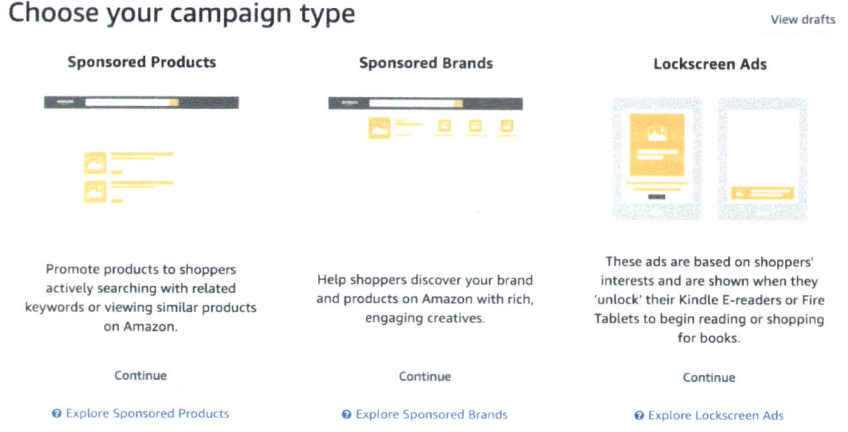

The three types of Amazon Ads available to indie authors.

Sponsored Products

Sponsored Products are, by far, the most popular type of campaign for advertising books and, in most cases, the most effective. They're what every first-time advertiser should start with before they go on to explore Sponsored Brands and Lockscreen Ads.

Where do Sponsored Products ads show up?

Sponsored Products ads appear in two different places:

1. In search result listings

Here's an example of two "sponsored" books that show up when I searched for *Lee Child* on the Kindle Store.

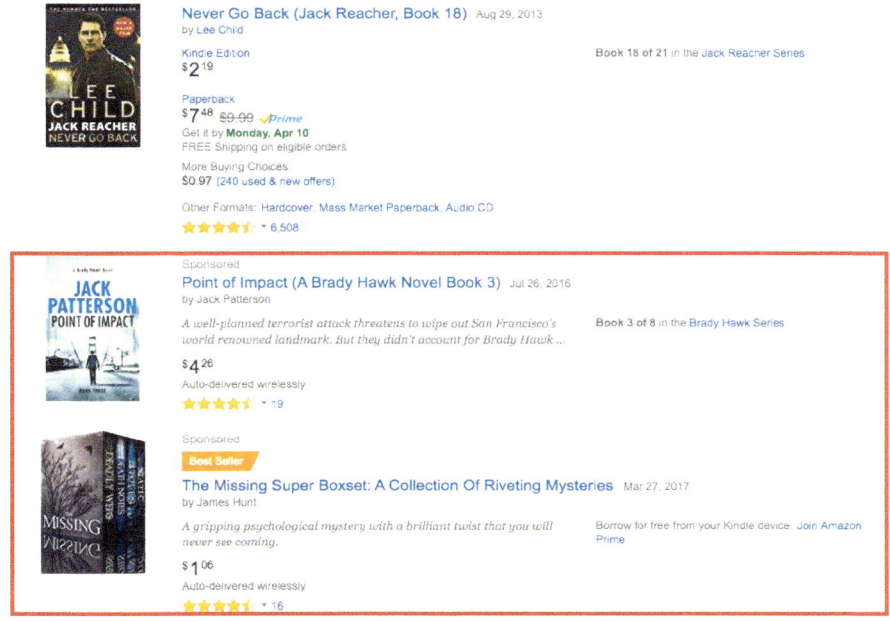

Sponsored Products ads in search results

As you can see, the only thing distinguishing the sponsored ads from an actual search result listing is the small tag saying, "Sponsored," which most readers won't even notice.

2. Below the "Also Boughts" on other books' product pages

Here's an example of the Sponsored Products that showed up when I visited the Amazon page for Lee Child's eighteenth Jack Reacher book, *Never Go Back.*

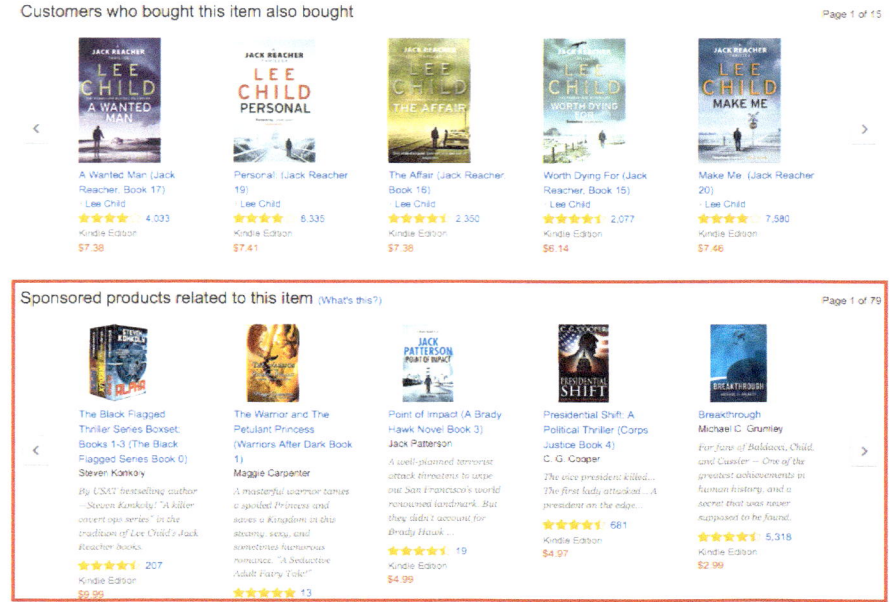

Sponsored Products ads on product pages

Again, only the header, "Sponsored products related to this item," distinguishes the Sponsored Products carousel on the page. Even then, the important bit that most readers will notice is that these items are related to a book that they're already interested in, not that they're Sponsored Products.

Sponsored Products targeting options

So how do you choose on which search results and product pages your Sponsored Products ads show up? By using the right targeting options.

I'll go more in depth into targeting in future chapters, but here are the four different ways you can control where your Sponsored Products ads appear:

- Automatic: If you choose "automatic targeting," Amazon automatically selects the keywords and products to target for you.
- Keywords: Under "manual targeting," keywords allow you to place your

ads in relevant search result pages, as well as on product pages related to the keyword. You can use either "broad," "phrase," or "exact" matches with keyword targeting.

· Products: Also under "manual targeting," and sometimes called "ASIN targeting," product targeting allows you to select all the individual product pages where you want your ads to appear. It's a good way to laser-target your ads.

· Categories: Instead of handpicking individual products, category targeting allows you to target all the products in any given Amazon category, all at once.

As you'll see, Sponsored Products ads offer the widest range of targeting options, which is handy as they allow you to start small and target a few select products, and then progressively widen your scope and scale your investment based on initial results.

Sponsored Products reporting

One of the reasons why Sponsored Products are the most popular type of campaign is that they offer, by far, the most in-depth reporting insights into their performance.

The Sponsored Products campaign dashboard will report on impressions, Top-of-search impression share, clicks, orders, sales value, as well as KENP read and Estimated KENP royalties generated by every single target in the campaign.

Now, the data aren't always as complete as we might want—more on that later—but they are certainly more exhaustive than the data Sponsored Brands and Lockscreen Ads can offer.

Sponsored Brands

While Sponsored Products ads are the right choice for any kind of au-thor—whether you're just starting out with one book, or are established with several pen names and series—Sponsored Brands are for authors who have a proper *brand.*

First, you need to have *at least three books* published in order to be able to use them, and not just any three books. To be effective, you'll want these books to have a strong crossover in readership and ideally to be in the same series.

Why? Because they'll be shown next to one another.

Where do Sponsored Brands ads show up?

Sponsored Brands ads allow you to access one of the most prominent pieces of real estate on Amazon search: the very top of the search result page.

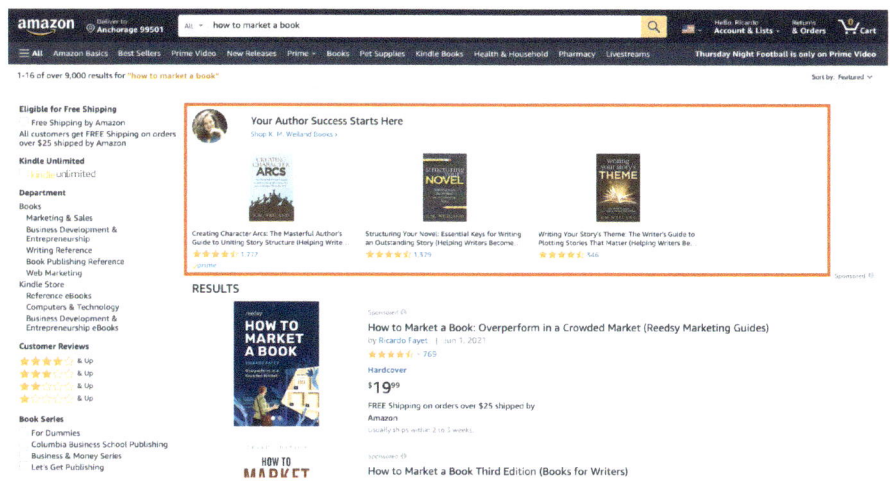

Sponsored Brands ad in search results

As you can see, Sponsored Brands ads display

- An image (as a default, your author photo, but you can customize that to have something else, like a logo), plus
- A headline (maximum 50 characters), and
- Three books.

Sponsored Brands targeting options

The targeting options for Sponsored Brands ads are similar to those of Sponsored Products, with the notable exception of automatic targeting, which is not available.

Still, you can manually target keywords (with broad, phrase, or exact match), individual products, and categories.

Naturally, because of the nature and placement of Sponsored Brands ads, the option that will generally bring the best results is keyword targeting, which will allow you to pick and choose the exact searches where you want your three-book ad to show up.

Sponsored Brands reporting

If you're a series author, I imagine that you'll be excited by now to try Sponsored Brands: they show up at the top, they feature several books, and you can customize the copy. But where's the catch?

First, since Sponsored Brands placements are naturally less abundant, they tend to be much more competitive than Sponsored Products, requiring higher bids and costs per click.

Still, I'd say that would probably be worth it, if it weren't for the main drawback—in my opinion—of Sponsored Brands ads: Amazon won't report figures for KENP reads or KENP royalties for Sponsored Brands campaigns.

If you're not in Kindle Unlimited, that won't matter to you. But if you are, and if an important part of your income comes from page reads, then using Sponsored Brands will be like advertising in the dark because you won't know whether they make you money and will therefore not be able to optimize your targeting, bids, and creatives accordingly.

Lockscreen Ads

Lockscreen Ads are least used by indie authors, mostly because their targeting options are too broad to be effective enough in terms of return on investment. However, they can be helpful for brand building, and, in some rare cases, they might even perform better than Sponsored Products.

Where do Lockscreen Ads show up?

Full-screen ad on locked Kindle E-readers

Banner ad on the Kindle E-reader homepage

Full-screen ad on Amazon Fire tablet in full-color display

The three places Lockscreen Ads show up for Kindle readers.

Lockscreen Ads show up directly on readers' Kindle devices—namely, on the home screen and on its screen saver. As you can see, the format grants a ton of visibility to the advertised product, which can be a boost for building your brand and getting eyeballs on your ads.

That said, this also means that Lockscreen Ads are served to readers at a time when they're not necessarily looking for a new book (as opposed to Sponsored Products and Sponsored Brands, which are served on the Store directly).

Lockscreen Ads targeting options

The main drawback of Lockscreen Ads, however, is the lack of precise targeting options.

With Lockscreen Ads, you can only target broad categories ("Interests"), which don't quite match up to the actual categories on the Kindle Store. Worse, "Interests" definitely don't have the same depth in terms of sub-categories as what you'll find on the Store. For example, there's no good category/interest to advertise this particular book. There's no "writing" or "publishing" interest. The best alternative I would have to use is the broad "Nonfiction" interest, or one of the "Business & Money" subinterests.

It is true that in some genres you have many more precise options—take Romance for example, where all of the following subinterests are targetable:

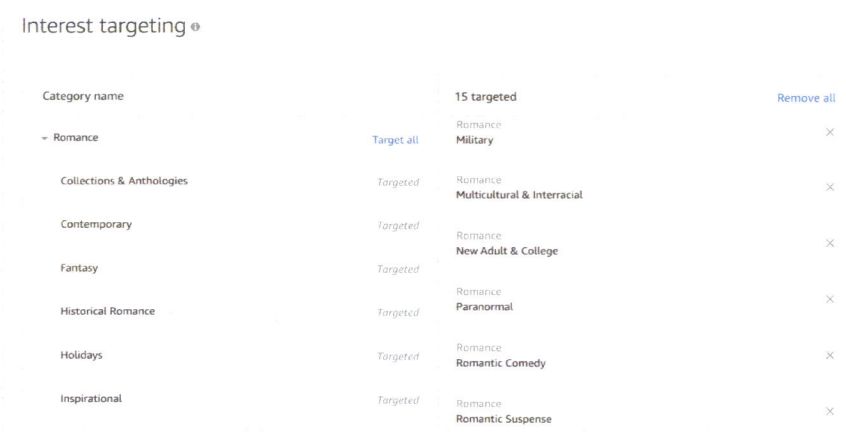

Romance offers many interest targeting options for Lockscreen Ads.

If there is a targeting interest available that looks like a perfect fit for your book, then it might very well be worth setting up a Lockscreen Ads campaign to test it. Otherwise, I'd recommend you only try Lockscreen Ads once you've mastered Sponsored Products and Sponsored Brands.

Lockscreen Ads reporting

In terms of reporting, Lockscreen ads are lacking, to say the least. First, despite being an ebook-only advertising avenue, they don't currently report on KENP reads and royalties—only Orders, Sales, and ACOS.

Worse, you can't see a breakdown by type of interest you targeted. For example, if you selected "Contemporary Romance" and "Holidays Romance" when setting up your campaign, you would only see aggregated results in the dashboard, which makes it impossible to see whether one interest is performing better than the other. For that, you'd need to set up two separate campaigns (with a minimum $100 budget each).

One thing in their favor is the inclusion of a "Detail Page Views" metric in the dashboard, which, in theory, should count the number of times a shopper spent a proper amount of time on your product page after clicking on the ad. In practice, however, the way Amazon decides what a detailed page view is seems to be a bit broken. My latest Lockscreen Ads campaign, for example, led to 3 orders out of 0 DPVs!

Detailed Page Views are measured for Lockscreen Ads.

In the rest of this book, we'll focus almost solely on Sponsored Products campaigns. The reasons for this are twofold: first, they tend to be the most effective and easily scalable campaigns for authors, and second, most of the advice I'll share for Sponsored Products will be applicable to Sponsored Brands as well, and to Lockscreen Ads (to a certain extent). What all three campaign types have in common, in any case, is the bidding system.

3

The open bidding system

Almost every advertising platform out there leverages some sort of bidding system to award their various advertising placements to the advertisers. In other words, advertisers compete for real estate on the site and bid against each other to get the best (or the most) placements.

In some cases (like Facebook Ads), the bidding happens behind the scenes, meaning you don't actually set manual bids, but Facebook automatically creates those based on your budget, your audience, and your ad relevance, among other factors. The more advertisers target the same audience, the higher the costs will rise, as they're bidding against each other behind the scenes.

In the case of Amazon Advertising, the bidding very much happens on stage. For every specific placement (or group of placements) you target via Amazon Ads, you need to set a specific bid. This bid corresponds to how much you're ready to spend to get one click on your ad—it's a bid amount per click. Amazon then compares your bid to those of other advertisers targeting the same placement—along with other elements such as ad relevance, which we'll examine further down the road—and consequently awards you a certain number of impressions.

Let's use a simple example. Lee Child just released a book, and you want your book to show up in the sponsored "Products related to this item" section of that book's product page. You create a Sponsored Products campaign targeting the ASINs of both the Lee Child ebook and paperback edition. For each of these ASIN targets, you'll need to set a specific bid. The higher the bid, the more impressions your ad will earn—that is, the more times Amazon will actually display your book in the "Sponsored Products related to this item" section when a customer browses it.

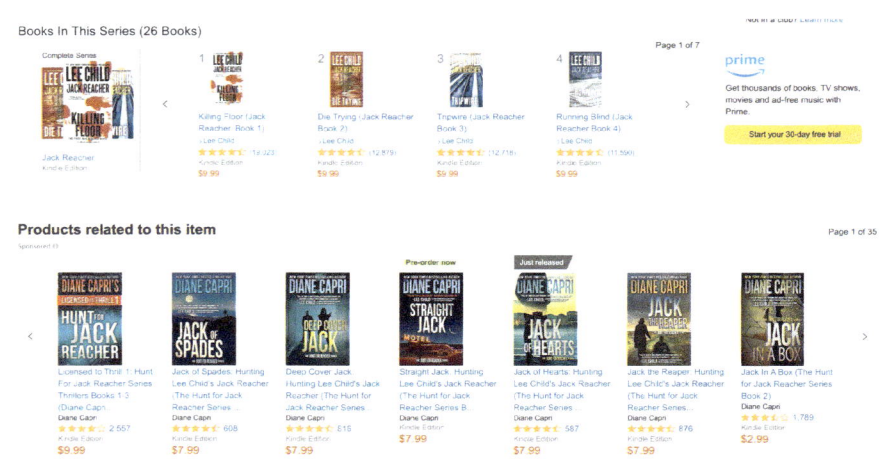

"Products related to this item" section on an Amazon product page.

It's not just a matter of quantity, though. The quality of the impressions can sometimes be just as important.

If your book shows up first in the carousel in the previous illustration, it's much more valuable than if it's on the far right or, worse, on subsequent pages of the carousel—because it's much more likely to be clicked on.

When you target keywords (rather than ASINs), your ads will show up both on product pages (like the previous example) and on search results. For search results placements, showing up at the top of the page is naturally much more valuable than placement at the middle or bottom—again, because it's much more likely readers will click on your book if it's at the top of the page. So much so that Amazon recently introduced a Top-of-search Impression Share metric on dashboards, which basically lets advertisers know how they're faring versus others specifically for top-of-search placements.

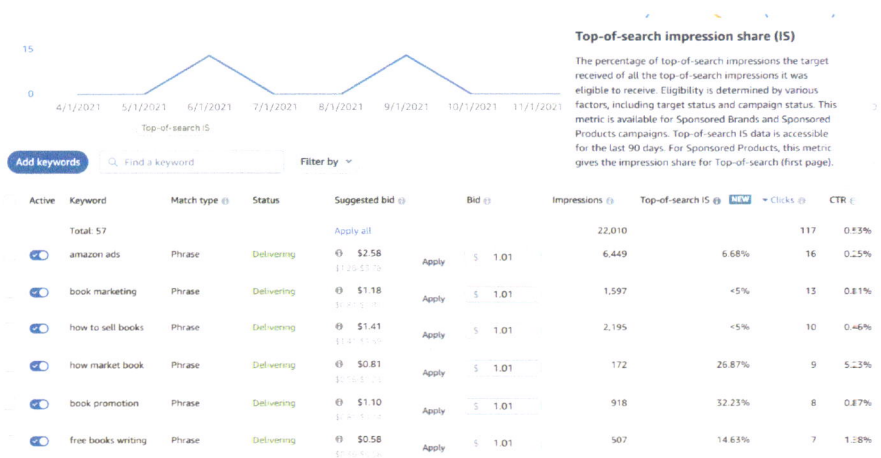

Top-of-search Impression Share metric on Amazon Advertising dashboard

Now, this metric is not yet available on all campaigns, but it probably will be in the future, and in any case serves to highlight the fact that not all placements (or impressions) are equal.

There are several factors that decide who gets which placements, and how often, but the most important one, by far, is the bid. The higher your bid, the higher your impression share, and the more qualitative the placements.

Bid versus cost per click

While the bid you set on a target represents the amount you're ready to pay for each click that target triggers, this doesn't mean that you'll actually end up spending exactly the bid amount for each click. In other words, your bid and the eventual cost per click (CPC) can be—and almost always is—different.

This is because of Amazon's bidding system, which sees bids not as the amount you want to pay, on average, per click, but as the *maximum amount* you're ready to pay for a click.

Imagine a secret auction in which the winner buys the prize not for the amount that they bid but for the amount of the second highest bid: that's a little bit how the Amazon Advertising bidding system works: it uses your bid to determine how many auctions you win against other advertisers, but only charges you for a click based on the bids of the other advertisers who lost the auction. So the amount you end up paying per click is therefore always lower or equal to your bid, and depends on the competition.

> Note: One notable exception to this is when using "Up and down dynamic bids," but I dedicate a whole chapter to dynamic bidding strategies in Part IV of this book.

In my experience, the difference between your bid and the eventual cost per click can be hard to predict. For highly competitive targets, you can expect your CPC to be close or even equal to your bid—because of the sheer number of other advertisers participating in the auction.

For less competitive keywords, your CPC can sometimes be two times or three times lower than your bid—and in my experience, it can be quite hard to predict. Here's an example from a campaign targeting search words for a paranormal cozy mystery:

Keyword	Suggested bid ⓘ		Keyword bid ⓘ	Impressions ⓘ	Clicks ⓘ	CTR ⓘ	Spend ⓘ	▾ CPC ⓘ
Total: 19				2,590	60	2.32%	$45.70	$0.75
witch cozy mystery series	ⓘ $1.02 $1.02-$1.04	Apply	$ 1.01	135	4	2.96%	$3.82	$0.96
paranormal cozy mystery	ⓘ $1.08 $0.46-$1.09	Apply	$ 1.01	488	7	1.43%	$6.64	$0.95
paranormal cozy mystery series	ⓘ $1.01 $0.65-$1.02	Apply	$ 1.01	141	3	2.13%	$2.76	$0.92
cozy witch and paranormal bo...	ⓘ $1.02 $1.00-$1.02	Apply	$ 1.01	93	5	5.38%	$4.49	$0.90
witch cozy mystery	ⓘ $1.01 $0.65-$1.07	Apply	$ 1.01	844	11	1.30%	$9.67	$0.88
paranormal cozies	ⓘ $1.01 $1.00-$1.02	Apply	$ 1.01	135	3	2.22%	$2.60	$0.87
paranormal cozy mystery kind...	ⓘ $1.03 $1.02-$1.53	Apply	$ 1.01	71	1	1.41%	$0.63	$0.63
witch cozies	ⓘ $1.27 $0.71-$1.34	Apply	$ 1.01	493	25	5.07%	$14.08	$0.56

The difference between the actual bid, as shown here as $1.01, and the eventual cost per click can be hard to predict.

While all the keywords use a bid of $1.01, the resulting CPCs vary from $0.96 to $0.56. In some cases, the difference is easy to understand: "paranormal cozy mystery" is a search term that's probably used much more often than "witch cozies," and therefore attracts the competition of more advertisers, resulting in a CPC much closer to the actual bid. In some other cases, it can be much harder to predict—for example, "witch cozy mystery series" at $0.95 while "witch cozy mystery" is at $0.88. Predicting the relationship between bid and resulting CPC becomes even harder when using phrase or broad match types, which can trigger search terms very different from the keyword itself, but we'll dig more into those later.

In the meantime, the one thing that always stays true is that the higher you bid, the higher your cost per click will be. And since higher bids not only deliver more impressions, but impressions on placements that are more likely to lead to clicks, these can very quickly drain your advertising budget.

At the end of the day, your biggest and most important challenge with Amazon Ads will be finding the right balance when it comes to bids and figuring out the perfect bid for each target—in other words, the bid that delivers the most and best exposure to your ad, while still earning you money.

Amazon knows this, which is why they try to make advertisers' lives easier by providing suggested bids.

Amazon suggested bids

I only have one simple rule when it comes to Amazon suggested bids: ignore them. I know, I know, they come from a good sentiment, but the reality is that they are often deeply flawed.

According to Amazon: "Suggested bid and bid range are calculated from a group of winning bids for ads that are similar to yours." And here comes the first problem: while all authors advertise similar products (books), they all have different situations and goals. An author with just one book out may not be ready to bid as high as a peer advertising a ten-book series. An author with a free book won't bid the same as one with a high-priced one. An Amazon-exclusive author won't bid the same as a wide one. You get the gist.

As a rule of thumb, copying other authors' bids is rarely a good idea, unless these authors are in the exact same situation as you, with the same types of books, and the same objectives—and if they actually know what they're doing too. But Amazon's suggested bids don't just look at other authors' bids, they also include bids from other industry players advertising books: traditional publishers. This further skews the data, especially for high-competition keywords or for print-oriented ones, as publishers earn infinitely higher margins than indie authors on print and can therefore afford higher costs per click.

All in all, the best strategy with suggested bids is to flat out ignore them, and only use your own data and your own objectives to set and adjust your bids over time.

The ad quality score

While bids are the core external factor of how Amazon Advertising allocates impressions across advertisers, there is another factor, an internal factor, that you can't quite control, but that is equally important for impression allocation: the ad quality score.

This is a score that Amazon Advertising's algorithms allocate to each ad, based on a variety of factors, and is computed together with the maximum bid to determine how the ad ranks versus other advertisers targeting the same search term or product.

In mathematical terms:

```
Ad rank = maximum bid x quality score
```

This means that you can afford to bid low on certain keywords/products if you're confident your ad will have a high quality score.

As always when it comes to internal algorithms, we can't be 100 percent sure of what these factors are, nor of their overall importance in the algorithm, but we do know that the main elements that factor into the ad quality score are these:

- **Relevance**: How relevant is your ad to the search, or product page, that you are targeting? Relevance is generally determined semantically based on your product's metadata (for example, if your product's title contains the search terms).
- **Historical data:** If a given ad has performed better than competing ads for a search term in the past (it may have attracted more clicks and led to more purchases), it's likely that Amazon will increase its quality score for that search term (and related terms). At the end of the day, it's in Amazon's interest to display ads that generate clicks and purchases.
- **Availability**: This is less important for ebooks and print-on-demand books, which are almost always in stock. But for other products, availability and shipping speed can play a role. That said, it's likely that Amazon Advertising will favor books that are available in multiple formats, and print books that are in stock.
- **Reviews:** We're entering into speculation territory here, but it's likely that reviews and review average play a role in the ad quality score, as they're a sign of social validation. That said, books with a high number of

reviews and high review average naturally tend to convert better, leading to better historical data, so it's possible that reviews only play an indirect part in the quality score calculation.

There are few resources out there on Amazon Advertising that mention the ad quality score—and you'll see that I won't mention it much throughout this book. The first reason is that, well, we know little about it—as I mentioned, this is what advertisers have been able to deduce through experiments and correlation analyses.

The other reason is that there is not much you can do to increase your ad's quality score for a particular keyword or product target. It's not like you can make your book more relevant, or improve its historical data, or get more reviews just like that.

What you can do, instead, is tweak the other part of the equation that you have direct control over: the bid. Even with a terrible quality score, you can get a lot of impressions for your book if you bid high. It'll cost you, but you'll get them.

It is, however, good to always keep the quality score in mind when choosing your targets. I'll delve deeper into the topic in Part II, but you can essentially afford to bid lower if you're targeting hyper-relevant keywords or products (for example, your own book title, author name, your own books/series) because your quality score will make up for the low bid.

You can also progressively lower your bids and still get the same number of impressions on targets if they perform well. Their performance will build positive historical data, which will increase the ad quality score and allow you to keep a similar level of impressions at a lower bid. This is why bidding higher and then progressively decreasing is usually a good strategy for first-time advertisers—provided you have the money to sustain the losses in the short term.

The open bidding system is what sets Amazon Advertising apart from the other major advertising platforms for authors. Most of your time on there will be spent adjusting bids based on results, so it's important that you understand and keep in mind the fundamentals of how the auctions work on the platform.

Speaking of results, the final pillar you need to have a perfect understanding of is the reporting one, which is how Amazon attributes and reports on the income generated by your ads.

4

Conversion attribution

One of the hardest and most crucial parts of advertising books on Amazon is understanding the data that Amazon offer you in the advertising dashboard. The most common mistakes related to Amazon Advertising have one root cause: misreading or misinterpreting the data in the dashboard, and making misinformed or wrong decisions as a result.

The great advantage of Amazon Advertising over Facebook or BookBub ads is that it is the *only* advertising platform that actually offers you sales data in the advertising dashboard. You don't have to guess how many of your clicks converted into sales; Amazon tells you directly. But this can be both a blessing and a curse, because, as with all things Amazon, getting accurate sales data is not that simple.

Ebook and print sales attribution

The first thing you need to understand is how Amazon attributes and reports on sales driven by ads. If you've never heard of the concept of attribution in marketing, it refers to the process of determining which conversions (in this case, book sales) can be attributed to a particular marketing channel (in this case, Amazon Ads).

For example, if Jim sees your ad, clicks on it, and immediately purchases your book, that's simple, right? We can attribute Jim's purchase to the ad.

But now take Dwight: He clicks on the ad and makes a note of purchasing it later (when he gets back to his farm). When he eventually purchases your book, it might be days or weeks later, and as a result of searching for the title directly on Amazon. Will Dwight's purchase get attributed to the ad?

And now take Pam: She sees the ad but doesn't click on it, instead she makes a mental note of the title and buys it later. What do you attribute Pam's purchase to?

By now you probably get the gist: Attribution is a complex topic with no right or wrong answers. And to make things more complicated, every advertising platform tries to "solve" it in a different way.

Let's take Facebook, for example. In order to take into account the fact that conversions can happen in a number of different ways, they've created different attribution settings for advertisers to choose from, with what they call conversion windows:

- 1-day click: Facebook will only report conversions from users who click on your ad and convert less than twenty-four hours after the click.
- 7-day click (default): Facebook will only report conversions from users who click on your ad and convert less than seven days after the click.
- 1-day click or 1-day view: Facebook will report conversions from users who click on *or* view your ad and convert less than twenty-four hours after the click.
- 7-day click or 1-day view: Facebook will report conversions from users who click on your ad and convert less than seven days after the click, as well as conversions from users who view your ad and convert less than twenty-four hours after.

By using one attribution setting or another, you might get entirely different conversion results and make entirely different decisions as a result.

By now, you should be curious enough to wonder how Amazon Advertising attribution works.

Well, I'm glad I forced you to ask! In the words of Amazon, found when you hover over the little "i" information icon next to "Sales" in the dashboard:

31

*"Sales is the total value of products sold to shoppers within the specified timeframe for a type of campaign **due to clicks on your ads.***

*Sponsored Products: Sales from advertised products as well as other products within your brand sold by Amazon **within 14 days.** This doesn't include third-party sellers.*

Sponsored Brands: Sales from advertised products sold by Amazon within 14 days. Where eligible, this also includes sales from all products within your brand sold by Amazon and third-party sellers.

For authors, your KDP sales reports will show you the final sales numbers, which may be different from the number you see here.

It can take up to 12 hours for your sales data to update. As a result, sales data may be delayed in the Today date range. We recommend waiting until all sales data is populated before evaluating campaign performance.

Payment failures and orders that are cancelled within 72 hours will be removed from sales totals." [**Boldface** is mine for emphasis and discussion]

Let's decipher this jargon. The first bit of vital information is in the first sentence: "Sales is the total value of products sold to shoppers . . . **due to clicks on your ads.**" This means that Amazon Advertising attribution is purely click based: it will not report any sales driven by views only. To go back to our previous examples, it would not attribute Pam's purchase to the ad.

Next, Amazon tells you what its conversion window is: 14 days. So in our Dwight example, his sale would get reported in the dashboard, but only when it actually happens, and only if it happens within fourteen days of his clicking on the ad.

Moreover, what Amazon doesn't tell you in this little information window, but which you can find if you dig through their support documents, is this:

· For Sponsored Products campaigns, the sale is attributed to the day of the most relevant click (click date reporting). So if a click led to a sale seven days later, that sale would show up seven days later in your dashboard, but attributed to the day of the click.

- For all other types of campaigns (Sponsored Brands, Lockscreen, Sponsored Display), the sale is attributed to the day of the sale (conversion date reporting). If a click leads to a sale seven days later, that sale would show up attributed to the seventh day.

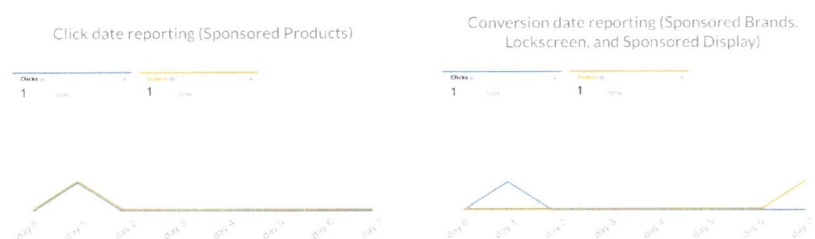

Click date versus conversion date reporting, on the hypothesis of a click that leads to an order seven days later.

Print sales attribution

Now, to get the full picture on Amazon sales attribution, there's one thing that Amazon doesn't mention in that guidance, which is absolutely crucial for print books: print sales are only reported when the book is shipped. Amazon doesn't bother to note this because the same is true for any physical product in the Store. Customers are charged—and the sale is registered—only when the item ships (until then, the customer has the option to just cancel the order).

Depending on the type of campaign, this sale will get attributed either to the day of the click (click date reporting), or to the day of the order (conversion date reporting). This might be a bit hard to wrap your head around, so let's take an example.

Phyllis clicks on your ad on Monday. On Tuesday, she purchases your paperback, which gets printed and shipped two days later (on Thursday). In the case of a Sponsored Products campaign,

- Phyllis's order will only appear in your Amazon Advertising dashboard on Thursday (shipping date), and
- It will be attributed to the day of the click (Monday).

So even if Phyllis's order happens on Tuesday, you'll see nothing in your dashboard until Thursday, and when you do, it'll show up as a Monday order.

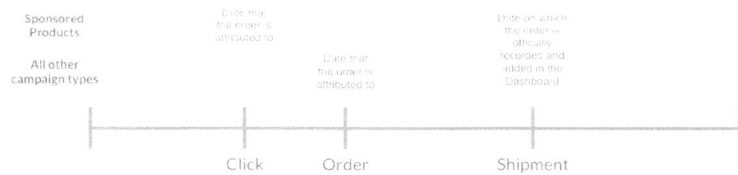

Print book attribution timeline

With print-on-demand (POD) books, the delay between the reader ordering and Amazon (or any other POD provider) is generally quite short, provided the book is in stock already. If not, it can take up to a week for Amazon to print and ship it—or in some cases, much longer.

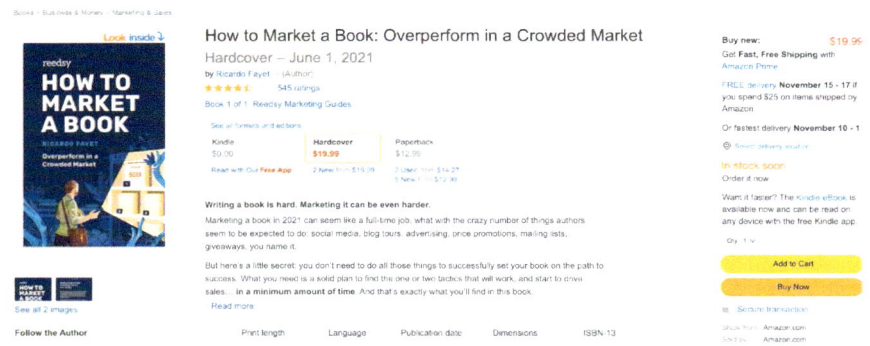

Note the ten-day shipping delay for the hardcover of my book.

At the time of writing this book (late 2022, with global supply chain issues), many POD books are taking up to a week or more to be shipped by Amazon, which means that it can take up to a week or more for print sales to show up in authors' KDP and Advertising dashboards.

This is why I always exclude at least the last week when looking at Amazon Advertising results—especially when advertising print. Many print sales generated by Amazon Ads in that time period just won't get reflected in the dashboard, so the data will be, at best, corrupted and, at worst, meaningless.

KENP read and royalties attribution

In 2020, Amazon Advertising introduced two new game-changing metrics in the Amazon Advertising dashboard for books enrolled in KDP Select:

- KENP read: The estimated number of pages read by Kindle Unlimited customers attributed to your ads, based on the Kindle Edition Normalized Page Count (KENPC).
- Estimated KENP royalties: Estimated royalties from pages read attributed to your ads (KENP read).

The second is a byproduct of the first: it's basically the KENP read multiplied by the current KENP rate (the Kindle Unlimited payout per page, rates per month vary). But what's important to highlight is this additional information from Amazon (emphasis mine):

> **"Pages read are reported on the date of reading.** *Pages read from off-line devices can take 1 week to be reported."*

Why is this important? Well, suppose Andy clicks on your ad and borrows your book through Kindle Unlimited—but only starts reading it after a week (after he's finished practicing his new a capella song). In this case, Andy's page reads and his associated royalties will only show up after a week and will gradually increase as he makes his way through the book. If you check your campaign before then, you wouldn't see his page reads reported.

If you want a real-life example, take a look at the screenshot below. It shows spend (clicks) happening on December 23 and 29, and page reads coming in ten days later, on January 9–11. Since there are no other clicks in this campaign after December 29, we can deduce that these page reads are the result of these earlier clicks—they just took a while to appear because the reader didn't start reading the book when downloaded.

Example of delayed KENP reads in the Amazon Advertising dashboard.

If you've been following so far, you'll have recognized from the graph that Amazon uses conversion date reporting for page reads—which is a bit counterintuitive considering KENP reads are only reported in Sponsored Products campaigns, and those use click date reporting for sales!

At the end of the day, however, it doesn't really matter which day Amazon attributes the sales/reads to—just note where the orange spike shows up in the graph—but that these are recorded and reported in the first place.

Which invites the question: How long does Amazon track the reading activity of Kindle Unlimited subscribers who click on your ads? This information isn't disclosed in the hover box on your Amazon Advertising dashboard, but is accessible through a "Learn more" link:

> *"We track clicks associated with your advertised titles, and attribute them to the reading events for the same titles **up to 14 days after customers click the ad.**"*

So in our example, Amazon would track Andy's page reads for fourteen days after he clicks on the ad—that is, for seven days after he starts reading the book. If he finishes the book in a week, then all of his page reads and associated royalties will show up in your Amazon Advertising dashboard (after fourteen days). But if he takes longer to finish, only a portion of his page reads will be recorded, because Amazon will stop attributing after fourteen days.

Depending on how long your books are (I'm thinking of you, epic fantasy authors), it may very well take your readers more than fourteen days to read your books in full. So the actual KENP reads and royalties generated by your ads will be higher, and sometimes much higher, than the ones reported in the Amazon Advertising dashboard.

Because of this, I always recommend that Kindle Unlimited authors also keep an eye on the page reads reported in their KDP dashboard. If you notice that there's a big jump in page reads there after starting the ads, and that that jump is not reflected in the Amazon Advertising dashboard, you can be fairly sure that the difference is due to the fourteen-day attribution window.

This is not generally a huge issue when you're advertising just the one book (even if it's a long one). But it can definitely become one if you advertise several books in a series within the same ad group. Which brings us to—

Multi-product sales reporting

So far, we've focused mostly on how Amazon attributes sales when you're advertising just one book. But what if you want to advertise several books (a series) within the same campaign?

You may have noticed the following bit from Amazon's information on sales attribution (emphasis mine):

> *"Sponsored Products: Sales from advertised products **as well as other products within your brand** sold by Amazon within 14 days."*

This means that Amazon reports orders and sales, in each campaign, for:

1. All the products advertised in the campaign; and
2. All the products "within your brand."

This means that Amazon reports Orders and Sales, in each campaign, for

1. All the products advertised in the campaign and
2. All the products "within your brand."

And here comes the slightly confusing part: authors don't technically have a "brand" on Amazon—at least not in terms of what Amazon considers a brand.

See, brands are reserved for Seller accounts. Think fashion brands, cooking brands, traditional publishers—all Seller accounts who register their brand on Amazon. Indie authors who access Amazon Advertising through their KDP account don't have the option of registering a brand in the first place. Instead, they have Author Central accounts.

Therefore, only products for which Amazon Advertising will report sales in the dashboard are the products advertised in your campaign. If your ad leads to a purchase of another of your books, but that book is not included in the campaign, that sale will not appear in the dashboard.

Inversely, let's say you include two products to advertise in your campaign. If a reader clicks on an ad for product one but then ends up purchasing product two instead, then that sale will get recorded. And if they buy both products (within the fourteen-day window), then both sales will get recorded.

This attribution happens not only on the campaign level, but on the ad level as well. For example, let's say your campaign advertises both the ebook and paperback version of your book—with the ebook at $0.99 and the paperback at $12.38. When looking at the "ads" tab of your campaign, you could end up seeing something like this:

Sales reporting for various versions of a book.

What this shows is that ads featuring your ebook have led to *one* orders of your book, for a total in sales of $12.38—and the same goes for the ads featuring your paperback. But considering your ebook is priced at $0.99, one orders should make for a total in sales of $0.99, not $12.38, so why the difference?

You guessed it: one of the ads featuring the ebook led to a sale of the paperback format instead. And since that format is also included in the campaign, Amazon is reporting it as well and attributing it to the ebook—since it's an ad for the ebook that led to that sale.

That's very important to keep in mind when looking at that Ads tab: the sales/page reads that Amazon reports for each product in the campaign are not the sales/page reads that each product has earned—but the sales/page reads that ads featuring this product have generated (for any product included in the campaign).

To give you another example, here's the Ads tab of a campaign advertising nine ebooks in the same series:

Product ⊙	Status	SKU/ASIN	▾ Spend ⊙	Orders ⊙	Sales ⊙	ACOS ⊙	Estimated KENP royalties ⊙
Total: 9			$111.21	10	$52.90	210.25%	$75.52
Book 1	Delivering		$92.26	10	$52.90	174.40%	$73.95
Price cannot be found							
Book 3	Delivering		$7.21	-	-	-	-
Price cannot be found							
Book 2	Delivering		$3.66	-	-	-	$0.00
Price cannot be found							

Results of a campaign advertising multiple books.

Unsurprisingly, most of the ad spend goes toward advertising the first book—which is the one generating all the orders and page reads. But these could be orders/page reads of book one, or of any of the eight following books, or a mix. The ten orders could be the result of ten different readers buying book one, or two different readers buying the first five, or five different readers buying two books—you get the gist.

The fact is this: the only thing we know is that these orders and page reads resulted from readers clicking on an ad for book one. Exactly what they bought/read afterward, we don't know—but at least we know the total value in orders and page reads that our ads generated (within fourteen days of the click).

Attribution for series authors

And this is precisely one of the main reasons why I usually favor Standard campaigns for series over Custom text ones (which limit you to one advertised product). By including all the books in your series in a Standard campaign, you get a much more accurate reporting picture.

Let me illustrate that with a counterexample: Meredith has a five-book series out (available through Kindle Unlimited) and is setting up her first Amazon Advertising campaign to promote it.

Now, Meredith hasn't read this book, so she creates a Custom text campaign advertising her first-in-series. After a week, she notices a solid bump in sales and page reads across her series, so she excitedly heads to check her Advertising account—only to find out that her campaign spent $50 and generated no more than five orders of book one, plus a few dollars in KU page reads. Surprised, she pauses the campaign, and for some mysterious reason, her sales and page reads go down again.

What happened to Meredith? You might have guessed: these five readers who purchased book one went on to purchase the following books in the series. But since the campaign only advertises book one, Amazon didn't attribute the sales of the other books to it. And the same goes for page reads. This was probably a profitable campaign, but Meredith killed it.

This is not to mean that Standard campaigns are perfect attribution-wise, far from it. First, the fourteen-day conversion window can be quite short for longer series. If you have ten or more books in your series, it'll probably take most readers longer than two weeks to go through them.

In terms of page reads, the two metrics Amazon offers are definitely useful but show an incomplete picture. For example, let's say that your Standard campaign advertising your five-book series shows 1,000 in attributed page reads. These could come from one single reader making their way through your series, or from dozens of different ones who just got started. A figure for "borrows" representing the number of readers who initially borrow your book in Kindle Unlimited would be a lot more helpful—but considering that metric doesn't even exist in KDP Dashboards right now, it's unlikely we'll ever get to see it in Amazon Advertising.

So you're still left with a healthy amount of guesswork and estimation when time comes to judge the performance of your campaigns and targets. More often than not, you'll need to wait at least a week or two until you can trust the data in the dashboard—and even then, the fourteen-day window will mean the data are incomplete.

But if you keep all of the above in mind (I've added a little cheat sheet that you can refer to if you forget about some of it), you'll already be light-years ahead of the competition, and in the best position to make the right decisions on your campaigns.

Amazon Advertising Attribution Cheat Sheet

✔ **Click-based attribution:** Sales and page reads are attributed to an ad only if they happen as a result of the reader clicking on the ad.

✔ **Click date reporting for orders** (on Sponsored Products campaigns): The order is attributed to the day when the click happened. For Sponsored Brands, Lockscreen, or Sponsored Display campaigns, the order is attributed to the day of the purchase (conversion date reporting).

✔ **Fourteen-day window:** Sales and page reads are attributed to an ad only if they happen within fourteen days of the reader clicking on the ad. Any sales or reads from the same reader happening thereafter will not show up in the Amazon Advertising dashboard.

✔ **Advertised product attribution:** Amazon will only attribute and report on the sales/page reads for the ASINs advertised in your campaign. If you include several ASINs, then sales/page reads for any of the products happening as a result of a reader clicking on an ad will be attributed to this ad. If the reader purchases/reads several advertised products (within fourteen days), Amazon will attribute all these purchases/reads to the ad. If the reader purchases/reads a book that is not advertised in the campaign, Amazon will not report that sale—even if you're the author of that book.

II

Setting up your first campaigns

Now you're familiar with the pillar principles of Amazon Advertising, it's time to go in and set up your first campaigns. In this section, you'll learn all the best practices to start on the right foot and give your first campaigns the best chances of immediately turning a profit.

5

Structuring your campaign

Most of the major advertising platforms have some sort of "architecture" when it comes to setting up advertising campaigns, with different hierarchy levels controlling different aspects of the advertising process such as budget, optimization goal, audiences, placements, bids, and ad copy.

Facebook Advertising and Google Ads, for example, are fairly similar in how campaigns are structured. They use a pyramidal structure with "campaigns" at the top, "ad groups/ad sets" below, and finally "ads" at the bottom—each controlling different elements of the campaign setup process.

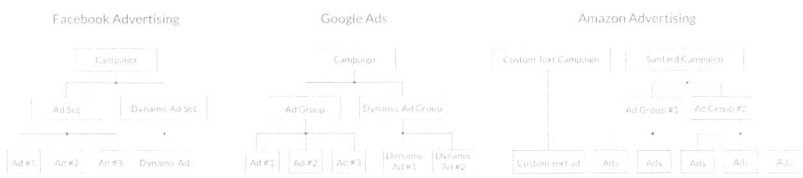

Facebook vs. Google vs. Amazon Advertising campaign architecture.

Understanding the structure of an advertising platform is not just important to set up your first campaigns, it is key to staying organized in the long term and quickly finding your way through the dashboard when you have dozens of campaigns running.

I have personally had access to over fifty different Amazon Advertising accounts, and it may have been a coincidence but the best-performing ones were always the most efficiently organized.

Here's how successful campaigns are structured on Amazon and how you should set up yours.

Standard vs Custom text

Until recently, the only campaigns authors could access on Amazon Advertising were simple ones with a horizontal structure: you just set up a campaign, and every aspect of it was managed under that main umbrella.

A couple of years ago, though, Amazon introduced Standard campaigns with Ad groups to authors as well (these had already been available to Vendor or Advantage advertisers on the Store).

The first task is to understand the structural difference between these Standard ad campaigns, and the legacy ones, now called Custom text ad.

Custom text campaigns

As their name indicates, Custom text ad campaigns allow the author to use custom advertising copy—in other words, you can customize the ad with a couple of lines of specific copy provided by the you, the author (up to 150 characters). This option is not available in Standard ad campaigns—instead Amazon will not display any copy on the Standard ad, except for the usual information: title, subtitle, series title, author name, and other elements of metadata.

The difference between a Custom text ad and a Standard ad.

Since their ads feature custom marketing copy, Custom text campaigns only allow you to advertise one book per campaign. Otherwise, you'd have to craft copy that could work for several interchangeable titles, which would probably be less compelling as a result.

That said, you can add different formats of the same book to a Custom text campaign—for example, Kindle edition, paperback, and hardback. As a side note, you cannot yet advertise audiobooks specifically through Amazon Advertising, though no doubt that'll come in the future.

Standard ad campaigns

Standard ad campaigns, on the other hand, allow you to advertise as many different products (ASINs) as you wish within the same campaign—whether they're related to the same book or not. They're a versatile tool, for example, to advertise all the books in a given series at once.

When running a Standard ad campaign advertising multiple ASINs, Amazon will pick and choose which product to show to which reader, based on historical performance and reader data. It'll also report sales and reads coming from the ads for all the ASINs included in the campaign, as we'll explore in the next chapter.

The biggest difference between Custom ad text and Standard ad campaigns, however, has to do with ad groups: Custom text campaigns don't feature ad groups, while Standard ones do.

The function of the ad group is to introduce a second level in the campaign architecture: a campaign can have several ad groups under it—all of which will share the settings of the campaign that governs them. This helps with keeping things organized, especially when it comes time to scale.

Campaign and ad group structure

Now you know about the two different types of campaigns, let's dissect them to see what each structure looks like.

As I mentioned, Custom text campaigns are simple: you have one campaign level that governs everything, from budget to bidding strategy, targeting, advertised products, placements, and copy.

A Custom text ad campaign can be used to advertise only one book, can only use one type of targeting, one type of bidding strategy, and so on.

If you want to advertise separate books using Custom text campaigns, or if you want to advertise the same book but using both ASIN product targeting and keyword targeting, you'll have to set up two different campaigns.

In contrast, here's what the structure of Standard ad campaigns looks like:

Custom Text Campaign Architecture	Standard Campaign Architecture	
Campaign Level	**Campaign Level**	**Ad Group Level**
Start & end dates	Start & end dates	Targeting
Budget	Budget	Negative targeting
Bidding strategy	Bidding strategy	Advertised products (unlimited)
Targeting	Placement bid adjustments	
Negative targeting		
Placement bid adjustments		
Advertised products (maximum one)		
Custom advertising copy		

Custom text ad vs. Standard ad campaign architecture.

As you can see, Standard campaigns can be a lot more versatile. While the budget and bidding strategy are decided at the campaign level (they will be shared by all the ad groups under it), everything else is decided at the ad group level.

This means that one Standard campaign can potentially

- Advertise different books across different ad groups, and/or
- Leverage different targeting types (keywords, products, categories) across different ad groups.

There is one exception to this, and it's in the case of using Amazon's automatic targeting. If you set up a Standard campaign with auto targeting, you'll be able to have different ad groups, each advertising different books, but all of them will have to use automatic targeting.

In the future, I do expect Amazon Advertising to roll out ad groups across all types of campaigns, as it makes for a more organized advertising experience, so I'd very much encourage you to get familiar with them right away. My experience has also shown that Standard campaigns, because of their ability to advertise several books at once, tend to be more effective and easier to scale, and I'll show you how in the next chapter.

Sponsored Brands campaign architecture

We've covered campaign architecture in Chapter 3, but that was for Sponsored Products. Sponsored Brands have a similar setup, with the following exceptions:

- **Advertised Products**: Here you need to select at least three different books (these can't be different formats of the same book, by the way). You can, however, select more, which is important for sales attribution, but more on that soon.
- **Creative**: In this section, you can customize what your ad will look like by selecting the three books you want to feature (and their order), adding your profile picture (or brand logo), and crafting the headline for the ad.

Since all Sponsored Brands ads feature a headline, there's no option to choose between Custom text and Standard campaigns. There's only one type of Sponsored Brands campaign at the moment, and it has a flat structure with everything nestled at the campaign level.

In other words, there are no ad groups when it comes to Sponsored Brands ads.

Lockscreen Ads campaign architecture

Lockscreen Ads are also quite different from Sponsored Products/Brands when it comes to the budget. Instead of setting up a daily budget for the campaign, you set up a total lifetime budget (with a minimum of $100), and then choose whether to spend it as fast as possible, or spread it evenly over the campaign dates.

As you'll see in future chapters, Amazon is terrible at spending your daily budget for Sponsored Products and Sponsored Brands campaigns. However, for Lockscreen Ads, Amazon will spend your lifetime budget reasonably quickly if you ask them to. This makes it the only kind of ad on Amazon where you need to be somewhat cautious when setting up the budget, dates, and bid, lest your money disappear with little to no return.

Moreover, since Lockscreen Ads appear on Kindle devices, they can only be used to advertise ebooks, not print. This makes sense, but also makes it less compelling to authors whose income stems predominantly from print sales.

Finally, Lockscreen Ads also have a creative side: you can customize the ad with 150 characters of text. This is the same length as the text you can use on Custom text Sponsored Products campaigns, and since Lockscreen Ads tend to spend your budget (and therefore get you data) much quicker, you can use them as a testing ground to find the best custom text to use for your book—the one that yields you the best click-through-rates.

Naming conventions

Whether you favor Standard campaigns or Custom text ones, chances are you'll be setting up several and running them concurrently, which means your dashboard will look something like this:

Campaigns ⓘ	Impressions ⓘ	▼ Clicks ⓘ	CTR ⓘ	Spend ⓘ	CPC ⓘ	Orders ⓘ
Total: 14	862,374	897	0.10%	$630.31	$0.70	207
HMB - Campaign 1	287,272	272	0.09%	$173.41	$0.64	69
HMB - Campaign 2	210,612	155	0.07%	$109.76	$0.71	32
HMB - Campaign 3	99,257	118	0.12%	$71.31	$0.60	37
HMB - Campaign 4	3,216	35	1.09%	$44.85	$1.28	9

A dashboard with poorly named campaigns.

Unless you want to lose a lot of time when going through your campaigns to optimize them, I highly recommend you don't name them as I did in the screenshot here. Instead, you'll want to use a simple naming convention consistently for all the campaigns in your account.

Figuring out the best convention will depend on the type of campaigns you run, as well as a number of other factors, but I'll share the main conventions I use so that you can take inspiration from them.

If I set up Custom text campaigns, I'll usually make sure that all the following elements are included in the name:

- Type of campaign: "SP" for Sponsored Products, "SB" for Sponsored Brand," and "LS" for Lockscreen
- Title of the advertised book (or abbreviation): "Harry Potter and the Chamber of Secrets" or "HPCS"
- Bidding strategy: "Down," "U&D," "Fixed"
- Targeting type: "Auto," "Keywords." "Categories"
- Something to identify the targeting keywords or ASINs (such as "Also Bought ASINs," "Fantasy search terms")
- In the case of keyword targets, the match type: "Broad," "Down," or "Exact"

For example, here's how I'd name a campaign advertising the first Harry Potter book, using down bidding strategy, and targeting popular YA fantasy search terms in broad match:

```
SP HPCS - Down - YA Fantasy Search Keywords - Broad
```

Optionally, if I'm running tests around the ad copy, then I would add a last identifier to the name of the campaign to identify the copy it's using, like "hook 1" or "review 1."

If I'm running a Standard campaign, the naming will be a bit different and depend on how I set up the ad groups. Generally, though, I'll try to include in the campaign name all of the elements that are common across all the ad groups of the campaign—and in each ad group's name, those that are specific to the ad group.

For example, if I set up a campaign advertising the whole Harry Potter series, with an ad group targeting author comps, another for title comps, and a last one for Also Bought ASINs, I'd name like this:

1. The campaign: *SP HP Series All – Down – Comps*
2. Ad group one: *Author comps broad*
3. Ad group two: *Title comps phrase*
4. Ad group three: *Also Bought ASINs*

The more different series, pen names, and types of ads you run, the more information you'll want to include in your campaign names. For example, if you advertise two different series, I'd include an acronym for each. This allows you to then filter the results in your dashboard to see only the data for one series or another. The same goes for different pen names and genres, and the like.

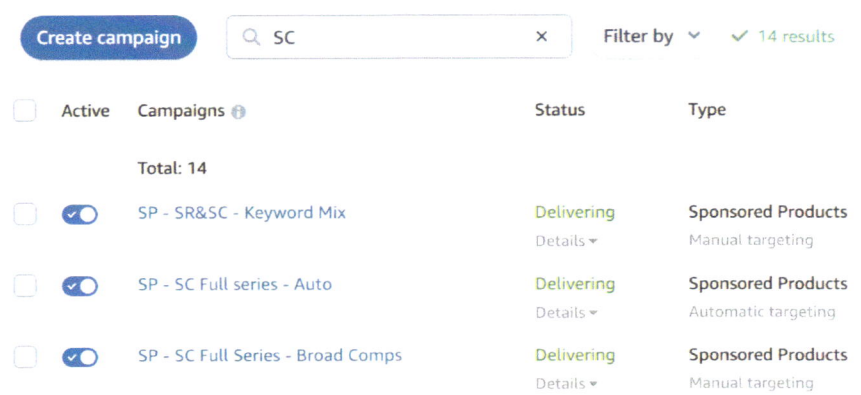

Filtering the dashboard to include only campaigns advertising my "SC" series.

Naturally, you don't need to follow this convention to the letter—what's important is that you find one that works for you and that allows you to immediately understand, at first glance, what every one of your campaigns and ad groups is about, and to visualize results efficiently in your dashboard.

6

Custom Text versus Standard Campaigns

As discussed in the last chapter, there are two types of Sponsored Products campaigns: Custom text (no ad group) and Standard (ad group).

For me, the advantages of both types of campaigns boil down to this:

- Custom text: you can add custom copy to your ads (obvious, I know).
- Standard: you can advertise several books in the same campaign (with the reporting/attribution advantages this implies).

And the problem here is the opposite of Frank Sinatra's view on love and marriage: you can only have one without the other.

Then the question becomes which one of these two advantages is more important to you? In some cases, it's easy. For example, if you have only one book out (like I do as I write this), then you don't need ad groups and can take advantage of Custom text. But if you have several books out, then the choice between Custom text and Standard campaigns becomes a solid conundrum.

Just how important is custom ad copy?

First, consider just how valuable it is to be able to add custom marketing copy to your ads. While that custom text shows up in a relatively small font, it does seem to help the ad stand out both in search results, as well as on product page carousels.

Compare the look of the Custom text ad with the Standard ad.

More importantly, though, being able to set the copy yourself allows you to run what we marketers call A/B tests. You create one ad with copy A, one ad with copy B, and run them both to see which gathers the best results—in most cases, the highest click-through-rate (CTR) and sales numbers. Once you've found a winner, you can run another test pitting that winning copy against a new and different one, and so on until you settle on the perfect ad copy to use for each book.

A/B testing ad copy in Custom text campaigns

Or at least, that's what would happen in an ideal world. Sadly, Amazon is far from an ideal world, and testing ad copy for Sponsored Products campaigns is a bit of a hassle, to put it gently.

First, to test two different ad texts, you need to create a separate campaign for each—you can't just have two ad creatives within the same campaign (that'd be too simple). And for the test to be meaningful, you need to set up both campaigns identically (same targeting, products, and bids) and run them at the same time (otherwise, you'd be comparing apples to oranges).

To keep the apples being apples, you would also need to make sure that you don't touch the campaigns over the course of the test; or if you do, that you make identical changes to both campaigns. Otherwise, you won't know if the winning campaign is the result of better ad copy or of the changes you made.

Finally, and this is where the biggest problem lies with A/B testing ad copy on Amazon, you need to wait long enough for the results to be meaningful. If you stop the test after a week and both campaigns only generated a few clicks and sales, then you will have learned nothing.

Then how many clicks/sales do you need for the test to be statistically meaningful, you might be asking about now. Excellent question. You'll find a chapter later in this book that is all about statistical significance (don't worry, it's not as scary as it sounds), but to give you a guideline, I'd want to wait until both campaigns have gotten at least 100 clicks each before making any conclusions in terms of ad copy. More often than not, that can take weeks, if not months (depending on your targeting and bids).

And what you'll often find if you follow these steps religiously is that there isn't that much difference between the two campaigns—or at least, that's been my experience so far. Which leads me to my main point about advertising copy on Amazon Sponsored Products: I just don't think it matters that much.

Do readers actually read the copy?

Let's think about it this way: I mentioned that custom copy helps your ads stand out on the Store. But here, standing out can be seen both as a good and a bad thing. Here's the logic: only Sponsored items feature such additional marketing copy on the Store. Organic search results don't, and neither do Also Boughts.

So while this additional, custom text might serve to grab the interest of a reader, it also flags your product as an advertisement. In search results, for example, the little *Sponsored* sign on top of the title might be invisible to most people browsing the Store, but a big chunk of text that is only present on sponsored results definitely isn't.

While Custom text ads do stand out, this may not necessarily mean they look more attractive to readers. It might mean they just look more like, well, an ad.

The fact that Amazon doesn't usually include any text when displaying books in search results, or on product pages, has shaped its customer purchasing behavior over the years.

Readers are used to browsing the Store and making click decisions based solely on the cover, title, and, to a lesser extent, price and review average. My theory is that most readers' eyes will just skim over the descriptions, or flat out ignore them, and instead focus on the elements that will actually inform their clicking decision. After all, if they want to find out more about the book, they have a whole blurb just one click away.

Now, I'm not saying that custom advertising copy is completely useless: there are certainly readers who will read it—provided their eye has been caught by the cover first. What I'm saying is that if their eye has already been caught by the cover, or they've been intrigued by the title, then there's already a high probability that they'll click on the ad. And whether you use Ad copy 1, Ad copy 2, or no copy whatsoever, you can only sway their decision so far in one way or another.

And by now you may be wondering: "But this is all conjecture. If you're writing a book on Amazon Ads, shouldn't you have actual data to share about whether Custom text ads perform better than Standard ones?"

You're right. I don't appreciate your rhetorical snarky tone, but you're right.

To test my theory, I set up two custom copy campaigns, both using automatic targeting and identical bids and placements, and both advertising my free book: *How to Market a Book: Overperform in a Crowded Market.* I used Custom text for both, but while one featured an editorial review by Bryan Cohen, I used the following copy for the other:

"I'm running a test to see if readers actually read this ad copy. I'll share the results in my next book."

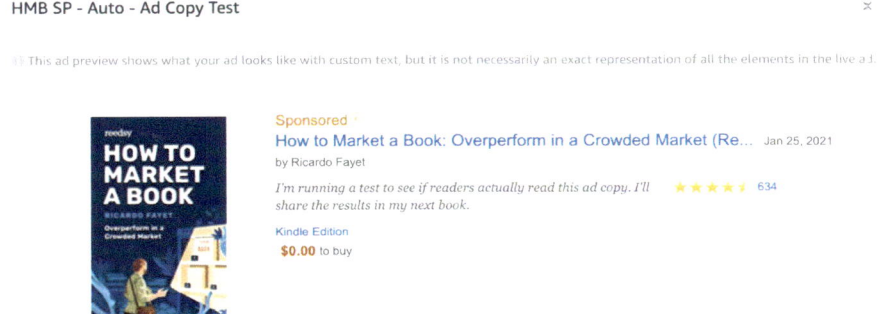

My little experiment in testing copy in Custom text ads.

Naturally, I kept everything else (bids, budgets, placements, bid optimization) identical across the two campaigns.

Want to guess which campaign performed better? None! The two are almost identical in performance, with Clicks, Spend, CPC, and Orders varying by less than 2 percent from one to the other:

Campaigns	Impressions	Clicks	CTR	Spend	CPC	Orders	Sales	ACOS
Total: 14	3,093,189	4,195	0.14%	$2,914.18	$0.69	1,218	$1,086.18	268.30%
HMB SP - Auto - Cohen Quote	473,505	907	0.19%	$641.37	$0.71	293	$25.98	2,468.71%
HMB SP - Auto - Ad Copy Test	487,614	896	0.18%	$642.13	$0.72	291	$38.97	1,647.75%

Results of A/B testing copy in Custom text ads.

This is only one test, of course, but it certainly seems to indicate that custom copy not only doesn't make a big difference, but might not actually matter at all.

When to consider using Custom text

All that said, there is one case scenario where I think it can be quite beneficial to leverage this small perk that is Custom text: when you're targeting a single, specific author (or book, or series) in your campaign.

For example, if you've found that Lee Child works particularly well as a target for your mystery/thriller books, then you could create a campaign specifically targeting his name, book titles, and series and using a Custom text piggybacking on his brand—for example, "for fans of Lee Child" or "Are you a Jack Reacher fan? Then you'll love [my character]."

This might help draw the right readers' eyes and boost the click-through-rate a bit, though don't expect spectacular results either: this will only work for targets that have already proven to work well for you. It's not a miracle solution to turn a low-performing target into a high-performing one.

The advantages of Standard campaigns

Now we're more clear on the real advantages of using Custom text for Sponsored Products ads, let's analyze the advantages of using the other type: Standard campaigns.

First, from an organizational standpoint, once you have several books, a series, or even pen names, you might find yourself drowning in campaigns every time you check out your Amazon Advertising account.

Using ad groups smartly allows you to structure and organize your advertising efforts in a more efficient way, reduce your number of campaigns, and thus spend less time looking at your ads every week.

For example, instead of having a campaign targeting your Also Bought titles, one targeting their ASINs, and one targeting their author names, you could have one single Also Boughts campaign with three separate ad groups for each targeting group. This will make it easier for you to check the results of targeting your Also Boughts as a whole on the campaign level, as well as to drill down into the results of each ad group.

The second big advantage is one I touched on already: Standard campaigns allow you to advertise several books at once, which offers you more attribution and reporting data. This, in turn, allows you to get a better picture of how effective your ads are being at not just selling the one book, but at pulling in readers who make their way through your entire catalog.

It's true that because of the fourteen-day conversion window, that data will always be incomplete, so there are actually two different schools of thought on whether having reported sales/reads for all the books in the series is better than having it for just book one. But that's something we'll explore more in depth in Part V of this book.

Personally, and you'll have probably guessed this by now, I largely favor Standard campaigns, especially when working with authors with several series out. First, because I don't think ad copy is that important, but mostly because I find the extra data (even if incomplete) and organizational structure invaluable.

I also believe ad groups and multi-product advertising are the future of Amazon Advertising, as it's likely they'll soon develop machine-learning algorithms to help them match the right product to the right consumer. I'll share my predictions for the future of Amazon Ads toward the end of the book, but for now, let's look at a type of automation already used by Amazon in their automatic targeting campaigns.

7

Automatic targeting

Automatic targeting campaigns are by far the easiest campaigns to set up and monitor, as you basically leave all the hard work—the targeting—in the hands of Amazon. Based on the products you advertise in the automatic targeting campaign, Amazon will choose which search results and product pages to place your ads on and will auto-optimize its targeting based on results.

In the words of Joseph Alexander, indie author and publisher of over 120 music books, who has been incredibly successful with Amazon Ads—

> *"It's creepy, but Amazon knows what you're shopping for, what you've been looking at, what your interests are, and how best to deliver the right advert at the right time. They've got years of experience here, and I know absolutely nothing! Are my keyword choices going to be better than Amazon's? Probably not.*
>
> *I guess this isn't necessarily true for fiction books, but that's not my area."*

Now, it's true that Joseph's books are in a highly specific niche, and all have titles and metadata that were carefully selected to make the books show up for the right searches—so Amazon Advertising's work is cut out in terms of figuring out the best targets for the auto campaigns.

This isn't going to be the case for everyone, and typically, nonfiction books in a specific niche tend to do much better with auto ads than novels. But whatever your genre, it is always a good idea to set up at least one auto campaign per book. Before I get into why, let's answer the question you're probably asking yourself right now.

How does Amazon choose what to target?

As with many mysteries related to Amazon algorithms, that's a question that we'll never really have the exact answer to: it's Amazon proprietary information. The only thing we can do is speculate based on experience, and based on the little information that Amazon makes public.

Now, Amazon has four match types for automatic campaigns—that is, four types of keywords/products that they'll go after:

1. Close match
2. Loose match
3. Substitutes
4. Complements

In their words,

> "With close match and loose match, your ad will be eligible to be shown in the shopping results if your product matches the shopping query closely or loosely, respectively."

This gives us a little bit more insight into how Amazon selects keywords to target in auto campaigns. Close and loose match types will target search terms that Amazon has determined are closely or loosely relevant to your book. This relevance depends on several factors, which are many of the same factors that Amazon's search algorithm uses to index and rank products for particular searches.

How does Amazon decide which products to display in search results? It's simple: it's going to look at the metadata of the book, in particular (and in this order):

- The title, subtitle, and series title
- The categories the book is in
- The seven meta keywords used by the publisher to describe the book
- The product description
- The title, subtitle, and series title
- The categories the book is in
- The seven meta keywords used by the publisher to describe the book
- The product description

This is why nonfiction books tend to perform better than novels with auto targeting: their titles and other metadata elements are generally strongly optimized for searches. For example, in the case of Joseph Alexander's music books, each book has a title that corresponds to a very particular search query (such as "blues guitar intros"). This makes Amazon's job of picking which search terms to target extremely easy.

But what about complements and substitutes, you may ask? From the same Amazon Advertising help page:

> *"With substitutes and complements, your ad will be shown to shoppers who view the detail pages of products that are similar to or complement your products, respectively."*

Therefore, while close and loose match targets are keywords, complements and substitutes are ASIN targets (specific products). In this case, your auto ad will appear directly on the product page of that ASIN (generally below the Also Boughts).

How does Amazon decide which ASINs to target? For substitutes, Amazon is looking for products that are similar to your products. What does "similar" mean? We can't know for sure, but I suspect that Also Boughts play an important role here—though Amazon may also target books with similar metadata (that is, books with related titles or meta keywords) or other popular books in your main categories.

Complements are products that "complement your products." Again, it's hard to know for sure what that means in Amazon-speak, but I believe it's a targeting type meant for products that have shown to have some sort of synergy or relationship with other products. For example, you might have come across this kind of "Frequently bought together" section on Amazon product pages:

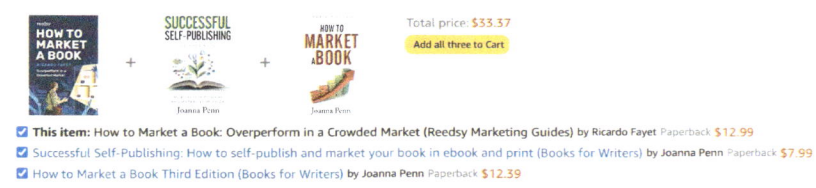

Amazon shows complementary products frequently bought together.

This is what complements are all about: products that Amazon has identified as often being purchased together with yours. If we exit the book world for a moment, a perfect example of two types of products being natural complements would be printers and toner, or hiking boots and hiking socks, or phone chargers and charging cables—you get the gist.

As you can imagine, complements are not always as relevant on the Books Store: it's rare that you have to buy one book in order to be able to read another. And yet, the Frequently bought together section is showing up on more and more popular books, even in the fiction realm:

Frequently bought together

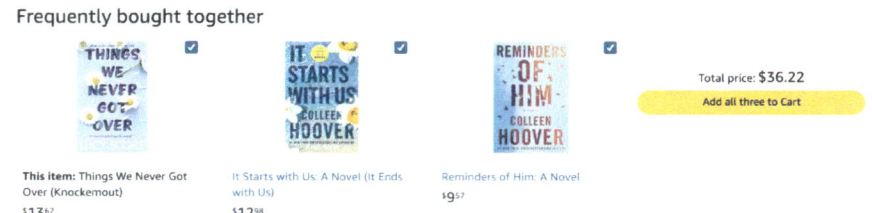

Frequently bought together books in contemporary fiction

If Amazon detects that readers of Lucy Score's *Things We Never Got Over* also tend to buy Colleen Hoover's books, then it makes sense for Lucy Score's automatic campaigns to target these Colleen Hoover titles, and vice versa.

In my experience, though, the targeting groups that tend to work best for authors in auto campaigns are close and loose match. If you're setting up an automatic targeting campaign for the first time, I highly recommend you customize your bids from the start, and bid highest for close match, lower for loose match, and lower again for substitutes and complements.

Finding your best-performing automatic search terms

One of the things I like the most about automatic targeting campaigns is that Amazon actually tells you which keywords and products your campaign targeted, as long as those keywords/products generated at least one click on your ad.

To view the results, you have two options. The first one is easy: just open the campaign or ad group and go to "Search terms" in the sidebar. There, you'll see all the targets with more than one click in the reporting window you selected, along with the other important metrics:

Customer search term 🛈	Impressions 🛈	▾ Clicks 🛈	CTR 🛈	Spend 🛈	CPC 🛈	Orders 🛈
Total: 283	65,887	507	0.77%	$332.05	$0.65	139
nonfiction best sellers	3,125	13	0.42%	$8.83	$0.68	7
nonfiction	530	10	1.89%	$7.09	$0.71	3
affiliate marketing	856	9	1.05%	$5.95	$0.66	1
ASIN: B08Y7Y93HJ Marketing Fastrack: The Little Book That Lau…	1,955	9	0.46%	$2.77	$0.31	–
free ebooks english	86	9	10.47%	$6.61	$0.73	2
free books on kindle	6,496	9	0.14%	$6.79	$0.75	1
writers market	337	8	2.37%	$4.94	$0.62	5
ASIN: B019H38JL2 Successful Self-Publishing: How to self-publi…	291	7	2.41%	$4.46	$0.64	4
ASIN: B091K5C6LR 3 Secrets to Landing Your Dream Literary Ag…	169	7	4.14%	$4.48	$0.64	3

Search terms of an automatic targeting campaign.

As you can see, my campaign above has targeted both search terms (via close match and loose match) and products/ASINs (via substitutes and complements). This view can be a great way to see which targets are performing particularly well for your book—and potentially "steal" them for your own manual targeting campaigns.

Another way to get a similar insight into your auto campaigns' actual targets is to run a "Sponsored Products Search term report." You'll find that option in the Reports section of your dashboard (accessible through the sidebar), which lets you download a spreadsheet of all the search terms and products with one click or more across all your campaigns.

These search term reports are particularly helpful if you're running several auto campaigns. Instead of having to go through each one's search terms individually, you can find them all at once, in bulk, in the spreadsheet. Of course, the report also includes search terms from manual targeting campaigns—but you can filter those out easily with some basic Excel or Google Sheets skills.

Now, the one major flaw of these two methods is that they only allow you to visualize search term performance from a maximum period of sixty-five days. As we'll see in future chapters, that's not always enough to be able to draw conclusions on a particular search term, so what I recommend instead is that you schedule a recurring search term report every thirty days and then aggregate the data.

If that sounds like gibberish to you, then fear not, I created a Google Sheet that will do this task automatically for you—you'll find a link to it and a short explanation on how to use it in the Bonus Resources (Sponsored Products Search Term Aggregator).

Brand searches and negative keywords

When checking out the search terms of your automatic targeting campaigns, you might find that Amazon tends to target your own title, author name, or other keywords related to your brand.

These are all considered close match search terms by the algorithms, and they can positively skew the results of your automatic campaigns, as they're much more likely to result in a click and sale. Case in point, here are some of the search terms of an auto campaign I'm running for *How to Market a Book: Overperform in a Crowded Market*:

Customer search term ⊖	Impressions ⊖	Clicks ⊖	CTR ⊖	Spend ⊖	CPC ⊖	Orders ⊖	Sales ⊖	ACOS ⊖	ROAS ⊖
Total: 3	3	3	100.00%	$2.37	$0.79	4	$25.98	9.12%	10.96
how to market a book	1	1	100.00%	$1.12	$1.12	2	$12.99	8.62%	11.60
how to market a book ricardo fayet	1	1	100.00%	$1.00	$1.00	2	$12.99	7.70%	12.99
reedsy how to market a book	1	1	100.00%	$0.25	$0.25	-	-	-	-

My own book shows up in close match search terms of an automatic targeting campaign.

We'll discuss the merits of using brand keywords (also called defense keywords) as part of your advertising strategy in Chapter 10, but it's important to be aware that automatic targeting will often trigger your ads on such search terms, especially if you set a high bid on the close match targeting group.

If you want to avoid targeting brand keywords in your auto-campaigns (whether because it's not part of your strategy, or because you're already doing so through a manual campaign), then you can simply add them as negative keywords.

Making smart use of negative keywords

Negative keywords are not specific to automatic targeting campaigns: it's a targeting feature that you'll find in all Sponsored Products and Sponsored Brands campaigns. However, since they can be particularly relevant to automatic targeting, I'll discuss how to make the best use of them.

But first, what are negative keywords exactly? They're the opposite of keywords. While keywords tell Amazon *what* to target, negative keywords tell Amazon what *not* to target. In other words, they can be used to exclude search terms from your campaign's targeting.

It's worth noting that negative keywords only prevent your ads from appearing in determinate search results: they have no impact on product targeting. So if you use *ricardo fayet* as a negative keyword, your ad will not show up on searches for my name, but it might still show up on my book's product page. To avoid that, you have the option to add negative products as well.

How and when should you use negative keywords? Well, there are different schools of thought on this. Some people recommend regularly monitoring search terms and adding any search term that is not performing well as a negative keyword.

Mine lie more on the lazy side of things: I usually try to guess beforehand which negative keywords would make sense for a given campaign. Generally, these will be words such as these:

- *free* (if advertising a paid book),
- *kindle unlimited* (if advertising a book that is not available in Kindle

Unlimited),

- *series* (if advertising a stand-alone),
- *print* or *kindle* (if you only advertise one format), and
- genre-related keywords.

For example, if you write across different genres with little to no crossover (say horror and cozy mystery), then you might want to use negative keywords to make sure your automatic campaigns for one genre don't end up accidentally targeting readers of the other (for example, use *horror*, *scary*, *thriller*, *gore*, and the like as negative keywords for a campaign advertising a cozy mystery).

Since romance is so prevalent across all commercial fiction genres (for example, in fantasy, science fiction, and thriller), I also like to use romance-related negative keywords when advertising a book whose main storyline isn't romance. For example, if advertising an epic fantasy, I'd add *romance*, *erotica*, *harem*, *alpha*, *shifter*, and similar descriptors as negative keywords.

Now, you have two match type choices for negative keywords: phrase and exact. I'll do a proper deep dive into match types in the next chapter, but basically know this:

- Phrase match negative keywords will exclude any searches that include your keyword. For example, *harem* in phrase match will exclude searches such as *reverse harem*, *scifi harem*, and *paranormal reverse harem fantasy*.
- Exact match negative keywords will only exclude searches that are your keyword or a close variation. For example, *harem* in exact match will only exclude the searches *harem* and *harems* (plural counts as a close variation).

I personally almost always use phrase matches exclusively for negative keywords because I want to exclude any searches that might include one of my negative keywords.

On the other hand, if you make a heavier use of negative keywords than I do, and regularly add to the list any search term or keyword target that isn't performing well in the campaign, then you might want to use exact match negative keywords instead.

8

Manual targeting

We've already seen that Amazon offers four main targeting options for Sponsored Products:

1. Automatic (which we just covered),
2. Keywords,
3. Products, and
4. Categories.

Before I discuss how you can find the best possible targets for your ads, let's analyze each of these options more in depth, as not all will make sense to start with.

1. Keyword targeting

Manual keyword targeting is the most common form of advertising on Amazon and the second easiest to start with (after auto-campaigns).

Contrary to popular belief, keyword targeting campaigns don't just get your ads to show up in search results—when readers run searches related to the keywords you're targeting. They also get your ads featured in product pages related to these keywords (in the "Sponsored products related to this item" section).

For example, if I target the keyword *harry potter*, then my ads may appear both in search results for *harry potter* and on the product pages of each Harry Potter book. If I target *yoga for beginners*, my ads may appear on search results for that query and also on the product page of any *yoga for beginners* title.

I'll get more into the different placements, their costs, and placement bid optimization strategies in Chapter 22, but for now just keep in mind that keyword targeting doesn't equate to just search results; it's search results *plus* product pages.

Now, which search results and product pages your ads will show on depends on two simple things: the keywords you target and the match type.

The three match types: Exact vs Phrase vs Broad

Match types allow you to both diversify and control the exact search queries and product pages that your ads are eligible to appear on. A reader could use hundreds of different ways and search terms to search for a particular book on Amazon, and advertisers can't be expected to think of them all. That's what match types are for.

You can choose from three match types when adding keyword targets to your Sponsored Products or Sponsored Brands campaign: exact, phrase, and broad. Let's analyze each of them.

Exact match

Exact matches are used when you know the exact search query (or product) you want to target. Close variations (plural or singular) will also be included, but the search terms need to include the full keyword phrase, in the exact same order, and not contain any additional keywords.

Here are some examples.

Keyword	Eligible search terms*	Ineligible search terms
children's adventure books	children's adventure books, children adventure books, children's adventure book	kid's adventure books, children's adventure books 8-12, adventure books for children
free epic fantasy book	free epic fantasy book, free epic fantasy books	free epic fantasy, free fantasy book, free high fantasy book, epic free fantasy book
inspirational stories	inspirational story, inspirational stories	inspirational story collections, inspirational books, inspirational stories for men, inspirational
addiction recovery memoir	addiction recover memoir, addiction recovery memoirs	memoirs about addiction, addiction recovery true story, addiction, recovery memoir

Eligible search terms are search terms that your ads are eligible to show up for based on your keyword targeting.

Phrase match

Phrase matches are useful when you have a precise idea of what you want to target, but want to include longer searches that contain the phrase in question. Only search terms and products that include your exact keyword phrase in the right order will be eligible, but these search terms can include other words before and after the targeted phrase.

Keyword	Eligible search terms*	Ineligible search terms
children's adventure	children's adventure books 8-12, children's adventure series	adventure books for children, kid's adventure books, children's travel adventure books
free epic fantasy	free epic fantasy kindle unlimited, best selling free epic fantasy, free epic fantasy like eragon	epic free fantasy, free high fantasy, epic fantasy books, epic fantasy books for free
inspirational stories	inspirational story collections, true inspirational stories for women, free inspirational stories	inspirational books, inspirational true stories, stories that will inspire you
recovery memoir	addiction recovery memoir, recovery memoirs about drugs, recovery memoir by david poses	best memoirs about recovery, addiction recovery true story, recovery biography, recovery drug memoir

*Eligible search terms are search terms that your ads are eligible to show up for based on your keyword targeting.

Broad match

Broad match is the match type that will allow you to target the broadest array of searches and products. These will still need to include all the individual words in your keyword phrase, but they can be in any order, as well as include other words before, after, or in between them.

Keyword	Eligible search terms*	Ineligible search terms
children's adventure	adventure books for children, children's travel adventure print books	kid's adventure books, children's books, adventure books
free epic fantasy	epic fantasy books for free, epic fantasy books available for free in kindle unlimited	high fantasy, epic fantasy books, free romantic fantasy books
inspirational stories	inspirational true story for children, how to write an inspirational story	inspirational books, uplifting stories, how to find inspiration
addiction memoir	addiction recovery memoir, memoirs about drugs and addiction, a memoir of panic and addiction	drugs recovery memoir, addiction biography, memoir

*Eligible search terms are search terms that your ads are eligible to show up for based on your keyword targeting.

A note on misspellings: Misspellings are not considered close variations and are therefore not included in any match type. For example, if you target *harry potter*, a reader searching for and mistyping *harru potter* will never see your ad, no matter the match type. This is why it's always a good idea to add misspellings of popular keywords to your keyword targeting list.

How to make smart use of match types

Now that you know the difference among the three match types, it's time to look into when you should use which.

Since exact match is quite limiting, I only recommend using it for short, popular keywords. If you target *cat cozy mysteries with strong female detective* as an exact match keyword, it'll probably get zero impressions. While many readers might be interested in a book like this, none of them will search for it using that exact phrase.

Instead, *cat cozy mystery* could make for a good exact match keyword—provided your book is a cat cozy, of course. It's short and popular enough to have a good number of exact match searches, while specific enough to be relevant to your book.

What about broader keywords such as *cozy mystery*, you ask? These can sometimes be good exact match targets if your book has a broad enough appeal. Readers searching for these broad keywords aren't looking for a specific book or subgenre, but this doesn't mean that they'll be interested in just any cozy mystery. If yours is in a very specific niche (say *British dog detective paranormal cozy mystery*), then it's unlikely that *cozy mystery* will be a good exact match target.

In summary, I'd reserve exact match targeting for short-tail keywords that either

1. Perfectly describe your book or
2. Have proven to work well as search terms in the past.

But how do you find these high-performing search terms in the first place? Through phrase and broad match campaigns.

Broad match in particular is useful for targeting a wide array of search topics without having to come up with every potential way a reader could be searching for them. To go back to our cat cozy author, cat cozy would be a great broad match keyword, as it would cover pretty much any search readers could make for books like this: *cozy cat mystery, cat cozies, cozy mysteries with cats, cozy mystery with cat protagonist*.

Finally, phrase match type is perfect for targeting author and product names (that is, book titles), because they allow you to capture all searches like [author name] + [book title] or [author name] + [series title]. For example, here's a phrase match campaign I'm running for *How to Market a Book* targeting author names:

Customer search term ⊖	Added as	Keywords ⊖	▾ Clicks	CTR ⊖	Spend ⊖	CPC ⊖
Total: 10			12	10.26%	$11.67	$0.97
joanna penn books	-	joanna penn Phrase Bid $1.09	3	17.65%	$3.15	$1.05
joanna penn	Keyword	joanna penn Phrase Bid $1.09	2	3.85%	$2.02	$1.01
angela ackerman	Keyword	angela ackerman Phrase Bid $1.01	1	7.69%	$0.95	$0.95
chris fox 5000	-	chris fox Phrase Bid $1.01	1	50.00%	$0.90	$0.90
chris fox books	-	chris fox Phrase Bid $1.01	1	100.00%	$0.94	$0.94
jeff goins books	-	jeff goins Phrase Bid $1.01	1	25.00%	$0.86	$0.86
joanna penn books for writers	-	joanna penn Phrase Bid $1.09	1	50.00%	$1.04	$1.04
k. m. weiland	Keyword	k. m. weiland Phrase Bid $1.01	1	6.25%	$0.90	$0.90
rob eagar books	-	rob eagar Phrase Bid $1.01	1	10.00%	$0.91	$0.91

Customer search terms for a phrase match campaign targeting author names.

As you can see, the phrase match targeting covers relevant author or book-related search terms.

If you find a specific search term that seems to perform particularly well, then that is one you can target as an exact match, with a slightly higher bid, to try to win as many impressions for it as possible.

Bidding and match type hierarchy

As you add more keywords across your campaigns and play with the different match types, it's inevitable that you'll create some overlap. In such cases, what happens?

For example, let's say you have a campaign targeting *how to market a book* as a phrase match, and another with *how to market a book ricardo fayet* as an exact match. If a reader searches for the latter, how does Amazon decide which ad to serve? It's simple, they'll just go to the highest bidder. If you're using a higher bid for the exact match, then Amazon will prioritize that one—and vice versa.

As a result, if you want your exact match targets to deliver impressions and clicks, you need to make sure that they're not overlapping internally with other phrase or broad match targets. If they do, make sure they use higher bids—otherwise, you might as well not bother having that exact match keyword in there.

To recap, here's my recommended strategy for using match types efficiently:

1. Start with broad and phrase match campaigns.
2. After a few weeks, dig into their search terms and identify any search terms that are performing particularly well.
3. Add these top-performing search terms as exact match keywords, with a higher bid.

In other words, you use phrase and broad match to scout for search terms with a broad scope, and then double-down on the most successful ones with exact match. This will ensure that you don't miss anything and that you're as competitive as possible for the search terms that really matter to you.

2. Product targeting

While keyword targeting allows you to place your Sponsored Products ads on both search results and product pages, Product targeting can only get you onto—you guessed it—product pages.

The idea is simple: instead of telling Amazon to target searches/products based on a keyword, you tell Amazon the exact product you want to target. In that sense, it's a bit like exact match, but for products. You do so by either searching for the products you want to target or entering their ASINs directly.

As such, it's a great precise targeting tool to get your ads to show up on the product pages most relevant to yours—and, similarly, to exact matches, to double-down on what works.

For example, let's say that *harry potter print* as a keyword is working well to promote your print book. You might want to create a specific campaign to target the ASINs of the print editions of all the books in the Harry Potter series.

Here again, you'll want to set higher bids for these ASIN targets than the one you used for *harry potter print*, as that keyword is already getting you onto these product pages. If you set a lower bid, the campaign probably won't even deliver.

Another simple trick, which I briefly mentioned in the last chapter, is to monitor your automatic targeting campaigns to see which products/ASINs Amazon is targeting, extract the profitable ones, and add them to your manual product targeting campaigns.

3. Category targeting

Category targeting is technically part of product targeting. When you set up a campaign or ad group, Amazon will prompt you to choose between keyword targeting and product targeting, and you'll have to choose the latter to get access to categories.

If ASIN targeting is a precise targeting strategy, category targeting is very much "spray and pray." Technically, an ad targeting a category is eligible to show up on product pages of any book in that category. This doesn't mean that it will though. Instead, Amazon will look for the most relevant product targets in that category (that is, the books that it identifies as closest to yours).

The main issue with category targeting is that most categories on Amazon are heavily "polluted," meaning they feature books that don't really have anything to do with that category. Authors and publishers are allowed to list each of their products in up to ten different categories—and many of them equate more categories to more exposure (which isn't really true, but that's another subject). As a result, it's hard to find a category on the Store that isn't riddled with books that don't realistically belong in it.

Because of this, category targeting generally isn't as effective from an ROI perspective as keyword or individual product targeting, since Amazon ends up placing your ads on a bunch of product pages that are not always that relevant.

One way to narrow your targeting a bit, or at least avoid targeting specific books that you know are irrelevant, is to add negative products to the campaign. Those will work just like negative keywords and exclude the products from the campaign's targeting. But excluding every single product that doesn't belong in a category would take an insane amount of time, which would be better invested in finding individual books to target through their ASINs directly.

Another option is to use the Refine feature before adding the category. This lets you restrict your targeting to products within a certain price range, or with a certain review average. But considering that 90 percent of books have an average of 4 stars or above, and are all generally within the same price range, this refining tool isn't all that helpful.

This is not to say that you should disregard category targeting directly. While I probably wouldn't start with it if you're on a tight budget, I do think it's a good way to scale your spend and identify product targets that you might not have thought of on your own—the same way you can use auto-targeting to find new search terms to target.

In the "Search terms" tab of a category campaign, Amazon will show all the "Matched products" where your ads received at least one click, as well as the campaign they're associated with. You can order the list by Orders, ACOS, or Sales and immediately identify the best-performing products that Amazon has targeted in each category.

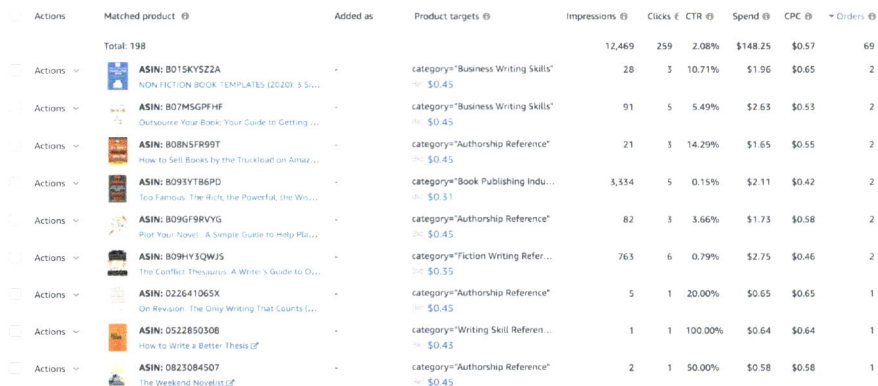

Matched products of a category targeting campaign.

Inversely, this is also a good way to spot the low-performing Matched products and potentially add them as negative products. For example, let's say I want to negate products who have generated 5+ clicks but no orders. I can filter the results by "Clicks > 5," check the boxes of all the products that have had zero orders, and "Add as negative product target."

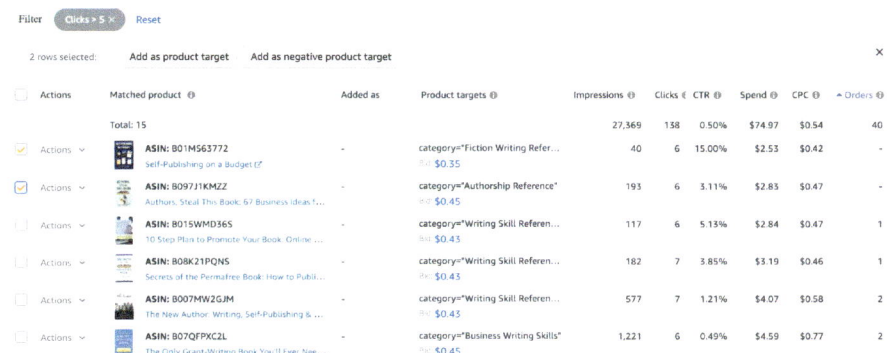

Weed out low-performing Matched products to add as a negative targets.

You can see that you also have the option of adding ASINs as product targets to the campaign. But while you can indeed have both product and category targets within the same campaign, this is not something I recommend. I'll explain why in the next chapters.

III

Testing the waters

So far, we've created some automatic targeting campaigns and looked into the different manual targeting options available. The next step is to find targets for your first manual targeting campaigns and learn how to properly test them.

9

Finding your first targets

Finding keywords and products to target in manual campaigns is my favorite part of Amazon Advertising because it's the only one that requires a tad of creativity—and creativity is what authors are known for, right?

In this chapter, I'll share some ideas for how to come up with these targets—and by targets I mean both keywords (which can be a search phrase, a book title, an author name) or products (ASINs).

What you should keep in mind above all, though, is that these are just ideas. There are many different ways you can go about finding good targets for your campaigns, so let your creativity run wild and don't follow my suggestions to the letter.

1. Also Boughts

This is one of the most popular ways of finding products and product keywords (such as author names, book titles, series titles) to target.

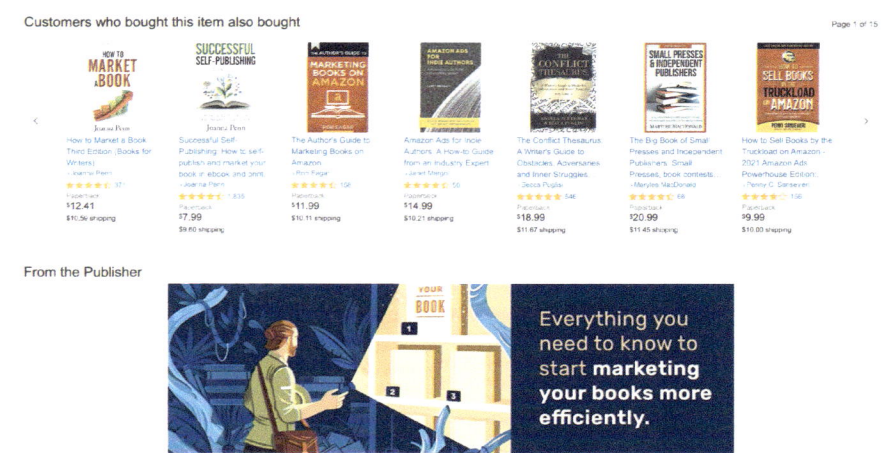

"Also Bought" products for How to Market a Book: Overperform in a Crowded Market.

The idea is simple: you scroll down the "Customers who bought this item also bought" section of your book's page and make a note of all the books that Amazon displays there. In particular, you'll want to gather the following formation for each product and build a spreadsheet with these elements:

· The book title
· The series title (if applicable)
· The author name
· The ASINs (of both the Kindle and print editions)

> Note: To save yourself some time, make sure to exclude all elements of punctuation when copying book titles to your spreadsheet, as well as overly long subtitles or series info like "Book 1 in the Cockier Spaniel Series." This will allow you to have a clean keyword list that you can directly import into Amazon.

Book Title	Series Title	Author Name	ASIN
Successful Self-Publishing		Joanna Penn	1912105853
How To Make A Living With Your Writing	Books for Writers	Joanna Penn	1514756633
How To Write Non-Fiction	Books for Writers	Joanna Penn	1912105780
Business for Authors	Books for Writers	Joanna Penn	150107833X
Self-Publisher's Legal Handbook		Helen Sedwick	0988302195
Your First 1000 Copies		Tim Grahl	1645010317
14 Steps to Self-Publishing a Book		Mike Kowis	0997994657
The Author's Guide to Marketing Books on Amazon	The Author's Guide	Rob Eagar	1729478492
The Successful Author Mindset		Joanna Penn	1533676807
Learn how to turn Amazon into your 24/7 sales machine	How to Sell Books by the Truckload on Amazon	Penny C. Sansevieri	1695420799
The Nonfiction Book Publishing Plan		Stephanie Chandler Karl W. Palachuk	1949642003
Audio For Authors	Books for Writers	Joanna Penn	1913321215
Your Author Business Plan	Books for Writers	Joanna Penn	1913321541
How To Self-Publish A Children's Book	How To Write For Children Series	Yvonne Jones	0997025492
Productivity For Authors:	Books for Writers	Joanna Penn	1913321139
#1 Best Seller		Bryan W. Heathman	1641462876
The 1-Page Marketing Plan		Allan Dib	1989025013
Writer's Market 2020: The Most Trusted Guide to Getting Published	Market	Robert Lee Brewer	1440301220
Romancing the Beat	How to Write Kissing Books	Gwen Hayes	1530838614

Example of a keyword spreadsheet for Also Boughts.

Why are Also Boughts such a great way to find good product targets? Because these are the books that customers who bought your book also bought. So readers who are actively searching for those books, or checking them out, are statistically likely to be interested in your book as well.

In other words, these are not just books that you think are close comparable titles, they're books that Amazon's internal data on customer purchases has identified as closest to your book in readers' tastes.

Sometimes, you'll see a "Customers who read this item also read" section instead of, or on top of, the usual Also Boughts section. These are ideal targets as well since they include page reads on top of purchases, which is particularly useful for finding solid book targets that are in Kindle Unlimited.

Naturally, there are caveats to all this, and cases in which a book's Also Boughts won't make for sensible Amazon Advertising targets. The main one is if your Also Boughts are "polluted."

I have a whole chapter on the risks of Also Boughts pollution in *How to Market a Book: Overperform in a Crowded Market* (which is still free on all retailers, by the way). If you're not familiar with these risks, I highly recommend you check it out, as this an issue whose impact reaches far beyond Amazon Advertising—and which David Gaughran had also explored in depth on his blog and books.[5]

But in short, if you promote your book to the wrong readers (meaning readers not in your genre/niche) and manage to get them to buy it regardless (maybe because it's deeply discounted or free), then your Also Boughts section is going to populate with the books that these readers have recently purchased. And since these readers don't usually read in your genre, these Also Boughts will have nothing to do with your book—hence the pollution.

While reverting a situation like this ("cleaning out" your Also Boughts) is difficult, identifying the problem is easy: just browse through your Also Boughts section and see whether the books in there are similar to yours (in terms of covers, titles, and other factors).

If they aren't, then simply don't add those to your Amazon Ads targets spreadsheet.

2. Series Also Boughts

If you're advertising a series (congratulations, your odds on making a positive return on your ads just increased significantly), then you can take Also Boughts targeting to the next level.

For example, if you're looking for super relevant targets, you could compile the Also Boughts of not just book one in your series, but books two, three, four, and so on.

These are books that only true fans of your series will get to, so their Also Boughts will be all the more relevant. More importantly, book one is often the title that you'll promote the most heavily, with price discounts, free promotions, Facebook Ads, and more. So book one Also Boughts are much more at risk of being polluted than those of the subsequent books in the series.

The opportunities don't stop there though. Not only can you target the ASINs of your books' Also Boughts, Amazon also has individual ASINs for

---

[5]   David Gaughran's excellent article on Amazon Also Boughts: https://davidgaughran.com/also-boughts-amazon-recommendations/

series.

If you navigate to a series page, you'll find that ASIN in the URL of the page. And if you scroll down to the bottom of the page, you'll find a Series Also Boughts section, featuring other series that readers of yours have also read.

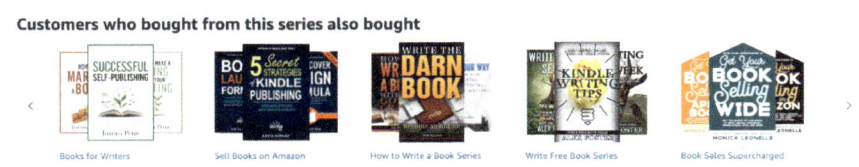

Amazon displays Series Also Boughts at the bottom of series pages.

You can note the series titles, author names, and series ASINs of all these, which will make for excellent targets for a Sponsored Brands campaign, for example.

3. Also Bought Authors

While the Also Boughts ideas are a strategic way to find close comp authors, there's an even simpler way to find your most closely related authors.

If you go to your Amazon Author page (if you don't have one, set it up via Author Central),[6] you'll find a section on the left titled "Customers also bought items by," which I like to abbreviate as "Also Bought Authors."

Similarly to Also Boughts, these are authors that Amazon has identified as most closely related to you based on customer purchases—in other words, they're the authors with whom you share the biggest reader base on Amazon.

---

[6] Article on setting up your Amazon Author Page via Author Central: https://blog.reedsy.com/amazon-author-central/

Customers Also Bought Items By section on my Amazon author page.

I imagine you'll already be familiar with several of these authors already, but you might find new ones there you hadn't thought of targeting.

In any case, I recommend clicking on each author's name to visit their author page and double-check that their books are indeed relevant to yours. It's also a solid way to check whether they write across different genres, in which case you might want to make a note of the books they authored that are not in your genre so you can add those as negative targets.

While Amazon only features a maximum of eighteen Also Bought Authors on any given author page, there is a simple way to find more: just click through to the pages of your Also Bought Authors and note *their* Also Bought Authors (after double-checking that these are equally relevant).

This is a quick and simple way to gather a working list of close comp authors. You won't have hundreds of them, but what they'll lack in numbers, they'll make up for in relevance.

4. Category lists

If you want numbers rather than relevance, then category lists are for you.

Again, the idea is simple: targeting the top books and authors in your main category. To do so, just head to Amazon's Best Seller lists—whether for ebooks or all books, depending on what you want to advertise—and then navigate through the sidebar to the best seller list in your category.

Alternatively, search for "Kindle bestsellers in [category]" or "Amazon best sellers in [category]" on Google, and click on the first result.

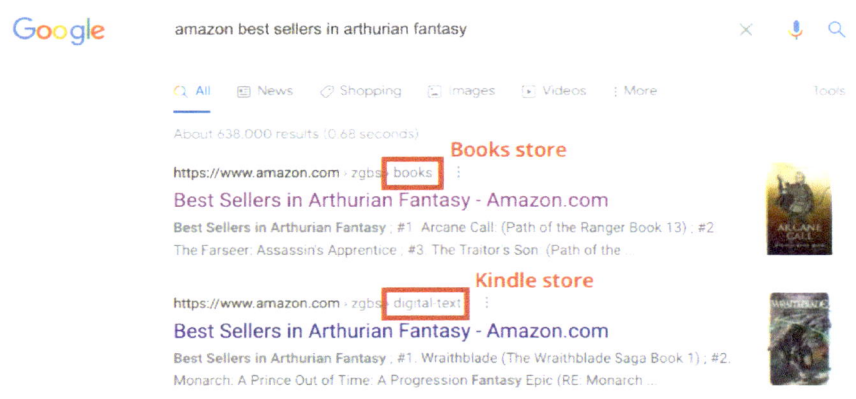

How to find Amazon best sellers with a Google search.

There, simply note down the titles, series, and author names of all the top 100 books in your category. Since these are best sellers, they will likely be popular targets, so you might have to bid higher to get impressions on such a campaign. On the other hand, if you manage to find one that converts well for you, it should lead to a healthy number of sales.

Similar to Also Boughts (and even more so), categories are often subject to pollution. Since publishers can list their books in up to ten different categories, rare is the Amazon category that only features books that are a natural fit for the category.

Depending on how polluted the top 100 list in your category is, you might want to manually exclude any books whose covers or titles don't look like they would draw in the same readers as yours. In some cases (yes, I'm referring to you, dear Dragons & Mythical Creatures category), that might mean excluding a lot of romance books, but that's a necessary extra step.

In a similar vein, another obvious but equally relevant list of books to target is the Hot New Releases list in your category. You'll find a link to it right on the top 100 best sellers page, usually under the top 6.

There will be some overlap between New Releases and Top 100 Best Sellers, but New Releases will also contain less obvious (and therefore less competitive) product targets that are trending right now because they were recently released.

This is also a way to find high-selling books that are still on preorder and can make for great targets to advertise your own preorder against.

Since a book is considered a new release for only the first thirty days after launch, Hot New Releases lists change constantly. Keep an eye on them and refresh your targets.

5. Goodreads/Listopia lists

While Amazon should be your main playground for target research, it sometimes pays off to look for good keywords and products to target outside of the Amazon realm.

One likely place is Listopia on Goodreads, which is famous for user-generated lists of books.

As we saw, the only lists of books you can find on Amazon are based on current top sellers, and in predefined, often polluted, categories. On Goodreads, however, you can find a wealth of user-generated lists for any subgenre, theme, character type, or other measure.

Writing a police procedural with a strong female lead? Here's a list for you:

Listopia

Female Detective Series

Please only add first-in-series books from series where the protagonist is a female detective or investigator of some type. Armchair detectives, mysteries, and thrillers are all acceptable genres.

All Votes   Add Books To This List

1. **The Girl with the Dragon Tattoo (Millennium, #1)**
by Stieg Larsson
★★★★½ 4.15 avg rating — 2,902,579 ratings
score: 815, and 9 people voted

Want to Read
Rate this book

2. **Murder at the Vicarage (Miss Marple, #1)**
by Agatha Christie
★★★★½ 4.06 avg rating — 168,736 ratings
score: 792, and 8 people voted

Want to Read
Rate this book

3. **The No. 1 Ladies' Detective Agency (No. 1 Ladies' Detective Agency #1)**
by Alexander McCall Smith (Goodreads Author)
★★★★½ 3.80 avg rating — 250,388 ratings
score: 590, and 6 people voted

Want to Read
Rate this book

4. **Now You See Me (Lacey Flint, #1)**
by Sharon J. Bolton (Goodreads Author)
★★★★½ 4.03 avg rating — 21,065 ratings
score: 587, and 6 people voted

Want to Read
Rate this book

4. **The Secret of the Old Clock (Nancy Drew Mystery Stories, #1)**
by Carolyn Keene
★★★★½ 3.98 avg rating — 72,905 ratings
score: 587, and 6 people voted

Want to Read
Rate this book

Listopia (Goodreads) list of Female Detective Series.

Listopia lists are user-generated and ordered based on member votes, so you can be confident that all the books featured on the top pages will not only be relevant to the theme at hand, but also popular enough to have some search volume on Amazon.

Now, let's say you're writing a grimdark fantasy with a dark elf protagonist. I couldn't find a Listopia list for that, but you can still rely on Goodreads tags to find some comps:

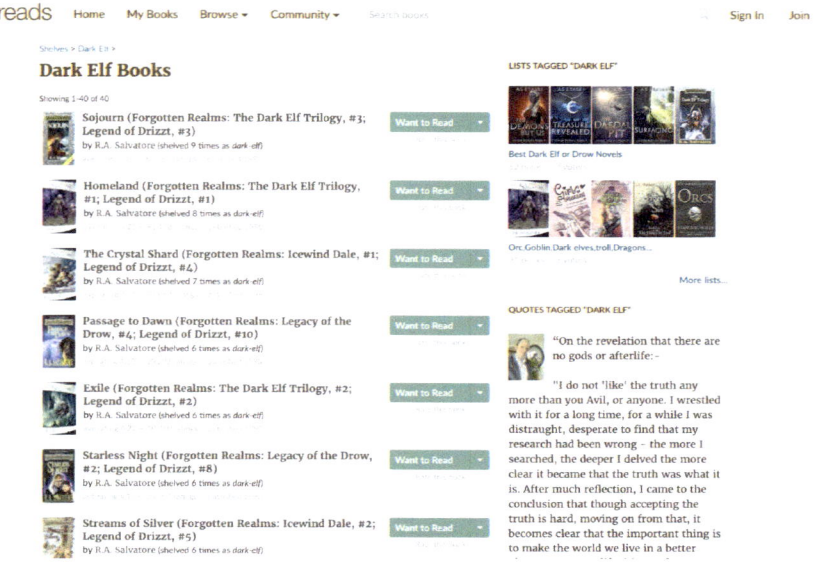

Goodreads tag list of Dark Elf Books.

This is a list of all the books and series that have been tagged with "dark elf" by Goodreads members. As you can see, it only featured forty books, because tags aren't that widely used on Goodreads, but it's better than nothing.

Since both Listopia and tags lists are user-generated, they won't be perfect. Not all the books they feature will be popular, or 100 percent relevant, and they probably omit other perfectly good books too. But they can still help you find targets that you wouldn't have thought of on your own.

Of course, these aren't the only two websites with lists. We have plenty of book lists on our Reedsy Discovery blog[7] as well, for example. So do BookBub's, or BookRiot's blogs. In all cases, your best bet for finding useful lists is as simple as running a Google search.

---

[7]   The Reedsy Discovery blog, with hundreds of lists of books: https://reedsy.com/discovery/blog/

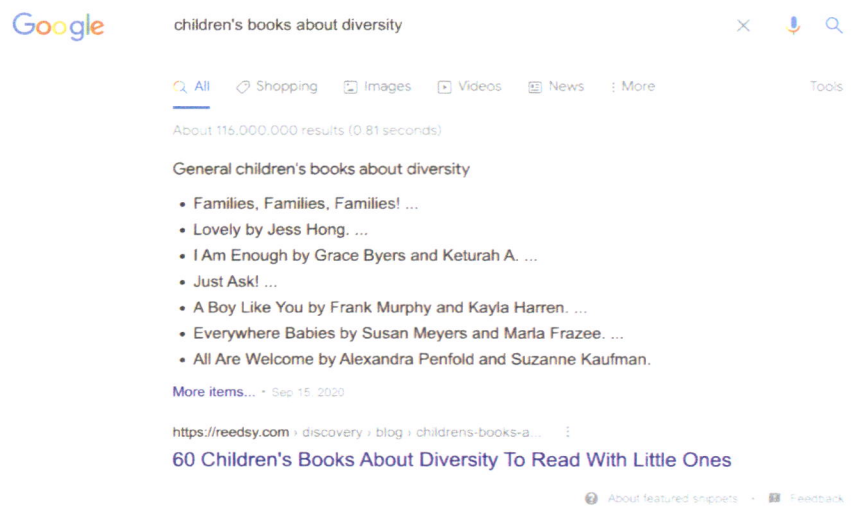

Searching on Google for "children's books about diversity"

6. Search keywords

So far I've focused on generating book-related targets for such elements as book titles, series titles, author names, and ASINs. These work well to reach readers while they search for, or browse through, books similar to yours.

But what about readers who're looking for a book in your genre/niche, yet don't have a particular title in mind? That's where search keywords come in.

Search keywords are essentially phrases that can be used to describe a book like yours or a book in your niche.

They can be related

- to your genre: for example, *urban fantasy books* or
- to your characters: for example, *badass female protagonist* or
- to your niche: for example, *19th century poetry* or
- to your theme: for example, *addiction recovery*—you get the idea.

These keywords will mostly get you search result placements (rather than product page ones), and as such will usually be more costly than book-related keywords. In many cases, however, they can be a lot more powerful and effective as well.

This is especially true for nonfiction reference books on specific topics. For example, if you've written a how-to book on Iyengar Yoga, it'll probably be more effective, and scalable, to target keywords like *iyengar yoga*, *iyengar yoga for beginners*, or *iyengar yoga for motherhood*.

Now, how can you come up with these keywords? There are several ways, but they all start with your brain. Think about your book and how you would describe it from a reader's perspective. Think about how you, as a reader, would search for books like yours on Amazon. Just by putting yourself in your prospective readers' shoes, you can already come up with a number of search keywords to test.

These first keywords can then be used as seeds to grow other search terms, with just a bit of sun and water and the following tools and tricks.

Amazon search bar auto-complete

One of the simplest ways to expand your search keyword list is to plug your seed keywords in Amazon's search bar and check the auto-complete options.

Amazon suggest auto-complete terms for iyengar.

Since the auto-complete only completes your searches, this technique won't help you find radically different keywords, but rather phrase match variations of your existing ones, which you can target as phrase or exact matches with slightly higher bids.

Amazon Advertising auto-complete

You can do the same thing within Amazon Advertising directly. When you use the enter list option for adding keywords, you'll see Amazon also offers auto-complete ideas as soon as you type or paste in a keyword.

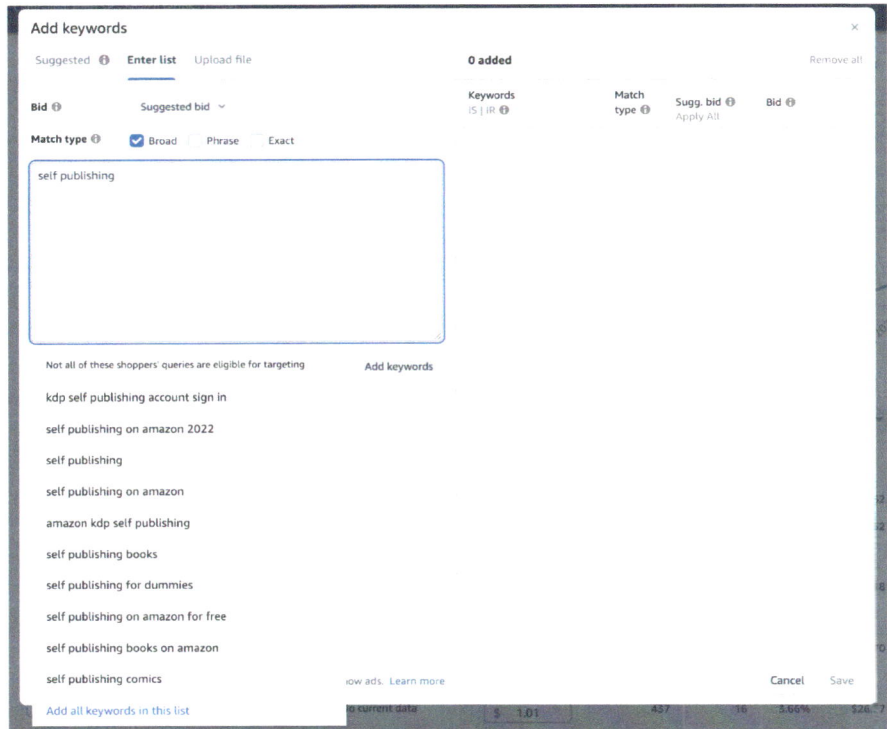

Amazon Advertising auto-complete suggestions for self publishing.

Google keyword planner

Here we start venturing into the world of keyword tools. Despite not being perfectly suited for Amazon, Google's own keyword research tool offers a massive advantage: it's free.

It does require you to create a Google Ads account and add your credit card—but you don't need to set up any Google Ads campaigns nor spend any money to get access to the Keyword Planner. Instead, you'll find it in the Tools and Settings section of your Google Ads account.

Once in the Keyword Planner, select the Discover new keywords option, and plug in one of your seed keywords. Google will then return a list of keyword ideas related to your seed keyword and ordered by search volume:

Keyword (by relevance)	Avg. monthly searches	Three month change	YoY change	Competition
Keywords that you provided				
viking romance	140	0%	+21%	High
Keyword ideas				
viking romance novels	480	+23%	+51%	High
viking romance books	140	+24%	+133%	High
best viking romance books	50	+29%	-80%	High
seven viking romances	20	-33%	0%	Medium
hot viking romance novels	20	0%	0%	High
viking time travel romance books	20	+67%	+150%	High
viking historical romance	30	0%	0%	High
best viking romance novels	10	+50%	+50%	High
viking fiction romance	20	0%	+100%	High
viking gay romance	10	0%	+∞	Low

Discovering new keywords using the Google Ads Keyword Planner.

One cool feature is that, on top of the monthly search volume data, you get some insights on current trends. For example, the screenshot shows that the interest in *viking time travel romance books* has more than doubled over the past year—and that the searches for *viking romance* keywords overall have grown a lot over the past few months. Maybe I should start a new pen name.

Of course, there's a trick here: this is Google's data, not Amazon's. It might be that searches for *viking romance* have grown on Google since last year, but that sales in the genre have actually dwindled on Amazon. It's unlikely, but it's possible.

In any case, regardless of whether the data are right or not, you can use the Keyword Planner to find a bunch of additional keyword phrases to add to your list.

> Note: When using Google's Keyword Planner from outside of the US, make sure to add the United States as a location for the search data, as that is the biggest market for English-speaking books.

Amazon Automatic Suggestions

Another way to find keyword and product ideas to add to your targeting mix is to leverage Amazon Advertising's automatic suggestions.

When setting up a new manual campaign, or when adding keywords to an existing one, Amazon will prompt you to add their suggested ones:

Add keywords				×

Suggested ⓘ Enter list Upload file

0 added   Remove all

Bid ⓘ   Suggested bid ˅

Keywords

Match type ⓘ   Sugg. bid ⓘ   Bid ⓘ
Apply All

Filter by ⓘ   ✓ Broad   ✓ Phrase   ✓ Exact

Keywords	Match type ⓘ	Sugg. bid ⓘ	Add all
marketing free books	Broad	$1.39	Add
	Exact	-	Add
book marketing authors	Broad	$3.97	Add
	Phrase	$3.97	Add
	Exact	$3.97	Add
how market your book	Broad	$3.07	Add
	Exact	$1.15	Add
free writing book	Broad	$1.09	Add
	Phrase	$1.25	Add
	Exact	-	Add
joanna penn	Broad	$0.83	Add
	Phrase	$0.83	Add
	Exact	$1.83	Add
ricardo fayet	Broad	$1.50	Add
	Exact	-	Add
bookbub ads	Broad	$2.00	Add
	Exact	$2.00	Add
facebook ads authors	Broad	$0.71	Add
	Phrase	$0.71	Add
	Exact	$0.71	Add
how advertise amazon	Broad	-	Add
	Phrase	-	Add

Amazon suggests keywords for a manual campaign.

These suggestions are compiled by Amazon based on the products you're advertising (through their metadata, categories, and Also Boughts) and on the performance of related search terms and products across your account.

In other words, Amazon might be recommending me to add *facebook ads authors* because that is present somewhere in my book's metadata (title, product description, keywords, categories, or elsewhere), or because search terms around Facebook Ads have proven to work well previously in campaigns advertising this same book.

As you can see, Amazon's keyword suggestions also come with a match type and, sometimes, a suggested bid. While I generally tend to ignore recommended bids, it's important to pay attention to the match type.

In the example, Amazon is recommending that I add *marketing free books* as a broad and an exact match keyword to the campaign. Why not a phrase match as well? Because I already have that keyword as a phrase match. In other words, Amazon is recommending that I add broad and exact match types for this keyword—and the same goes for the *ricardo fayet*, *how market your book*, or *bookbub ads* suggestions.

If you're like me and you like keeping match types separate across ad groups, then you can simply uncheck the boxes (in the filter area) for the two match type suggestions you're not interested in.

What about product or category targeting campaigns? These also come with their own Amazon automatic suggestions, which are also compiled based on your product information and your campaigns' historical performance.

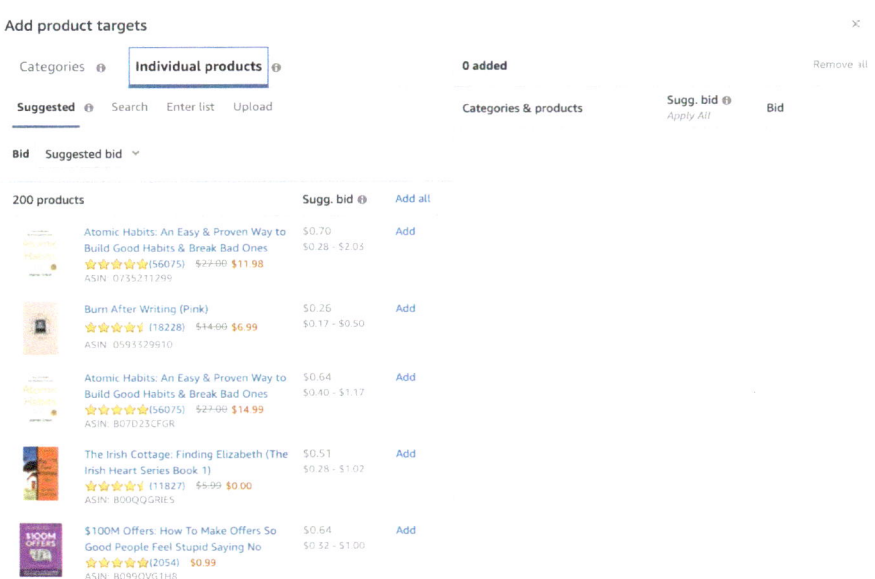

Amazon suggests products for a manual targeting campaign.

Now comes the million-dollar question: how relevant are these automatic suggestions?

As you can see in the screenshot, it's generally a mixed bunch. While *Atomic Habits* and *$100M Offers* could be relevant targets for me, *Burn After*

Writing makes a lot less sense, and *The Irish Cottage*, a fiction first-in-series, even less.

So more often than not, you'll have to sift through these automatic suggestions and separate the wheat from the chaff, based on how relevant these instinctively feel.

One positive note is that Amazon's auto-suggestions tend to get better over time, both in terms of quality (relevance of the suggestions) and quantity. This is because the more time (and money) you spend advertising your books on Amazon, the more data Amazon will gather, and the better informed their suggestions will be.

Because of this, I never really pay attention to auto-suggestions when first setting up ads for a new author or pen name: Amazon will have zero data about them, so their recommendations will be generic (title, author name, etc) or misinformed.

Once I've had a few campaigns running for a few months, though, I make a habit of regularly checking the auto-recommendations across all campaigns. It's a great way to make sure you haven't missed anything obvious, spot new products you hadn't thought about, or just generally scale your targeting while keeping it relevant.

Auto-campaigns and search term reports

I mentioned this in the previous chapter on automatic targeting, but auto-campaigns can also help you find new keywords and products to target in your manual targeting campaigns.

For that, just make sure to establish a routine of checking the search terms of your auto-campaigns every once in a while—or, even better, schedule a monthly search terms report from the Reports section of your dashboard, and then scour through it to identify winning search terms.

> Remember: I created a free Google Sheet (Sponsored Products Search Term Aggregator) to automatically aggregate your search

term data—you'll find a link to it in the Bonus Resources. Make sure to use it as the sixty-five-day lookback window limit on these will otherwise make it hard to find search terms or products that produced any meaningful results.

7. Paid Amazon keyword and product research tools

As you can see, there are dozens of different ways to find hundreds, or even thousands, of potential book titles, author names, ASINs, or search terms to target and test in your Amazon Advertising campaigns.

What all these tactics have in common is that they are free and slightly time-intensive. And as with most things in life that are free and time-intensive, there is an alternative: paying someone—or in this case, using a tool—to do it for you.

Publisher Rocket

If you've read *How to Market a Book: Overperform in a Crowded Market*, you'll already be familiar with Publisher Rocket.

It's a paid tool (one-time $97 fee) that helps authors carry out keyword and category research, both for metadata and Amazon Advertising purposes.

One of its flagship features is AMS Keyword Search, which I like to use to expand my list of search keywords. The functionality is simple: you just plug in your seed keyword, select whether it's for a Kindle book, audiobook, or print, and let Publisher Rocket come up with a list of potential keywords to target.

For example, here are the results for the *portal fantasy* seed keyword:

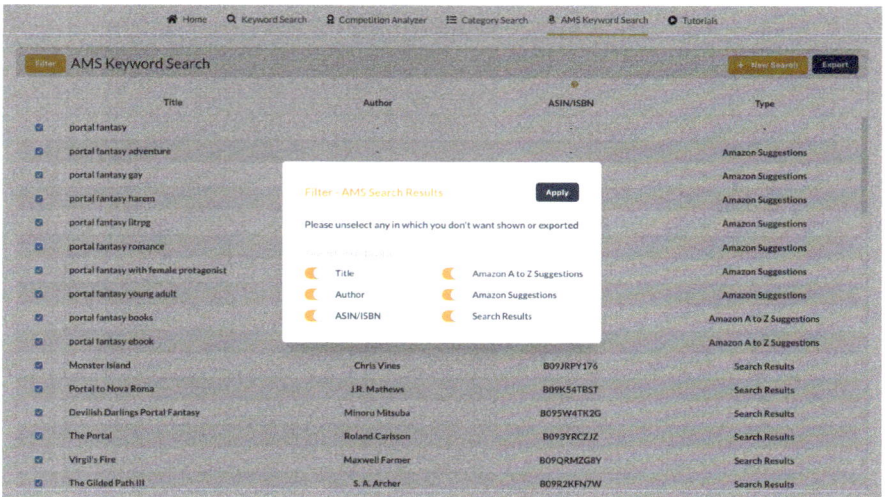

Title	Author	ASIN/ISBN	Type
portal fantasy			
portal fantasy adventure			Amazon Suggestions
portal fantasy gay			Amazon Suggestions
portal fantasy harem			Amazon Suggestions
portal fantasy litrpg			Amazon Suggestions
portal fantasy romance			Amazon Suggestions
portal fantasy with female protagonist			Amazon Suggestions
portal fantasy young adult			Amazon Suggestions
portal fantasy books			Amazon A to Z Suggestions
portal fantasy ebook			Amazon A to Z Suggestions
Monster Island	Chris Vines	B09JRPY176	Search Results
Portal to Nova Roma	J.R. Mathews	B09K54TBST	Search Results
Devilish Darlings Portal Fantasy	Minoru Mitsuba	B095W4TK2G	Search Results
The Portal	Roland Carlsson	B093YRCZJZ	Search Results
Virgil's Fire	Maxwell Farmer	B09QRMZG8Y	Search Results
The Gilded Path III	S. A. Archer	B09R2KFN7W	Search Results

Publisher Rocket can generate additional keywords from a seed keyword.

As you can see, the results are a mix of Amazon auto-complete suggestions (search terms) as well as search results (books).

The auto-complete suggestions are gathered by Publisher Rocket in much the same way that you would gather them manually.

The search results are the books that Amazon displays when you search for the seed keyword in the market you selected (currently, the US, UK, and German markets are available on Publisher Rocket).

So these are targets that you could gather manually yourself—it would just take a lot more of your time. The other advantage with Publisher Rocket is that you can filter the results. For example, if you want search terms only, you can uncheck everything except Amazon Suggestions and Amazon A to Z Suggestions. If you want to build a list of ASINs for product targeting, you can uncheck everything except ASIN/ISBN. Publisher Rocket can help you build a list of targets, in bulk, in a minimum amount of time.

MerchantWords and Helium 10

As you know, Amazon is not just a book retailer, it is the everything store. As such, authors are far from the only advertisers, and the best tools for Amazon Advertising are found not in the publishing world, but in the broader world of Amazon vendor/seller tools.

Two of the most famous Amazon keyword research tools are Merchant-Words and Helium 10. Because they're meant for professional advertisers (such as the big brands and agencies), they're not cheap. That said, they are definitely your best bet to scale and automate your keyword research and, in particular, to expand and diversify your list of search keywords.

They work in a similar way to Publisher Rocket: you plug in a seed keyword (or ASIN) and these programs return a bunch of related keyword ideas, with search and competitor data for each one. However, their results tend to be more numerous and varied, and their data more accurate than what you can get through Publisher Rocket.

For example, let's compare what these two tools return for the seed phrase *portal fantasy*:

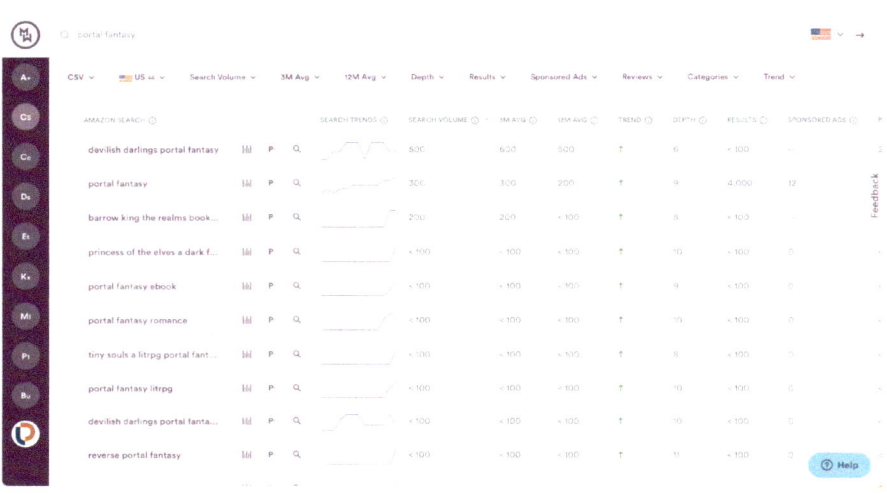

Classic Search results for portal fantasy *in MerchantWords.*

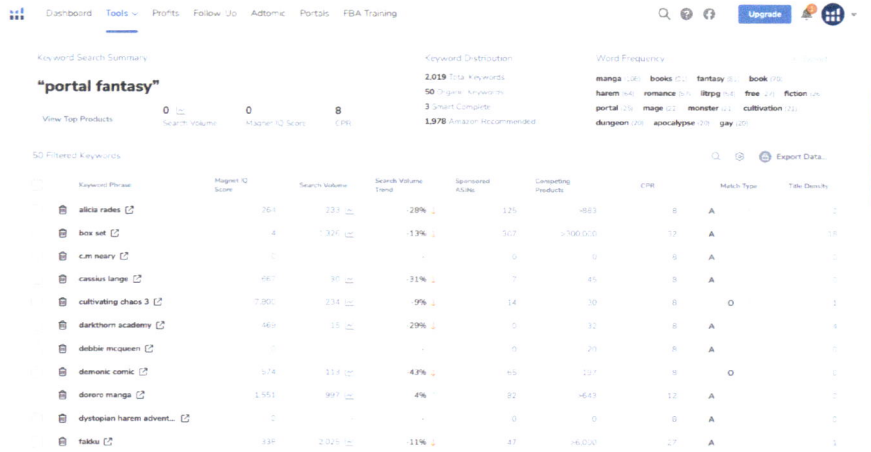

Magnet search results for portal fantasy *in Helium 10.*

As you can see, both Helium 10 and MerchantWords return a mix of search terms, book titles, and author names. At first glance, it looks like MerchantWords' results are a lot more relevant, but their data look less accurate (with most search volumes being <100, which is not particularly helpful to sort them by popularity).

The advantage with such tools is that they include a bunch of additional features on top of the classic "plug in your seed keyword and get more keyword ideas." For example, Helium 10 offers a Cerebro tool where you can use a seed ASIN to reverse-engineer its related keywords. I gave it a try by entering the ASIN for the Kindle edition of my first book:

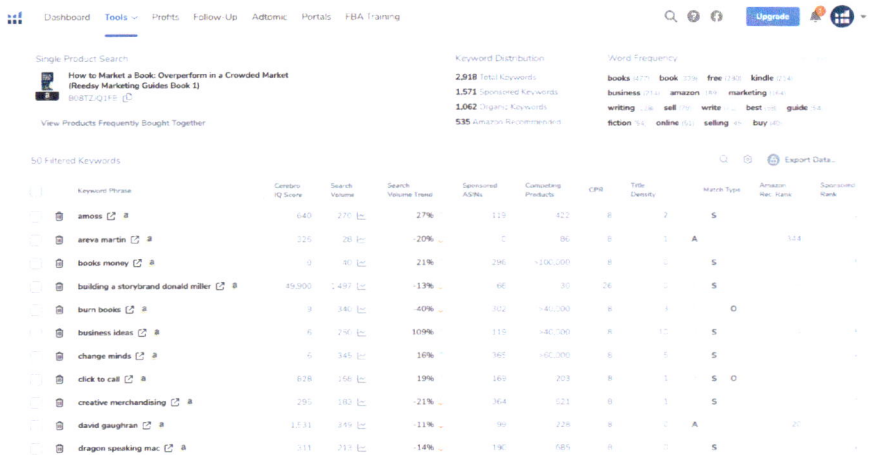

Cerebro results for an ASIN search in Helium 10.

As shown in the example search, the results are somewhat underwhelming, as only a couple of keywords from that list could actually make sense for a book on author marketing—but this could be due to the fact I'm on the free plan, and results are randomized rather than ordered by relevancy.

One feature I found more interesting, which is also available on Helium 10's free plan, is the Black Box, which allows you to view the products frequently bought together for any particular ASIN.

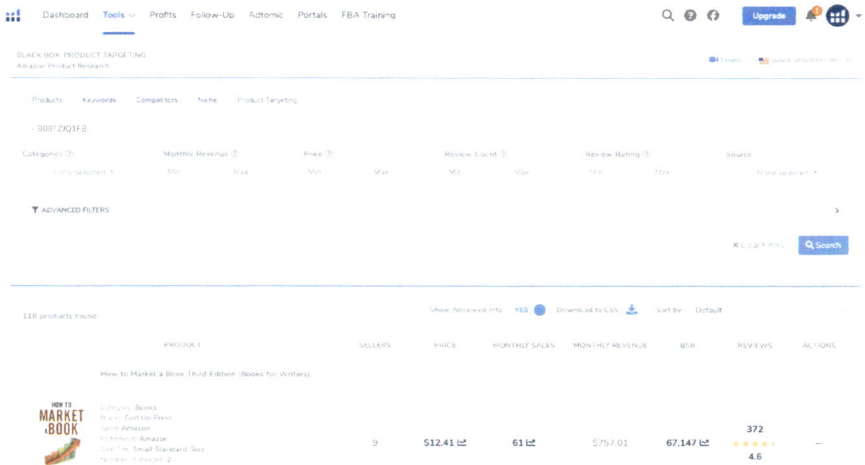

Black Box results for an ASIN search in Helium 10.

This returned a list of 118 books, most of them similar to mine, along with their price and sales trends. Even better, Helium 10 lets you filter these results based on their estimated monthly revenue, price, review count, or review rating.

Overall, I'd say that MerchantWords is a lot better for finding search terms, while Helium 10 has more accurate data and makes it super easy to build a good list of product targets.

One big benefit of Helium 10 is that it offers a free plan that allows you to play around with its features and find some helpful targets without a commitment to pay. MerchantWords, on the other hand, offers no free plan or trial, and the entry-level plan starts at $35 a month.

I've personally used both tools in the past for research purposes, and for building lists of potential Amazon Advertising targets, and they can both be worth it. It depends on your strategy, your level of spend, and your experience with Amazon Advertising. I certainly wouldn't recommend you invest in either if you're just starting out. Instead, use the free methods to build your first lists of targets, and only invest into automated tools once you know what you're doing.

Ahrefs and Semrush

While MerchantWords and Helium 10 are tools specific to Amazon research, there are other, generalist, keyword research tools you can use as well. For example, we use Ahrefs at Reedsy for Google keyword research and SEO, which also offers some (limited) options around Amazon keyword research.

The idea is always the same: you use a seed keyword to find keyword phrases related to it:

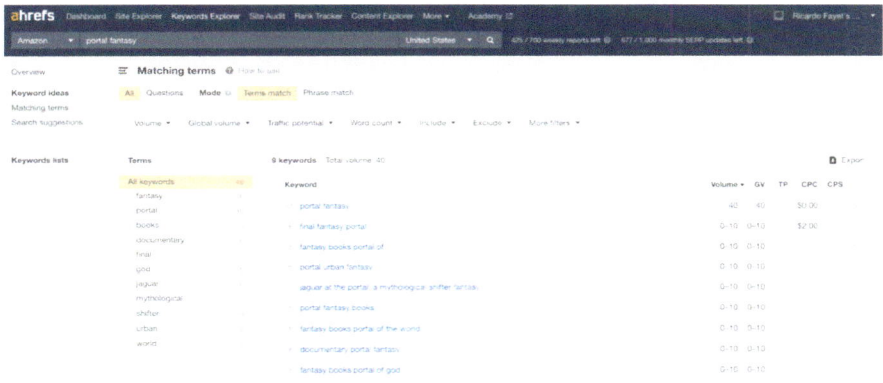

Amazon matching terms for portal fantasy *in Ahrefs.*

As you can see, the results are quite limited, but all relevant, which makes sense considering this is already a niche search. Moreover, I've found that the estimated search volumes that Ahrefs reports for Amazon tend to be more trustworthy than those of other tools.

Similarly, the other popular Google SEO tool Semrush also offers a Keyword Magic Tool for Amazon keyword research, which looks and works in a similar way to others.

So if you have a blog or nonfiction business that you're hoping to grow through SEO, I'd definitely recommend investing in a hybrid keyword research tool like Ahrefs or Semrush to cover both your Google SEO and

Amazon Advertising needs.

Now we've explored all the different ways to build long and varied lists of targets, there is one last step left before setting up the campaigns.

8. Avoid target overlap

As you may remember from the last chapter, you should *absolutely not* put all these keywords and product targets inside the same campaign or ad group. Instead, you want to create different campaigns and ad groups for each type of target—both for organizational and deliverability purposes.

Here's an example of what that targeting could look like.

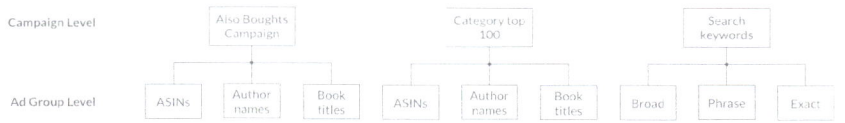

The only downside of this type of structure is that you can end up having quite a bit of overlap in targeting across your campaigns.

For example, let's say you have a campaign target the top 100 in an Amazon category (say Arthurian Fantasy), and another for the top 100 in another, similar category (Sword & Sorcery Fantasy). The two lists will have a huge number of books in common, since books can be in more than one category.

While this is not a huge issue per se—campaigns competing against one another within the same advertising account won't raise the cost per click that much—it can make it harder to judge a specific target's performance. Instead of having all the data in one campaign, it'll be split across several and you will need to manually aggregate it.

There are two simple ways to avoid this, though, and both rely on a section of the Amazon Advertising dashboard that I haven't touched on so far: the Targeting tab.

The Targeting section was only introduced in 2021, so few authors use it, and yet it can be a huge time saver when monitoring and optimizing your campaigns. It basically gathers all your targets (keywords, products, and categories) across all your different campaigns, in one single place.

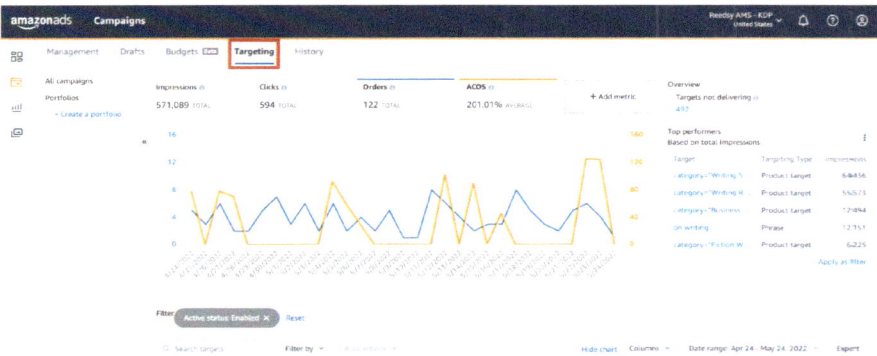

The Targeting tab in the Amazon Advertising dashboard.

Once there, you can filter the list of targets by Active status = Enabled, and order that list by keyword name (alphabetically). Then, just make your way down to spot all the keywords that are duplicated across campaigns/ad groups.

You can choose to pause any duplicate targets directly from the Targeting tab, in which case I recommend keeping the one that has the highest amount of data (clicks).

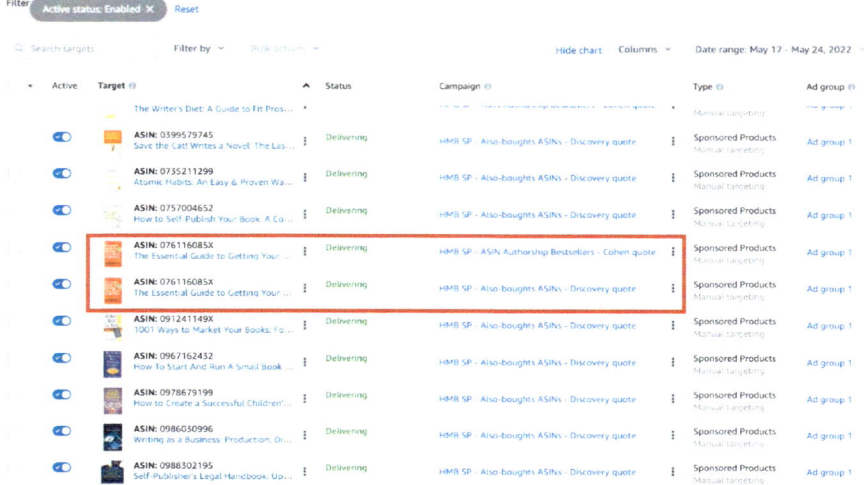

Identifying a duplicated target across two different campaigns.

While this only lets you spot existing duplicates in your Amazon Advertising dashboard, you can also leverage the Targeting tab to avoid introducing new duplicates when creating new campaigns or when adding new targets to existing ones.

The idea is simple: you take your list of potential new targets and check it against a list of all the keywords/products you're currently targeting in the account (which you can export through the Targeting tab), using some low-level spreadsheet skills.

Since I love playing around with Google Sheets, you guessed it, I created one that does this automatically for you. You'll find a link to download the Amazon Advertising Target Deduplicator in the Bonus Resources section at the end of this book.

The second method requires zero spreadsheet skills, but only serves to identify and remove duplicates that are already present in your account.

Remember: Target duplication won't hurt your overall account performance that much, and in some cases it can make sense to have a target in two campaigns at once (for example, if you're running Custom text campaigns and testing two different sets of copy). But if you're like me and you like to keep your campaigns as clean and separate as possible, then these are two simple tricks to achieve that.

10

Testing your targets

Back when I started playing around with Amazon Ads five or six years ago, a common piece of advice on the block was to run giant campaigns with hundreds of different keywords in them, or even a thousand (the upper limit per campaign).

The rationale behind it was simple: you only needed to run one or two campaigns, and they were big enough to allow you to test as many keywords as possible, as fast as possible. Once a keyword had gathered enough impressions and clicks to make a decision about it, you could then either dismiss it, keep it, or adjust the bid, based on its performance. And so on until you'd filtered your huge keyword list down to the successful ones.

This was not a terrible tactic in the early days of Amazon Advertising, when competition was scarce, clicks were cheaper, and impressions easier to garner. Now, however, such strategy is deeply flawed.

The popular takes it all: impression monopolies

First, such mega campaigns can quickly blow through your budget. But more importantly, they're not even effective at properly testing the targets. If you've run such a campaign in the past, you may have noticed that, out of the 1,000 targets you included, only a few hundred actually received any impressions and clicks from the algorithm.

The reason for this is simple: Amazon Advertising doesn't allocate impressions evenly across targets in a campaign. Instead, it identifies the ones most likely to receive a high number of clicks, prioritizes them, and sort of forgets about the rest. As a result, you end up with a small number of targets eating up all the impressions and leaving the rest to never gather any actual data.

I call this phenomenon impression monopolization, as the big targets essentially monopolize all the impressions in the campaign.

How can you avoid running into that problem? It's simple: you start with smaller campaigns, each focusing on a limited number of targets, so that Amazon distributes impressions across as many of them as possible, which allows you to quickly identify all the potential winners.

How small should the campaign be? you may ask. It depends on your targeting mix, and a little bit on personal preference. As a rule of thumb, I avoid having more than 100 targets (keywords or products) per campaign—and can sometimes have as few as five or ten.

The number of targets in a campaign is not the only factor of impression monopolization, though. Even smaller campaigns can suffer from this, especially if they group together targets that are widely different in size.

For example, let's take a category target and a single product (ASIN) in that category. The category is an infinitely larger target because it makes your ads eligible to show up on any product page in the category—while the ASIN only targets the one product page.

At the end of the day, Amazon Advertising's goal is to generate as many clicks as possible, so their algorithms will naturally focus the spend on the largest targets in a campaign.

If you target both a whole category, and a single product, within the same ad group, you can expect the algorithms to deliver impressions and clicks solely for the category and ignore the ASIN. This is why I never group categories together with anything else than, well, other categories.

This can happen with keywords too. If you target both an author name and one of their book titles in the same ad group, it's likely that the author name will monopolize the impressions. Not only do author names usually get more searches than their corresponding titles (except in rare cases like Harry Potter), author name keywords also make your ads eligible to appear on any of their books' pages; whereas, a title keyword will only target that particular book page.

Leveraging ad groups

So far, I've just been talking about number and size of targets within campaigns. But that's not entirely correct. You can have hundreds of different targets in a campaign, with widely different sizes, and still get impressions on most of them—if you use ad groups smartly.

Amazon Advertising's algorithms treat each ad group independently when it comes to allocating impressions across targets. So if you spread your targets across ad groups, and group the bigger ones together, you can maximize the impression distribution and avoid monopolization.

Let me give you an example: Let's say you want to target the top 100 Hot New Releases in a category. Instead of putting all the titles, subtitles, series titles, and author names into one big Custom text campaign, I would set up a Standard campaign and do this:

- Group all the titles together in one ad group,
- Group all the series titles together in one ad group, and
- Group all the author names together in one ad group.

This is not only a handier organizational structure, it will also maximize your reach and allow you to properly test all those keywords.

Now, it's important to realize that, despite your best efforts, your ad groups will always have some keywords that just don't get many impressions. In most cases, this is a sign that these targets are just too small: they hardly get any searches or product views.

However, if that happens with a keyword that you're certain should be big enough, then you can try to take it out of the ad group and isolate it into its own ad group. That's actually an effective way of growing your spend and scaling your campaigns, which I'll analyze more in depth in Part V of this book.

Sprinklers versus lasers

Wait a second, you are wondering. If you spread targets across ad groups so that all of them get impressions and clicks, isn't that going to eat your budget even faster?

Absolutely, but that is actually a good thing: you want to be able to get data on your targets so you can then optimize their bids. How much data you get, and how fast, depends on your budget and on your strategy.

Roughly speaking, there are two types of strategies when it comes to testing targets in Amazon Ads: sprinklers and lasers.

A sprinkler strategy consists of taking hundreds or even thousands of different keywords and throwing them all at the Amazon wall to see which stick. Of course, you'll want to spread these targets intelligently across campaigns and ad groups to make sure they all get a chance to stick in the first place—or else you'll run into the monopolization issue.

The sprinkler strategy remains the best way to test targets en masse, while maximizing your chances of boosting sales in the short term. The downside, of course, is that it'll deplete your budget just as effectively, as you waste a big portion of your spend and clicks on nonprofitable keywords.

You might have heard this referred to as "spray and pray" advertising, because you spray your targeting as widely as possible—like a sprinkler—and pray that your ads will hit some relevant people in the process.

The laser strategy is—you guessed it—the opposite of the sprinkler strategy. Instead of going after as many keywords as possible, you focus your targeting on a few hyper-relevant keywords/products. For example, Also Bought titles with similar covers/themes, close comp author names, and niche search terms.

The upsides of laser targeting are obvious:

· You don't waste money on targets that are unlikely to work.

- You only show your ads on searches/product pages where you think readers are most likely to click and buy. Because of this—
- Your account's click-through-rate will likely be high and encourage Amazon to prioritize your ads.

One downside, however, is that your campaigns will be very slow to take off. Highly targeted keywords/products tend to get few searches/views, so it can take several weeks until you start seeing results and getting the kind of data you need to make decisions on those targets (pausing them, lowering bids).

The other downside is that you'll miss out on good keywords/products that you didn't think about or initially dismissed as not relevant enough. As I mentioned, it's impossible to know in advance exactly which targets will produce the best results—otherwise anyone could make a killing with Amazon Ads. I've seen broad, tangentially related comps outperform niche, hyper-relevant ones many times.

	Sprinkler targeting	Laser targeting
PROS	Allow you to gather data on a vast amount of targets in minimum time.	Cost-effective: you don't waste advertising budget on targets that are unlikely to convert.
	Immediate influx of impressions, clicks, and potentially orders, which can be particularly helpful at launch or when trying to maximize rank.	The extra relevance ensures a high click-through-rate, which encourages further delivery of your ads.
CONS	You risk creating impression monopolies if you don't spread the targets well across campaigns and ad groups.	Depending on the size of your targets, the campaigns may be slow to start, gather data, and produce results.
	Requires a high daily budget which you are unlikely to recoup in the short term (the campaigns won't be profitable).	Misses out on non-obvious targets that could potentially be highly profitable.

Pros and cons of sprinkler versus laser targeting.

What's the best strategy? It depends on your budget and your goals.

If you just released your book and are looking to get as many sales as possible in the first thirty days, you might want to go broad with the sprinkler strategy to make sure Amazon gets you as many clicks as possible and allows you to find those money-making targets quickly.

If you're conscious of budget, however, you'll want to start small with hyper-relevant targets that won't blow through your budget.

Choosing the right strategy will also depend on your book, where it fits in the market, and your knowledge of said market.

If your book straddles genres or doesn't fit well in a specific niche—or if you don't know any close comparable titles out there—then you'll have to go broad to find the targets (if any) that will bring in the types of readers that would potentially be interested in your book.

If you write in a well-defined niche where you're familiar with all the top names, then it will be easy, and probably more profitable, to go for the laser approach.

In most cases, though, there's no black or white answer: your strategy doesn't need to be as extreme as the sprinkler or the laser ones I depicted. As with anything, there are middle grounds, and you can try to borrow the best of both worlds.

For example, you could have high-bidding campaigns targeting the few keywords/products that are clear laser targets, and a low or mid-bidding sprinkler campaign targeting a wide array of keywords/products that you want to test over time. You can then progressively move the high-performing targets from the sprinkler campaign to the laser one.

11

Building your defense

One of the advantages about Amazon Advertising is that it allows you to virtually place your book next to, or in the search results for, any other book on the Store.

The other side of the coin, however, is that it allows any other publisher to do the same to your books. In other words, there's a good chance that readers searching for your name, or one of your titles, on Amazon will see ads promoting other authors at the top of the search.

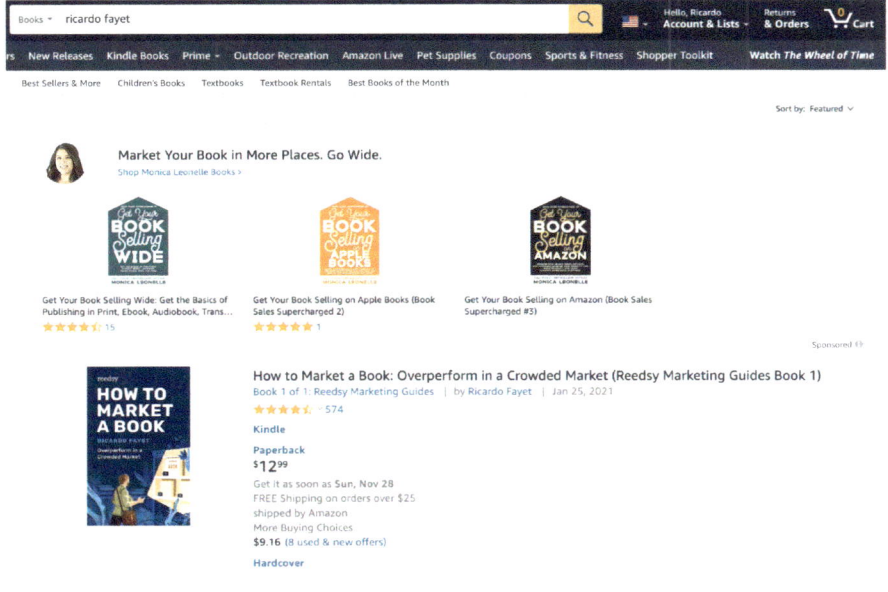

Well played, Monica, well played.

How can you avoid another author one-upping you? By setting up a defense strategy.

Targeting your brand and products

There is no way for you to control what other authors are going to do, so you can't prevent them from targeting you and your books. What you can do, however, is prevent them from taking this valuable real estate on the Store by occupying it yourself. And the only way to achieve that is by targeting your own name, titles, and products.

These are what I call defense targets, because your main purpose in targeting them is defending yourself from other advertisers who want to show up above you on searches and product pages related to your brand. Naturally, if you're the one owning these advertising spots, you will have to pay every time readers click on them.

"Wait, are you saying I have to pay Amazon for them to show my books to

readers searching for them?"

Well, yes and no. As you can see on my screenshot, Amazon will generally show at least one of your titles at the top of the search. There can be, however, a Sponsored Brands ad right above it, and Sponsored Products ads below. If you don't want other authors/books to capture these spots, then, yes, you will have to pay for them.

This might sound unfair, but that is how advertising works. And while you need to pay to secure these brand spots, the good thing is that you don't have to pay as much as other advertisers would, because your ad quality score (remember that one from Chapter 2?) on such targets will be much, much higher.

You can therefore afford to bid a lot lower than any other authors and still get the lion's share of impressions (unless you have a big-pocketed competitor bidding crazy high on your brand, of course).

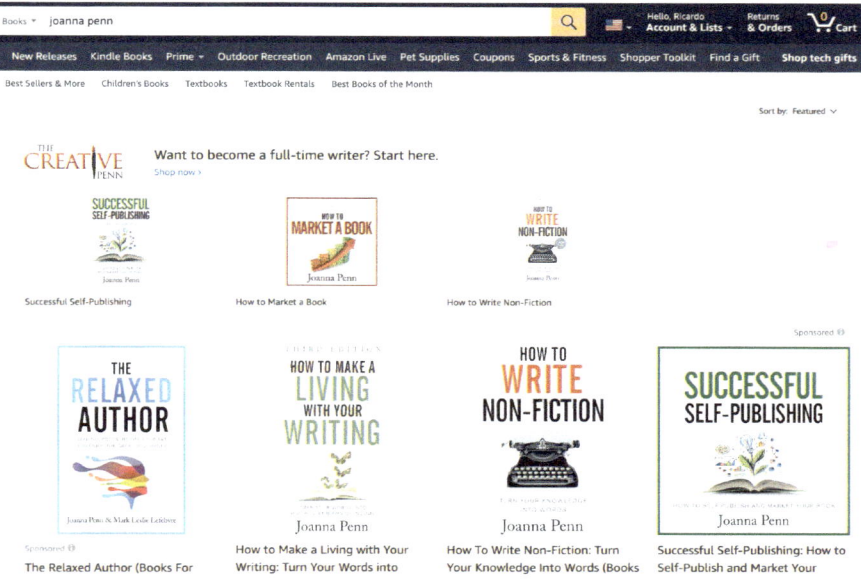

A perfect defense by Joanna Penn shows her books in ad space a competitor might grab.

Now, there are two schools of thought when it comes to defense targets: some authors like to use them, for the reasons I just explained, while others refuse to—trusting that readers who search for them on the Store, or visit their titles' product pages, will ignore ads promoting other books.

As you might have guessed, I belong to the first one and regularly use defense keywords as part of my advertising strategy. The only reason why Monica Leonelle's books (all of which I highly recommend, by the way) are showing above mine in the screenshot is that I can't compete for Sponsored Brands placements myself as I only have the one book out (at the time of writing this, and you need at least three). And, I'll be honest with you, this one of the main factors motivating me to write more books!

It's not just a question of pride, or brand protection, though—there are several other reasons that I believe justify the use of defense targets.

Also Boughts consolidation

If you have several books out in a series, or in the same genre, then one of your objectives from a branding perspective should be to make sure that they always show up first in each other's Also Boughts sections.

This not only increases the chances that readers pick up and read several of your books, and discover your other series, but also contributes to building strong brand awareness. Take the Also Boughts in this screenshot. They immediately convey the impression that this is a prolific, well-reviewed author, making it much easier for readers to want to take a chance on them.

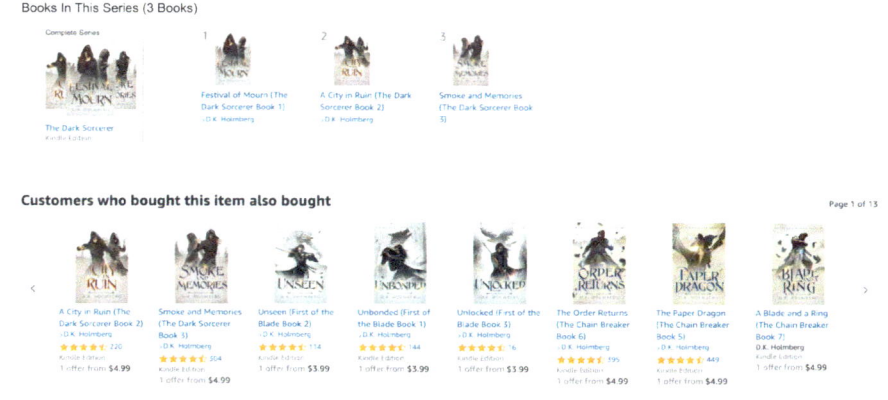

Perfect Also Boughts consolidation by D.K. Holmberg.

One of the best ways to consolidate your Also Boughts in such a way is to make sure that every reader who buys one of your books is aware that you have other books that they might like. This can be achieved in a number of ways (back matter mentions, newsletter, social media, among others), but a simple way to speed things up is to advertise your other books directly on that book's product page.

Sponsored sections often show up above Also Boughts on product pages nowadays, so if you leverage defense targets well, you can get your own books to feature in both sections, and both increase your brand awareness and reinforce your Also Bought consolidation. For example, take a look at the first Sponsored book on the same product page from the previous screenshot—it is another book by the same author.

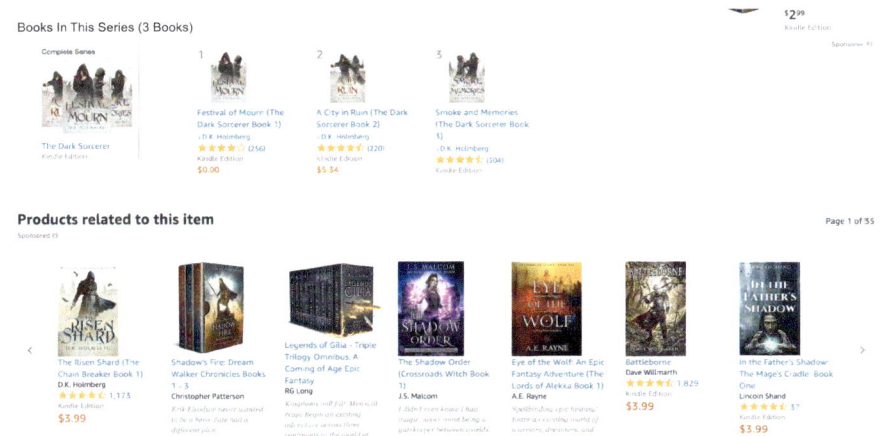

D.K. Holmberg owns the first slot in the Sponsored Products section of his product page.

But defense targets aren't just useful for branding and consolidating Also Boughts, they're also intrinsically great for inbound discoverability.

Inbound discoverability

You might be familiar with the concept of inbound marketing. If not, it's basically used to describe marketing strategies used to reach an audience that you already own or have access to. For example, sending a newsletter to your mailing list or posting in your Facebook reader group.

I see defense targets as another form of inbound discoverability. Most of the readers searching for your name, or your titles, on Amazon, will already be familiar with you—most likely, they'll already be readers of yours—even if it's not necessarily an audience you own per se. By targeting defense keywords, what you're doing is basically advertising to this existing readership.

But what's the point if they're already my readers? Well, they might have read one of your books, or several, but have they all read all your books?

Let me take a nonpublishing example. Let's say you buy some shoes online from a well-known brand. Do you think you'll see fewer ads online from that brand after that, or more? When that brand releases its next shoe model, who do you think will be the first to get their ads about it? That's right: existing customers (that's you).

It's the same in the book world. If a reader has already bought (and potentially read) a book of yours, it makes them all the more likely to pick up another book of yours—provided they know that you have another book out in the first place.

And while there are hundreds of different ways to let your readers know about that other book (mailing list, social media), none of those will reach your entire readership. Which is why it makes sense to promote that other book to them via Amazon Advertising, so that the next time they search for you on the Store, or check out your first book's Amazon description page, they immediately see your other book.

The more books and series you put out there, the more important inbound discoverability becomes. One thing I particularly like to do when it comes to defense targeting is cross-advertising series. Say you have two series out, A and B, in the same genre. One of your goals to increase revenue should be to maximize the number of series A readers who also purchase series B, and vice versa.

Here's what I like to do:

- Set up a campaign advertising series B's first book and targets series A keywords and ASINs; and
- Set up another campaign advertising series A's first book and target series B keywords and ASINs.

This way, I make sure that every reader who checks out one series on Amazon becomes immediately aware of the other series—while at the same time preventing other authors from taking these advertising slots away from me. You both defend and counterattack, if you will.

Ok, but what if I only have the one book out? In that case, defense targets will only serve to, well, defend. You might still want to use them to protect your brand (especially if you're thinking of writing more books), but it certainly won't be as beneficial to you. It's one of the rare case scenarios where I would contemplate staying away from defense targets, or even adding them as negative targets.

Organizing your defense

Even if you want to delve into defense targeting, you might not want every single one of your campaigns to potentially target brand keywords and products. For example, you might want to have one campaign dedicated specifically to defense targeting and exclude defense targets from the other campaigns (through negative keywords and products). Or you might want to have a specific ad group for defense targeting within each campaign.

This wouldn't just serve organizational purposes, but also goes back to the impression monopolies issue I discussed a couple of chapters ago. If you have a well-established brand already, and your pen name and books receive a lot of searches and visits, then you run the risk of your defense targets cannibalizing other keywords and products if they are together in the same ad group.

This is something I've seen happen quite often on automatic campaigns. Under close match, Amazon will often target keywords like your author name, book title, or series title, among other metrics. If these have a high search volume, then all your automatic campaigns' daily spend might go exclusively to these brand targets, which is a waste since you can think of those and target them on your own.

If you see that happening with one of your automatic campaigns, set up a specific campaign for defense targets, and exclude them from your auto-campaign with negative keywords. This will force Amazon's automatic targeting algorithms to be a bit more creative and widen their scope.

Playing with book titles

I touched on one counter-attacking tactic already, but I want to finish this chapter on a tactic that goes even further and turns defense targets into offense ones: including popular search terms as part of your book titles.

This is a common tactic used by most indie authors, and especially by big publishers, often with the objective to get the books to rank organically for these searches.

For example, if you've written a dark psychological thriller, you might want to include that in the subtitle of your book (*A dark psychological thriller*). This used to drastically increase the books' chances to show up in the first results for that search—and still does, but since everyone is using this tactic now, you're competing with a bunch of other titles that also have a variation of that in their subtitle. And to rank ahead of them, you need to outsell them.

But while this tactic may not be as effective as it used to be to increase your organic visibility on the Store (organic searches are natural searches, not paid through ads), it can still be incredibly effective when it comes to Amazon Advertising. Think about it this way: if your book's subtitle is *A dark psychological thriller*, then keywords like *dark thriller* or *psychological thriller* can be considered defense targets.

Of course, they won't be from a brand protection perspective—you don't own these terms—but they will from an ad quality score perspective. Amazon will detect a strong semantic relevance between your target search term and your product, since your product's subtitle will effectively contain the search term. This extra relevance increases your ad quality score and therefore makes it easier and cheaper for your ad to get the most impressions, and the best advertising slots. Case in point:

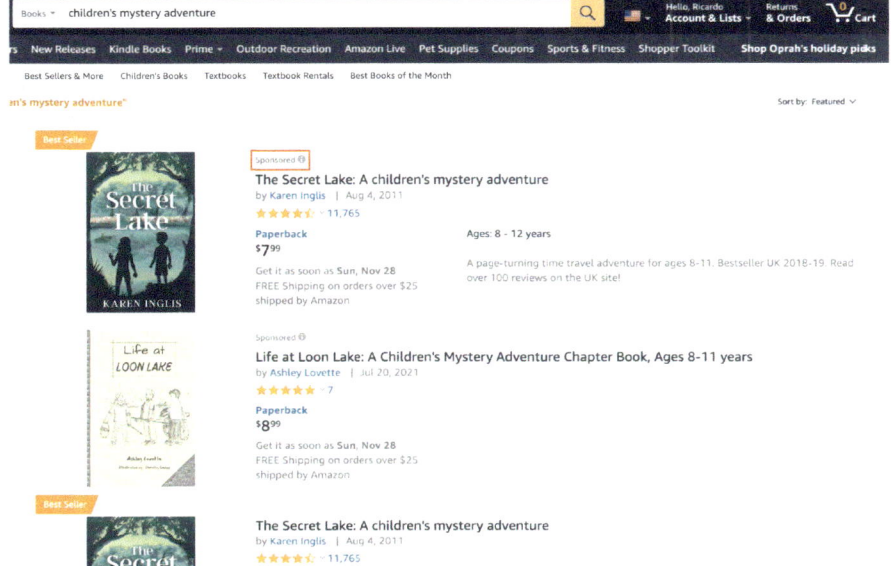

The Secret Lake by Karen Inglis shows up first in both sponsored and organic search results for the keyword phrase children's mystery adventure.

The beauty of this tactic is that it doesn't just improve your advertising results for these search terms, it also improves your organic ranking.

See, one of the main factors that decides how high a product ranks on Amazon search results is sales. The better a product sells, the higher it'll rank on all search results pages it is indexed for. Even better, there is some correlation data that show that the sales that have the most impact on search rankings are those coming from searches for the same search term (post-search sales).

In other words, if a customer searches for *children's mystery adventure* and buys your book as the result of that search, your book will rise in the rankings for that search term.

Advertising your book and placing it in the top sponsored results for these searches is a simple yet extremely effective way to not only increase your overall sales, but also drive these valuable post-search sales, thus propelling your book to the top-of-search results. Which explains why, in the screenshot, *The Secret Lake* is not only ranking #1 among sponsored results, but also among organic ones.

If you want another example, search for *how to market a book* on the Books Store. You'll find Joanna Penn's book and mine not only among the first sponsored results, but at the top of organic results as well. In this case, we're not achieving this through our subtitles, but, since our books are nonfiction reference, through the titles themselves.

And that's one of the great advantages of nonfiction: you can easily turn popular search terms into defense-offense keywords by using unimaginative, SEO-friendly titles (and subtitles). Such titles will also make Amazon's auto-targeting job easier and make your automatic targeting campaigns all the more effective.

12

Your first five Amazon Advertising campaigns

You now know everything you need to know—and probably a lot more—to set up your first campaigns on Amazon. But knowing the theory and putting it into practice are two different things. In this chapter, I am going to take everything I've discussed so far and apply it to five examples of actual campaigns that I generally like to set up when I take over an advertising account.

Not all these examples may apply to your situation, and there are other types of campaigns and targeting I'm not mentioning here that might work much better for you, but you can use these examples as inspiration to come up with your own first campaigns to set up.

1. The automatic targeting campaign

Automatic targeting campaigns have been performing increasingly better in recent years—a result of Amazon honing their targeting algorithms—and are also a way to find new keywords and products to target manually, so the first campaign I always set up is auto-targeting.

I generally like to set up one per series, include all the books in the series in it (in all formats), and trust Amazon to show the right one to each reader.

As we saw in Chapter 7, Amazon splits the targeting options for auto-campaigns into four categories: close match, loose match, complements, and substitutes. The first two target keywords, while the latter two target products (ASINs).

Since auto-campaigns are just as likely to suffer from impression monop-olization as manual ones, you'll often find that your automatic campaign ends up allocating most of its daily spend on one or two targeting categories only, sometimes three, but very rarely all four of them.

If that happens, it can be a smart idea to set up another, duplicate automatic targeting campaign, focusing solely on the targeting categories that your first one is ignoring. For example, you could have one auto-targeting campaign for close and loose match, and another for substitutes and complements.

2. The Also Boughts campaign

I always like to start my manual targeting with Also Boughts because these are the books that Amazon's data on customer purchases has identified as being closest to mine. Unless the Also Boughts are polluted, they should make for the most natural targets to start testing.

First, I compile the book titles, series titles, ASINs, and author names of all the Also Boughts of the book or series I want to advertise—as discussed in the last chapter. In the case of a series, if I see that the first book's Also Boughts are polluted, I note down those of book two, or three, instead. If the books have a "Customers who read this book also read" section, I make note of the books in there as well.

Then, I separate my Also Boughts campaign in four different ad groups:

1. **Author names (broad).** I like targeting author names as a phrase or broad match as I want to capture all searches including the author name. I also keep those separate in their own ad group as they'll usually have a much higher search volume, so they can easily monopolize impressions if mixed with other keywords.

Bid: Since author names tend to be competitive keywords, this is where I use the highest bids. Depending on the fame of these authors, and competitiveness of your niche, that might mean bids ranging from $0.50 to $1, or sometimes above.

2. **Book titles (phrase):** When adding book titles to this ad group, I'm first careful of removing any punctuation or unnecessary words or elements. I also don't include subtitles that are purely SEO-focused. For example, in the case of *The Secret Lake: A Children's Mystery Adventure*, I'd only target *The Secret Lake*. Finally, I'm careful not to add any short titles that could be confused with other books, or more generic search terms. For example, if one of the Also Boughts is titled *Fury*, I won't include that title in the ad group (I might, however, include the series title if it's more specific).

    Bid: Here you can afford to bid a little lower, in the $0.30 to $0.50 range, unless these titles are particularly well known. As a pro tip, when noting down Also Boughts in your spreadsheet, you can make a note of those that have more than 100 or 500 reviews, and make sure to use slightly higher bids for those.

3. **Series titles (phrase):** This will be a smaller ad group, since not all your Also Boughts will have series titles, and several of them might share the same series title. However, many readers search by the name of the series rather than by the name of book one, so it's always helpful to have those in.

    Bid: I set similar bids as for the book titles ($0.30–$0.50), unless a particular series name is highly popular.

4. **ASINs:** While all the previous ad groups are keyword targeting ad groups, this one is product targeting, in which I group the ASINs of all the relevant Also Boughts and their series' ASINs. If I'm advertising both ebooks and print books in my campaign, then I will include the ASINs of both the ebook and print editions of the Also Boughts. This ad group will naturally overlap in its targeting with the ones above, but it'll help me earn even more impressions on the Also Boughts' product and series pages.

Bid: Since this ad group will directly compete with the other ad groups, I set slightly higher bids for the corresponding ASINs. For example, if I used a $0.50 bid for a book title keyword, I'll bid $0.51 to $0.55 for the corresponding ASINs.

I personally like to make sure that each ad group in this campaign advertises the same group of products — i.e. either the ebook and paperback of book one, or all the books (in both formats) in the series. That said, nothing prevents you from having certain ad groups advertise only one edition of the book(s), or only specific books in the series.

3. The Top 100 campaign

This is another obvious and simple campaign to set up. The first step is to identify the one Amazon category that your book best fits in. Then, you go through it to note down the titles, series titles, ASINs, and author names of all the books in the top 100 of that category.

The main difference with Also Boughts is that you need to be very careful and exclude all the books whose covers and titles indicate they're not a natural fit in the category. Alternatively, only note down the books in the list whose covers are similar to yours.

Again, I like to separate this campaign into ad groups in much the same way.

1. **Author names (broad):** Since this a list of best sellers, you'll want to be careful about the author names, as it's likely many of them will write across different genres. For example, if you're targeting the Satire category, you might find J. K. Rowling's *The Casual Vacancy* in the top 100 list—but I would definitely not recommend that you target her author name in your campaign.
2. **Book titles (phrase):** Here I don't discriminate and add all the titles as keywords, unless, again, it's a one-word title that can be confusing or attract the wrong searches.

3. **Series titles (phrase):** Same as for the Also Boughts.
4. **ASINs:** Same as for the Also Boughts.

In terms of bids, I recommend setting similar bids as for the Also Boughts campaign, but adapt them on a case-by-case basis for those authors or book titles that are extra famous. You need to keep in mind that popular keywords are more competitive and thus require higher bids (think $1 or more) to get the top visibility spots. At the same time, bidding high on high-volume keywords is a surefire way to rapidly deplete your budget and monopolize impressions in the ad group.

That's why I'm generally cautious on such keywords and bid a bit below what I'd bid for an Also Bought, unless I feel the author or book is a perfect match for the one I'm advertising. It's easy enough to raise bids after a week or so if the target isn't delivering.

4. The Hot New Releases (HNR) campaign

Here, you apply the same principle as for the top 100 campaign, but for the HNR list in your main category.

There will be some overlap (which you can always exclude with negative keywords, or by deduplicating targets), but what I like about the HNR list is that it is more current than the top 100; it excludes the legacy bestsellers from traditional publishing (for example, all the Harry Potter books in Fantasy) and includes more indie authors who are not necessarily big enough to make the top 100, but who are starting to amass a wide enough following to hit the HNR list.

This is a list that you can refresh every month, either by adding the new monthly keywords/products to each ad group or by creating a new campaign.

It is, however, a category list that tends to be even more polluted than the top 100, so you'll need to be picky and careful when selecting which titles and authors to add to your campaign.

5. The search keywords campaign

I explained how to come up with a solid, exhaustive list of potential keywords and phrases readers could use to search for books like yours, in Chapter 10. Once you have that list, setting up the campaign is easy: just select manual targeting, then keyword targeting, and paste in all the keywords from your list.

Since most of these keywords will have dozens of close variations, I always target them with broad match, except in the case of vague or one-word keywords.

For example, a keyword like *historical romance* encompasses multiple centuries and subgenres, not all of which will have crossover appeal. Similarly, a broad or phrase keyword like *growth* could target all kinds of different searches, from *personal growth* to *growth hacking* or *hair growth*.

For keywords like this, I either target them with exact match—if they're truly relevant to my book—or else skip them altogether and stick to longer-tail keywords instead, so as to qualify searches enough to make them relevant to my book.

To go back to my example, if my book was titled *Growth*, then I'd want to target that keyword with an exact match. But if my book were on startup growth, I'd target *startup growth, company growth*, and *growth hacking* instead.

Of course, not all search keywords are created equal, and it's important to adapt your bidding strategy accordingly. To do so, you need to get a sense of the competitiveness of each keyword. Generally, most search keywords tend to fall into one of two categories:

- **Short-tail keywords:** These are short, highly popular keywords that naturally receive a lot of searches and are therefore usually more competitive as more advertisers target and bid on them. For example, *urban fantasy, cozy mystery series, yoga books, lgbt fiction, young adult romance*.
- **Long-tail keywords:** These are longer phrases, more niche, and with a

much smaller search volume—meaning they're usually less competitive. For example, *urban fantasy series for adults, british cat cozy mystery, chair yoga books for seniors, free lgbt kindle unlimited books, young adult werewolf romance.*

Of course, some search keywords have a high search volume and haven't yet become that competitive—either because the genre is nascent, or because it's a keyword few advertisers have thought of. But as more and more publishers advertise their books on Amazon, such untapped keyword opportunities become scarcer and scarcer, and as a general rule, you can consider that any keyword with a high search volume is going to be competitive.

Understanding whether a keyword is short tail or long tail is important to inform your bidding strategy. If you set a low bid (under $0.30) on a short-tail, competitive keyword, you're unlikely to get any impressions, because you'll be outbid by thousands of other advertisers.

Inversely, if you group both short-tail and long-tail keywords within the same ad group, and use high bids ($1 or more) for all, the short-tail keywords are likely to monopolize impressions.

My recommendation, then, is to divide your keyword list into at least two categories, depending on the search volume and competitiveness of each keyword. Tools like Publisher Rocket, Ahrefs, Helium 10 or MerchantWords, discussed in Chapter 10, all offer estimates for the search volume of a given keyword on Amazon, as well as a competition score. You can use those to separate your keyword list, and then create a specific ad group for each category.

For short-tail keywords, you'll want to bid relatively high to start with (around $0.75 if you can afford to take a small hit in the testing phase), while you can afford to be more conservative on bids for long-tail keywords ($0.40 or below).

> **Pro tip**: Setting up a search keywords campaign is not only beneficial from a paid advertising perspective, it can also help you

identify the search terms that convert best for your book and lead to the most purchases—which you can then in turn incorporate into your seven KDP keywords to boost organic visibility.

While these are the main five types of campaigns I'd recommend starting with, I'm all about offering added value and Bonus Resources in this book, so here are two other campaigns that I sometimes like to set up as well, depending on each author's situation and budget.

6. (Bonus) The top comp authors campaign

The idea is simple: you apply the "Also authors" technique mentioned earlier to find your top ten to twenty comp authors in terms of relevance (as identified by Amazon's algorithms). You can also add any names of authors you know are close to you in genre and style—if you know your market well—even if they don't show up among your "Customers also bought items by."

This is a campaign that is likely to overlap with the authors ad group of the Also Boughts and top 100 campaigns. That is intentional, however, as its purpose is to isolate these super comps and put them into a small ad group so they don't monopolize impressions and aren't cannibalized by others.

You'll want to bid relatively high again on this one (in the $0.50–$1 range) and target their author names in either phrase or broad match. If this campaign does overlap in targeting with the Also Boughts or top 100, you'll need to make sure you bid higher in this one so that Amazon prioritizes it. You can also potentially remove or negate these author names from your other campaigns.

Since you're keeping this number of targets small (you should have no more than thirty in total), you can afford to keep them all in the same ad group. You can always isolate one (or several) later in a separate ad group if they seem to be monopolizing impressions.

7. (Bonus) The category campaign

I mentioned before that categories are generally not the best targeting option to start with, but if you write in a highly specific niche that has a dedicated, targetable category, it can make sense to test it.

I've had several authors for whom Also Boughts and search keywords performed a lot worse than categories—so while that's not the norm, it can happen, which is why I generally like to set up one categories campaign with a few targets and see what happens.

I tend to lump all categories into the same ad group (it's rare that you'll find more than five or so categories to target, even when adding both Kindle Store and Books categories), and set low bids (in the $0.20 to $0.30 range). Since categories are such a vast targeting option, even bids as low as $0.10 can sometimes suffice to get a lot of impressions. That said, if you group together a big category and smaller ones, you'll again run the risk of impression monopolization. If that happens, just lower the bid on the high-spending category target, or split it into a different ad group.

As mentioned before, one of the main reasons for running a category campaign is that it allows you to identify products to target directly that you wouldn't have thought of on your own. So make sure to regularly check the Search terms tab of any category campaign you set up, and then add those high-performing product targets to your manual product targeting campaigns.

Now that you've set up a solid first set of Amazon Advertising campaigns, the hard work is not over! That said, make sure to leave them running for a good week or two before checking any results—you'll see later that patience is one of the most important virtues for advertising on Amazon. After that, go in, and optimize them for delivery.

IV

Optimizing for deliverability

"Help! I've set up a bunch of campaigns on Amazon Advertising, but I'm barely getting any clicks, let alone sales! What's happening?"

First, take a breath. This is much more common a problem than you might think. The challenge with Amazon Ads is to get them to spend some money in the first place. More importantly, such a conundrum is usually easy to fix by just adjusting your bids and optimizing your campaigns' click-through-rate. Let's talk about how to optimize for deliverability.

13

The advertising funnel

The first step to understand why a campaign—or a whole account—isn't producing the results you're looking for is to identify where exactly the problem lies.

We can deconstruct the funnel that leads to sales in the following way:

```
impressions -> clicks -> sales
```

An impression is tallied when a customer views your ad on Amazon. For that to happen, Amazon Advertising simply needs to display it—in technical jargon, deliver it—on the page the customer is looking at. Every time an ad is displayed to, and viewed by, a customer, one impression is recorded.

For each impression, two things can happen: either the reader clicks on the ad, or they don't. If they do, then a click is recorded. It's worth noting that a reader can, in theory, click on a particular ad several times, in which case several clicks would be recorded. The ratio from impressions to clicks is what we call the click-through-rate, and that is possibly the single most important metric in Amazon Advertising. But more on that later.

Finally, after the click comes the sale (or Order). Here again, not every click will lead to an order, and yet one click might yield several orders (for example, if a customer buys several of your advertised books). The ratio from clicks to orders is called conversion rate.

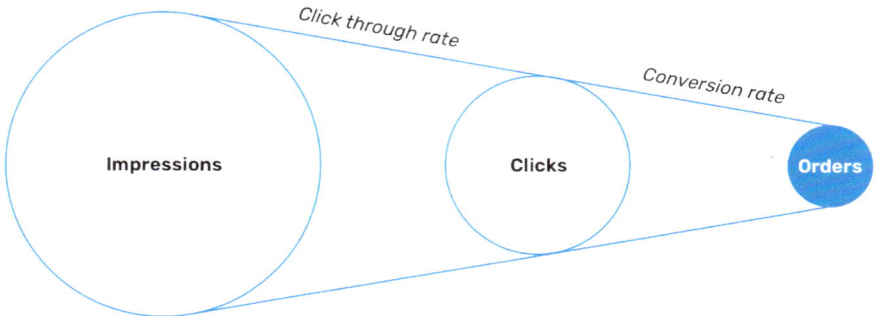

Every time an Amazon Advertising campaign is not performing well, meaning that it is not leading to sales, or at least not to the level of sales you expected, the problem lies somewhere along the funnel. There is a leaking point, or several leaking points, through which your impressions or clicks escape, making it impossible for them to turn into sales.

When we talk about optimizing an Amazon Advertising campaign, our objective is to find the leaks and fix them. Over the course of the next chapters, I'm going to identify all the places where such a leak may be happening and offer different ways to fix the leaks.

The start of the funnel

One of the particularities of the Amazon Advertising platform is that it is relatively common to experience a leak at the very entrance of the funnel. You create your first few campaigns, set them live, and . . . crickets. No sales, hardly any clicks, and few impressions.

This leak is very easy to identify because you'll see next to no activity on your Amazon Advertising dashboard, even several weeks after starting the campaigns. The dashboard might look like something like this:

Dashboard with a campaign deliverability problem.

This account here has only generated 6,000 impressions in the last thirty days, which is extremely low. The problem is not so much that it only got two clicks, and no sales, it's that it's hardly getting enough impressions in the first place.

In other words, there is an issue with campaign deliverability. And that is not an isolated or rare scenario. It is an incredibly frequent issue—if not at an account level, at least at a campaign level.

At any point in time, all the Amazon Advertising accounts I've managed had one or two campaigns that just failed to deliver impressions. This is fine as long as you have other campaigns that are doing well, but if the whole account suffers from low deliverability, then that's the number-one issue you need to fix. Generally, the only immediate fix is to raise your bids.

14

Raising your bids

As you may remember from the early chapters of this book, Amazon Advertising is an auction marketplace, where impressions are awarded to advertisers based on their ad rank. This ad rank is a combination (sum) of the bid and the ad quality score.

If a campaign is not generating many impressions, it means that it is not winning many auctions, as a result of a low ad rank.

How do you get this ad rank back up? It's simple: you need to either increase your bid or your quality score (or both). And since you don't have a lot of control over your quality score, the easiest thing you can do is raise your bids.

Invariably, the most frequent reason for a campaign not delivering is excessively low bids. And it makes sense: most independent authors are budget-conscious and focused on ROI, so they tend to start with low bids and are loath to raising them—especially if the campaigns are not producing the kinds of results (sales) they'd hoped for.

But the only immediate, surefire solution to solving a campaign deliverability issue is to raise the bids. You don't need to do it in a radical way; you can do it incrementally and stop once the campaign starts delivering well.

Which raises the question: "How high do my bids need to be in order for a campaign to deliver?"

That unfortunately depends on a number of factors, like the type of target.

In the last section, I gave you some ballpark figures for bids for each of the main types of targets, so I recommend you start there, and only increase if a target, ad group, or campaign, fails to deliver.

That said, bids will also vary greatly from one genre to another, or even from one niche to another, based on the competition. Since this is a bidding auction, the more advertisers are involved, or the more money these advertisers can afford to bid, the higher the auction will go.

Bids and genres

As with many quirks in publishing, romance is a bit of an outlier here. It is, by far, the genre with the most competition, both in general and on Amazon Advertising specifically. If you write in a big, mainstream romance genre (such as romantic comedy, historical romance, paranormal romance), it's likely you'll have to bid way above $0.50, and sometimes even above $1, in order to get your ads to deliver.

Why? Because successful romance authors tend to be savvy businesspeople. They write long series, with strong read through, and know exactly how much a sale of book one is worth to them—which, in general, is a lot. They know they can afford to pay up to $5 or sometimes $10 for a sale because that reader will make them double that in the long term. Which, in turn, means they're able to bid up to $1 per click—or more—and still make a good profit.

Now, I'm not saying that indie authors in genres other than romance aren't savvy, or don't write in long series, but they generally are more of a mixed bunch and tend to be more conservative with their bids.

For example, in YA fantasy, a genre where traditional publishing is still dominant, you can get impressions on most targets (even big ones) for under $0.50 (or even $0.25, in some cases).

Even within the same genre, you can have strong differences between niches. For example, cozy mystery overall is less competitive in terms of bids than romance, but some cozy mystery niches also require romance-level bids. These tend to be niches dominated, again, by savvy indie authors who can afford such bids because of the length and read through of their series.

As a general rule, if you know that your market is dominated by the types of smart indie authors or publishers I mentioned, you can expect to bid high to get your campaigns to deliver.

The one thing I recommend against, when starting out, though, is asking other authors in your niche about their bids. If they have been advertising for a while, they'll be able to get away with lower bids than you could when starting out. How come? They've built their ad quality.

Building your ad quality

The ad quality score is not a metric that is set in stone. It evolves over time, mostly based on the performance of the campaigns. What's quality ad for Amazon? It's an ad that leads to clicks and purchases because that's where Amazon makes its money.

The issue when you're starting up is that Amazon has zero historical data on your ads, so it can't really score your ads' quality.

In contrast, an author in your niche who's been advertising their books successfully for some time will have a high ad quality score—because Amazon has historical data showing that these ads are working.

So if you, Amazon Advertising rookie, use the same bid as the experienced author and savvy marketer, you will invariably lose the auction.

This is why you should never compare your bids with those of other authors, even close comps in your niche, unless you've both been advertising for an equivalent amount of time. This is also why you generally need to bid higher when you start out, to make up for your nonexistent quality score, and to start building that score. In other words, you need to pay a bit more in the beginning to prove yourself worthy to the Amazon Advertising gods—or at least as worthy as the experienced competitors in the auction.

Therefore, don't be afraid to overbid if you see that your campaigns aren't delivering. It's something that is easy enough to revert if it gets out of hand and is often the only way to win your first auctions and get some data into the account.

Once you've proved yourself—that is, once your targets have generated a good amount of clicks—you can usually afford to gradually decrease your bids without killing their delivery, as Amazon will have attributed a quality score to your ads.

Unless, of course, that quality score is low—or much lower than your competition's. How can you know that? It's simple: you need to monitor your click-through-rate.

15

Monitoring your click-through rate

The click-through-rate (or CTR) is one of the most important indicators of a campaign's health and a prime component of the ad quality score. I defined it a couple of times in this book already, but if you hate marketing jargon, just think of it as the percentage of people who click on your ad after seeing it. For example,

- If 100 people see your ad, but only one person clicks on it, that's a 1% CTR (and that's actually pretty high, in Amazon Advertising standards).
- If 2,000 people see your ad and only one person clicks on it, that's a 0.05% CTR (which is on the low side, but definitely not unusual).

As you can imagine, the CTR is an important metric to monitor on any advertising platform because it's essentially a sign of whether people like your ad or not. On Amazon, though, the importance of the CTR takes on a whole new dimension. Why? Because, as you may remember from the first chapter, Amazon Advertising only charges for clicks, so it doesn't make any money until someone clicks on your ad.

If your ad takes up precious advertising real estate, but earns Amazon zero dollars because no one clicks on it, Amazon is effectively losing money by displaying it.

As a result, which ads do you think Amazon Advertising prefers to display to customers? To which ads do you think it will attribute the highest quality score? You got it: the ones with the highest CTR.

Optimizing your campaigns' click-through-rate

What can you do to effectively improve the CTR in your advertising campaigns? It's simple: regularly monitor your campaigns and remove the targets with a low CTR.

If you don't, these targets will lower your campaign's overall CTR, which will lower your ad's quality score, which will, in turn, lead you to win fewer auctions, thus earning fewer impressions and so on until your campaign barely delivers anymore.

The first step toward optimizing your campaign's CTR is to decide what a low CTR looks like for you. If you've already been running ads on Amazon for a while, then you can look at your historical data to see the average CTR of your campaigns.

If you're just starting out (or don't have a lot of data yet), I've found that a good CTR to aim for on most keyword and ASIN targets is 0.20%. This doesn't mean that you should just pause all targets with a CTR under 0.20%, as many of these see their performance improve with time and rise above that threshold. But you can use this 0.20% threshold as an objective to optimize your campaigns.

> Note: The 0.20% CTR objective does not apply to all campaigns. For example, if you run a purely defensive campaign targeting brand keywords, you should aim for a much higher CTR (above 1%). On the other hand, category targeting campaigns, because of their broad and vague targeting, will generally earn a lower CTR (in the 0.10% range, or even below).

Here's an example of how I regularly optimize my campaigns to increase their click-through-rate. I go through all the targets in the campaign and apply the following rules:

- If a target has a CTR above 0.20%, I don't touch it.
- If the target has a CTR between 0.20% and 0.10%, I lower the bid.
- If the target has a CTR under 0.10%, I pause its delivery.

Now, there are two notable exceptions to these rules:

1. First, targets that have generated a sale (or significant KENP reads). If a target with low CTR has generated a sale, you might want to keep it going anyway. Sales/reads are just as important as clicks (if not more), and you can afford for that target to slightly hurt your overall CTR if it brings in money.
2. Second, targets that have not accrued enough data (impressions) to be statistically significant (you'll see this concept come back as a recurring theme throughout this book). If a target hasn't generated more than 1,000 impressions, then it's probably too early to judge its CTR, as it could double or triple overnight.

Consider this example:

Active	Keyword	Bid	Impressions	Clicks	▼ CTR	Spend	CPC
	writer's market 2020	$ 0.50	1,890	4	0.21%	$2.53	$0.63
	romancing the beat	$ 0.50	782	1	0.13%	$0.48	$0.48
	sin and syntax	$ 0.50	784	1	0.13%	$0.60	$0.60
	writers	$ 0.41	34,803	38	0.11%	$22.53	$0.59
	a manual for writers	$ 0.50	1,197	1	0.08%	$0.57	$0.57
	on writing	$ 0.45	107,973	74	0.07%	$46.16	$0.62
	the chicago manual of style	$ 0.50	4,556	1	0.02%	$0.69	$0.69

Here, following my logic, you might be tempted to reduce the bid on *romancing the beat* and *sin and syntax*, simply because their CTR is below 0.20% (at 0.13%). But consider this: if the next reader who viewed the corresponding ad clicked on it, these targets' CTRs would suddenly jump to over 0.25%! So it's really too soon to even look at the click-through-rate metric for these keywords.

Inversely, let's take the example of *the chicago manual of style*. That keyword has had 4,500+ impressions already, which is enough to make its CTR statistically significant. Even if it were to generate another two clicks with its next impression, its CTR would only jump to 0.07%, which is still under our 0.10% threshold—so we can safely pause it.

With these two exceptions in mind, here are my final guidelines for going through a campaign's targets to optimize the overall click-through-rate.

Condition 1	Condition 2	Condition 3	Action
Under 1000 impressions	—	—	Don't do anything
Over 1000 impressions	1+ orders	—	Optimize for profit
Over 1000 impressions	$1+ KENP royalties	—	Optimize for profit
Over 1000 impressions	No orders	CTR over 0.20%	Don't do anything
Over 1000 impressions	No orders	0.10% < CTR < 0.20%	Lower bid
Over 1000 impressions	No orders	CTR under 10%	Pause target

I recommend going through all your targets across all active campaigns every few weeks (at least once a month) and follow these guidelines.

In order to maximize the number of targets with 1,000+ impressions, I generally look at lifetime data, unless a campaign has been running for several years, or has gone through important changes (such as different products being advertised) in its lifetime.

Your new favorite CTR dashboard filters

"Wait, you want me to examine all my keywords/products every month and look at every single click-through-rate?"

I hear you, but that shouldn't take nearly as much time as it sounds, if you

157

make a smart use of filters and of the Targeting tab.

As you may remember, this section of your Amazon Advertising dashboard allows you to visualize the performance of all your targets in one single place. Even better, you can filter and order this dashboard based on the available metrics. Thanks to this, spotting underperforming keywords in terms of CTR only takes a few minutes.

First, make sure that your dashboard view includes columns for all the metrics I discussed so far: impressions, clicks, CTR, and orders. If it doesn't, use the Customize columns option and check all the relevant boxes.

Next, use the Filter by option to set up the following filters:

- **Active status: Enabled**: This will exclude any targets that you've paused or archived, thus not delivering.
- **Impressions: greater than 1,000**: This will exclude any targets whose results aren't yet statistically significant.
- **Orders equals 0**: This will exclude any targets that have generated sales or downloads.
- **Clickthrough rate less than 0.2**: This will show only keywords whose CTR is below our objective.

Finally, order your dashboard by CTR score, from lowest to highest, so that the worst-performing targets show up at the top.

	Active	Target ⊕		Bid ⊕	Impressions ⊕	Clicks ⊕	CTR ⊕ ∧	CPC ⊕	Orders ⊕	Sales ⊕
	⬤	on writing well	⋮	$0.61	5,304	0	0.00%	—	0	—
	⬤	draft no 4	⋮	$0.61	2,140	0	0.00%	—	0	—
	⬤	2k to 10k	⋮	$0.61	1,702	0	0.00%	—	0	—
	⬤	a writer's diary	⋮	$0.61	1,015	0	0.00%	—	0	—
	⬤	david gaughran	⋮	$1.01	1,123	0	0.00%	—	0	—
	⬤	the story grid	⋮	$0.75	1,487	0	0.00%	—	0	—
	⬤	how to sell books on amazon	⋮	$0.95	1,245	0	0.00%	—	0	—
	⬤	stefan zweig	⋮	$0.55	1,250	0	0.00%	—	0	—
	⬤	ready set novel	⋮	$0.61	3,403	1	0.03%	$0.85	0	—

Filtering and ordering your dashboard to spot low-performing CTR targets.

Here, just go through the targets one by one and either pause them or reduce their bid (depending on their CTR and impressions).

Of course, you don't need to follow these guidelines to the letter. For example, you might feel that 1,000 impressions is not enough to ditch a target if its CTR is just below 0.10%—in which case you can leave it running a little bit longer, or just lower its bid. Or you might want to just pause a keyword that has a CTR of 0.15% if you've already lowered its bid several times and it isn't bringing in many sales.

If you set up your targeting well and don't go too broad, this little filtering exercise shouldn't return more than fifty or so keywords—especially if you do it regularly. So you can afford to go through them all one by one and make the necessary adjustments.

If, for some reason, you end up with a filtered list of 100 keywords or more, you can automate things further with the bulk actions menu. For example, you change the CTR filter to less than 0.10%, raise the impressions threshold to 1,500 or 2,000 (just to be on the safe side), and then select all the remaining targets and bulk-pause them. This will remove all the obvious worst performers and let you focus your manual work on those that need bid adjustments.

Doing this regularly is the most effective way to raise your campaigns' click-through-rates and, in turn, your quality scores. While it may sound less important than optimizing for profit (which is what Part V of this book is all about next), it can actually save you money down the line. Remember, the higher your quality scores, the lower your bids need to be—so the lower you'll end up paying per click.

Not only will this little exercise improve your campaigns' deliverability, but it'll also lower your overall cost per click, and therefore increase your profit, in the long term. It is the very first thing you should do, even before you start looking into orders, sales, and profitability.

V

Optimizing for profit

Once your campaigns are delivering well and getting you clicks every day, the next step in the optimization funnel is to make sure these clicks turn into sales. And, more importantly, that the money you earn on these sales offsets what you paid for the clicks. This is what profit optimization is all about, and it starts by figuring out exactly how much a sale is worth to you.

16

Are your campaigns profitable?

Let's face it: the first campaigns you set up on Amazon Advertising are rarely going to be profitable from the get-go. It generally takes weeks or months of adjusting targets, bids, and placements to get to a place where your ads are turning a nice profit every month.

The first step to achieving that is to figure out when your campaigns are earning you money in the first place—which is trickier than it sounds.

As I mentioned in Chapter 4, one of the benefits of Amazon Advertising is that the platform actually gives you data on how many Sales and KENP reads your campaigns generated. The catch, however, is that these data are often incomplete. So the first thing we need to do is to complete them and figure out exactly how much money each campaign, ad group, and target, is making us.

The problem with Sales

Broadly speaking, you can earn two different streams of revenue through advertising your books on Amazon:

1. Royalties on book sales (ebook and print), and
2. Royalties on page reads by Kindle Unlimited readers.

> *Note: I don't count audiobook sales here as Amazon Advertising does not allow for audiobook advertising at this point.*

Both are reported in separate columns in the Amazon Advertising dashboard, but while the Estimated KENP royalties represents the actual net royalties (estimated) that you earn through Kindle Unlimited, the Sales metric can be a bit misleading, as it includes a lot of extra money that doesn't end up in your bank account.

What Amazon reports as Sales is the total retail value of the products sold as a result of the ads. Since this figure is based on the price of each product, it includes not only the royalties distributed to the author, but also the printing, shipping, and distribution costs.

In other words, **you only earn a fraction of what Amazon reports as Sales**.

This fraction (which I will call net royalty rate going forward) can be higher or lower, depending on the royalty rate and production costs. For most ebooks, royalty is generally either 70% (for ebooks priced between $2.99 and $9.99, and except in the case of heavy files that incur important delivery costs), or 35% (for ebooks outside of that price range).

For print, the net royalty rate tends to be a lot lower, considering that you need to factor in printing costs. If a paperback distributed by KDP Print retails for $10, but costs $4 to print per copy, the KDP Print royalty rate of 60% needs to be applied on the price minus printing costs. So the net royalty (that is the actual revenue that ends up in your bank account) earned by the author per copy is 60% x ($10-$4) = $3.60—which gives us a net royalty rate of 36%.

```
Net royalty = Sales x net royalty rate
```

Calculating your net earnings out of the Sales figure reported by Amazon Advertising may seem simple once you know your net royalty rate—but it can become a challenge once you start advertising several products with different royalty rates.

Before we get into this, let's touch on two dashboard metrics that are directly related to Sales, and which add to the confusion authors often feel when looking at their campaigns.

The limitations of the ACOS and RoAS

The ACOS, or Advertising Cost of Sale, is a simple metric: it's the ratio of spend (or cost) divided by sales.

```
ACoS = Spend / Sales
```

This is probably the most popular Amazon Advertising metric among advertisers, and the one you'll see discussed in most blogs, courses, and books on the topic. And for good reason: it's the only metric available in the Amazon Advertising dashboard that establishes a correlation between spend and sales, with the aim to estimate profitability.

Now, the Return on Advertising Spend is effectively the exact inverse of the ACOS.

```
RoAS = Sales / Spend
```

Some advertising dashboards (those of Vendor, Seller, or Advantage accounts) will include the RoAS. Even if you have a regular, KDP-accessed advertising account, you'll come across the RoAS on any reports you run and download.

In the broader advertising world, these two metrics are extremely useful because they tell you, at a glance, whether a campaign is making or losing you money:

- If the ACOS is under 100% (meaning the RoAS is over 100%), sales are higher than spend, so the campaign is profitable.
- If the ACOS is above 100% (meaning the RoAS is under 100%), spend is higher than sales, so the campaign is losing money.

However, on Amazon Advertising specifically, they are far from being as helpful, as they are calculated based on the total Sales value, not your actual revenue. As such, an ACOS of 100% actually signals that you're losing money—not breaking even.

Worse, these two metrics don't take KENP royalties into account, making them effectively meaningless for Kindle Unlimited authors who earn the majority of their income through page reads.

For non-KU authors, the ACOS can still be a good indicator of campaign performance, as long as you know what your net royalty rate is. For example, if you're advertising a full-price ebook (with a net royalty rate of 70%), you should aim for a 70% ACOS, as that's the point at which your campaigns break even. This figure is often referred to as a target ACOS.

Similarly, if you know that you earn 36% on your paperback sales, then you can optimize your campaigns for that paperback with the aim to achieve a target ACOS of 36%.

But what if you're advertising both the ebook and the paperback within the same ad group? Since you earn different royalty rates on these products, it becomes much harder to estimate your net revenue and work out a target ACOS.

Sales breakdown per advertised product

Let's take the following example, where the author is advertising both a $5.39 ebook and a $13.37 paperback within the same ad group.

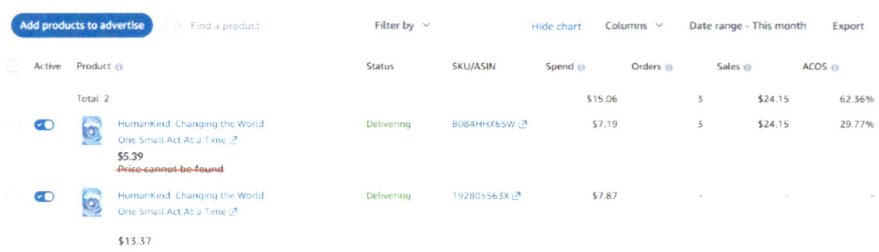

As you can see, the ad group generated $24.15 in total sales. Since there were only three orders, and we know the prices of both products, we can work out that these three orders were distributed as follows:

- Two for the ebook; and
- One for the paperback.

"Wait, if one of the orders was for the paperback, why isn't it showing in the row of the paperback in your screenshot?"

It seems that you, dear rhetorical reader, weren't paying attention to Chapter 4. If you did, you'd remember the Orders and Sales reported in the dashboard are not the sales that each product received, but those that each product generated.

If a reader clicked on an ad for the ebook but ended up buying the paperback, this sale worth $13.37 was attributed to the ebook product line.

In other words, you can't immediately see, by looking at your Amazon Advertising dashboard, how each of your advertised products sold. You can work it out, like I did here, if the total number of orders is low.

However, once you start accumulating more orders, working out their distribution quickly becomes impossible. If we look at year-to-date data, for example, it becomes a lot harder to work out what the proportion of ebook versus print sales is.

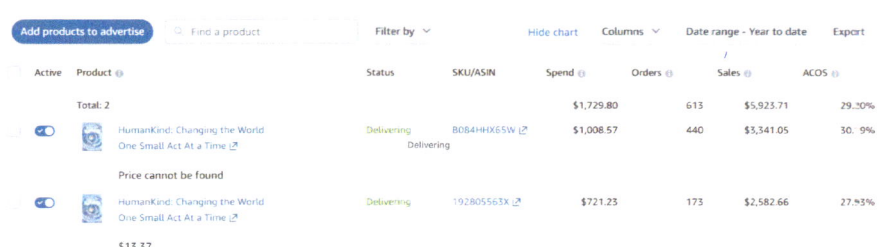

In cases like this, there are two methods you can use to estimate your net earnings. The idea for both these methods is the same: comparing the historical sales of your different advertised products, and working out an average.

Method #1: The average net royalty rate

For example, let's say you're advertising both the $10 paperback (with the 36% royalty rate), and a $3.99 ebook, within the same ad group.

After a month, your dashboard shows $611.37 in sales. It'll be almost impossible for you to figure out what percentage of ebook sales versus paperback sales are comprised in that overall figure. You probably could, with a smart mathematical model, but if we were all math geniuses, we wouldn't really struggle with Amazon Ads, would we?

Since you can't figure out that proportion, you have no idea how much actual money you're earning out of that sales figure. If 90% of those sales were ebooks, then you'd be earning over $400 in net royalties. But if 90% of the sales were paperbacks, your net earnings would be almost half that—which is a massive difference.

So how do you solve this problem? It's simple: you take an estimate. You look at your historical sales data, see what your proportion of sales is per format, and then use that to work out an average net royalty rate.

```
Average net royalty rate = % ebook sales x ebook royalty + %
print sales x print royalty
```

Okay, I get how horribly abstract this just sounded, so let me give you some scenarios based on the example.

Scenario 1: 65% of your sales come from the ebook. In this case, your average net royalty rate is

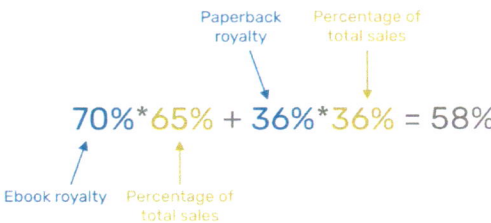

In other words, you know that, on average, when you manage to sell a book, your net royalty rate is around 58%—so you're earning 58% of the total sales figure reported in the Amazon Advertising dashboard.

This is a number that you can directly plug into your ROI calculations and actually use as your target ACOS. If a campaign, ad group, or target, has an ACOS below 58%, then you can be fairly sure that it is profitable. Inversely, if the ACOS is above 58%, then you can be confident you're losing money.

Scenario 2: 30% of your sales come from the ebook. Your average net royalty rate is

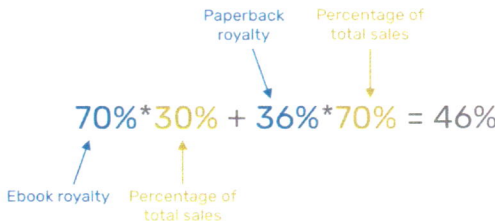

In this second scenario, you should aim for a much lower target ACOS (46% instead of 58%), because you're selling a higher proportion of the format with the lowest royalty rate.

Working out your average royalty rate is a simple solution, but it is not always the most elegant, so let's look at the second method.

Method #2: The average revenue per order

Let's take another example. This time, we're advertising an ebook priced at $3.99 and a paperback priced at $8, with printing costs of $3.50 per copy.

While these two formats have wildly different royalty rates (70% for the ebook vs. 33.75% for the paperback), they actually net you a similar amount of money when sold:

- For the ebook: 3.99 x 70%= $2.793 per copy sold, and
- For the paperback: ($8-$3.50) x 60% = $2.70 per copy sold.

So while their royalty rates are different, their net revenue per order is almost identical.

If a campaign, ad group, or target generates orders at a cost per order below $2.70, you know for a fact that the campaign is profitable—no matter what proportion of sales comes from one format over the other.

So instead of using a target ACOS, you can use a target cost per order. In simple terms, the cost per order represents how much you need to spend on clicks to generate one order of one of your advertised products.

```
Cost per order = Spend / Orders
```

You can then compare that cost per order to your net revenue per order:

- If the cost/order is lower than your net revenue per order, you're making money.
- If the cost/order is equal to your net revenue per order, you're breaking even.
- If the cost/order is higher than your net revenue per order, you're losing money.

It's worth noting that Amazon Advertising does not actually have a column in the dashboard for the cost per order. Instead, you have to calculate it yourself (either manually, or using a spreadsheet)—but I'll come back to that in a second.

Now, our example is handy because both products generate an almost identical revenue per order. But what happens if that's not the case? For example, let's say you're advertising two ebooks, one at $0.99 and one at $5.99. These would net you $0.35 and $4.20 per order respectively.

If you wanted to use the revenue per order method, you would need to figure out what your average revenue per order is, based on the proportion of sales of one ebook versus the other. This is basically the same as what we saw in Method #1, but focusing on the revenue per order, instead of the net royalty rate.

Let's run a few scenarios again using this example.

Scenario 1: 80% of your orders come from the ebook at $0.99. In this case, your average revenue per order is

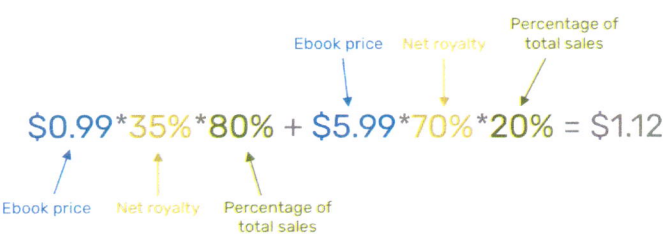

Scenario 2: 50% of your orders come from the ebook at $0.99. In this case, your average earnings per order are

How to choose the right method

As you can see, both methods are fairly similar, in that they consist of

- Looking at your historical sales data to estimate the percentage of total sales of each product, and
- Plugging that percentage into your average revenue or royalty rate calculations.

Is one method better than the other? Well, it depends.

Since we're working with estimations and averages here, one of our goals should be to reduce the discrepancy risk as much as possible.

If we take our latest example, the net revenue from the two advertised products is widely different ($0.35 vs. $4.20). So while you can estimate the sales percentage of each format based on your historical sales pattern, there is still a risk that a campaign, ad group, or target in particular will generate sales that won't follow the pattern. This is what I call the discrepancy risk.

For example, let's say we are in the Scenario 2 where, historically, your ebook and paperback sales have been split evenly.

If you target a keyword like *cozy mystery kindle* (or any *[genre] kindle* keyword), and this keyword generates 100 orders, it would be risky of you to assume that these 100 orders consist roughly of 50 ebooks and 50 paperbacks—because the keyword indicates a search intent geared toward Kindle books. As a result, there is probably a high discrepancy between your overall historical sales and the specific sales generated by this particular keyword.

If you were to use your historical sales distribution to estimate your net revenue on that keyword, you'd likely be grossly overestimating it—as you earn a lot more on the paperback than on the ebook.

How do you mitigate this risk? You pick the method that best suits the group of products you're advertising.

For example, if your ad group advertises products with similar net royalty rates, then you should use method #1, as the average net royalty rate you'll work out won't be far from that of either of the products.

Product 1	Product 2	P1 Net Royalty Rate	P2 Net Royalty Rate	P1 Revenue per Order	P2 Revenue per Order	Recommended method
Ebook at $2.99	Ebook at $5.99	70%	70%	$2.09	$4.19	Net Royalty Rate
Ebook at $0.99	Paperback at $8.99 with printing costs of $3.50	35%	36.64%	$0.35	$3.29	Net Royalty Rate

Two examples of when you should definitely use the net royalty rate method.

Inversely, if you're advertising products with different royalty rates, but a similar revenue per order, you should use the revenue per order method.

Product 1	Product 2	P1 Net Royalty Rate	P2 Net Royalty Rate	P1 Revenue per Order	P2 Revenue per Order	Recommended method
Ebook at $3.99	Paperback at $7.99 with printing costs of $3.50	70%	33.72%	$2.79	$2.69	Revenue per Order
Ebook at $8.99	Hardback at $22.99 with printing costs of $12	70%	26.39%	$6.29	$7.79	Revenue per Order

Two examples of when you should use the Revenue per Order method.

To be on the safe side, you can even pick the lower revenue per order as a target for the whole ad group (that is, $6.29 in our second example).

Of course, things won't always be as clear cut, and you might very well end up in a situation where you're advertising several products, all with different royalty rates and revenues per order.

Product 1	Product 2	P1 Net Royalty Rate	P2 Net Royalty Rate	P1 Revenue per Order	P2 Revenue per Order	Recommended method
Ebook at $0.99	Ebook at $3.99	35%	70%	$0.35	$2.79	???
Ebook at $3.99	Hardback at $22.99 with printing costs of $12	70%	26.39%	$2.79	$7.79	???

What do you do in cases like this?

If that's the case, then I'm sorry to say there's no elegant solution to mitigate the discrepancy risk. The only thing you can do is use either of the methods and assume that there will be a factor of risk involved.

Since method #2 does require calculating an additional metric—the cost per order that does not naturally exist in the Amazon Advertising dashboard—I tend to favor method #1 for all cases where there is no clear winner. That way, I can directly compare the estimated net royalty rate to the ACOS of each target (which Amazon Advertising does give me in the dashboard).

Feeling overwhelmed? I can understand—so here goes a simple recap:

· **Use method #1 (average net royalty rate) if** the net royalty rates of the products you advertise are not far apart. Otherwise,
· **Use method #2 (average revenue per order) if** the revenues per order of

the different products you advertise are not far apart.

· **Use method #1** if both the net royalty rates and revenues per order are too different.

Now you know how to estimate the revenue generated by your campaigns' sales, so it's time to look at the second revenue stream: KENP royalties.

Factoring in your Kindle Unlimited page reads

The good news is this: you don't need to work out any estimates, make any calculations, or create any spreadsheets to know exactly how many KENP reads (and corresponding royalties) your campaigns generate because Amazon actually discloses that to you, right in the dashboard!

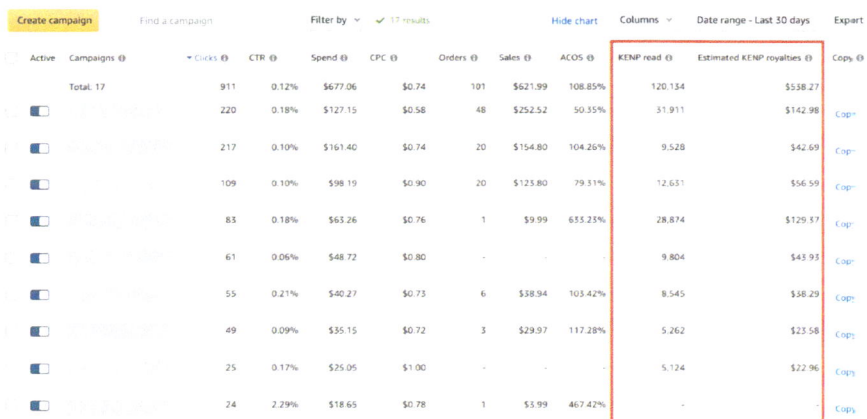

The Amazon Advertising dashboard shows KENP pages read and royalties generated from those page reads.

If your books are enrolled in KDP Select, and therefore earning royalties on page reads, then you need to add these KENP royalties to your sales royalties, to work out the total revenue of each campaign.

```
Total Revenue = Sales x royalty rate + KENP Royalties
```

Or if you're calculating your sales earnings using the revenue per order method:

```
Total Revenue = Orders x Revenue per order + KENP Royalties
```

This Total Revenue figure is the one you should be comparing to the Spend of your campaign, ad group, or target, to determine their profitability.

Once you have this figure, you can use it to calculate what I call your true ACOS, that you'll also find referred to elsewhere as KU-adjusted ACOS or revised ACOS. In a nutshell, it is the actual Advertising Cost of Sale of your campaigns—so the same as the regular ACOS, but instead of dividing Spend by the Sales figure reported in the dashboard, you divide it by your actual revenue.

```
True ACOS = Spend/revenue
True ACOS = Spend/(Sales x royalty rate + KENP Royalties)
```

If this true ACOS is under 100%, you'll know your actual revenue is higher than your spend, and therefore your campaign/ad group/keyword is profitable. Inversely, if it is higher than 100%, you're spending more than you're earning, meaning you're experiencing a loss.

I know these formulas may look scary, so I'll be sharing some spreadsheets with you in the Bonus Resources — the Break-even Bid Calculators — at the end of this book that will do all the mathematical work for you (like magic!). But at the end of the day, what you need to remember here is that we're simply adding up what you earn through sales and what you earn through page reads and comparing it to what you spent.

Let's do a quick example. In the following screenshot, I'm advertising a series of ebooks, with some at $0.99 and others at $9.99. I've worked out that around 50% of my sales come from the $0.99 ebooks, so I know that my average net royalty rate on these sales is 50%.

From, there, I can work out my total revenue from Sales and KENP royalties and use that to calculate the true ACOS of each campaign.

Campaigns ⓘ	Spend ⓘ	CPC ⓘ	Orders ⓘ	Sales ⓘ	ACOS ⓘ	KENP read ⓘ	Estimated KENP royalties ⓘ
Total: 17	$677.06	$0.74	101	$621.99	108.85%	120,134	$538.27
Campaign 1	$127.15	$0.58	48	$252.52 *50% = $125	50.35%	31,911	$142.98 Revenue: +$125 = $255 Real ACoS: 48%
Campaign 2	$161.40	$0.74	20	$154.80 *50% = $75	104.26%	9,528	$42.69 Revenue: +$75 = $115 Real ACoS: 140%
Campaign 3	$98.19	$0.90	20	$123.80 *50% = $60	79.31%	12,631	$56.59 Revenue: +$75 = $115 Real ACoS: 85%
Campaign 4	$63.26	$0.76	1	$9.99 *50% = $5	633.23%	28,874	$129.57 Revenue: +$75 = $135 Real ACoS: 46%

True ACoS calculation.

What's particularly interesting about this screenshot is that, if I didn't go through the trouble of making these calculations, I could easily have misinterpreted the data.

For example, if I'd only looked at Sales and ACOS as provided by Amazon, and ignored KENP reads, I could have been tempted to stop Campaign 4, while in reality it's the best performing one of all (thanks to the page reads).

Or if I'd omitted the fact that I only make 50% royalties on Sales, I would have missed the fact that Campaign 2 is clearly operating at a loss and needs to be adjusted.

But how do you go in and adjust a loss-making campaign? That's what we're going to look at next. Before that, though, there is one last thing we need to touch upon: series and read through.

17

Series advertising & read through

Note: This chapter is only for authors writing books in a series—whether in fiction or nonfiction. If you only write stand-alone books with no crossover to one another, or if you only have one book out, you can feel free to skip this chapter. That said, you should know that authors who write and advertise series have a huge advantage when it comes to marketing—and advertising in particular.

If you're not familiar with the concept of read through and its importance for series writers, I highly recommend you read the two chapters dedicated to the topic in my free book: *How to Market a Book: Overperform in a Crowded Market.* They will prepare you for the head-swirling calculations that come next.

In a nutshell, when you advertise a series, each sale of book one is worth more to you than what you earn on the sale itself because there is a probability that the reader will then pick up book two, book three, and more, thus earning you significantly more money in the long term.

This probability is effectively your read through, and you need to factor it into your revenue calculations. There are two methods to achieve that, depending on the type of campaign you set up and the number of products you advertise.

The first method is to estimate how much a sale of book one is worth to you, and then use that for your revenue calculations and campaign optimization. With this method, you can only advertise one book in your campaign—the first book in the series—which makes it ideal for authors who want to run Custom text campaigns.

The second method is simpler, involves fewer math skills, but requires that the author advertise all the books in their series within the same Standard campaign ad group, therefore ruling out Custom text campaigns. It's by far my favorite one (as you might have guessed by the number of times I've recommended the use of Standard campaigns over Custom text), but it might not be ideal for very long series.

Let's go through both and analyze how to use them, as well as the advantages and drawbacks of each.

Method #1: Using the lifetime value of book one

The idea for this method is relatively simple: you only advertise book one in your series and calculate your true ACOS based on the estimated lifetime value (LTV) that this sale represents for you.

To calculate this LTV, you need to know what your read through is throughout your whole series; then simply multiply that by the royalties you earn on each book.

Let me illustrate with an example. Say you have a five-book series, and your ebooks are all priced at $2.99, and you lose around one-third of readers from one book to another (on average). This would mean that

- Your read through from book one to book two is 66%,
- Your read through from book one to book three is 44%,
- Your read through from book one to book four is 30%,
- Your read through from book one to book five is 20%.

In other words, if you manage to sell 100 copies of book one, you know that this will generate, on average,

- 100 sales of book one, worth 2.99 x 70% = $2 each (rounding down), so $200 in total,
- 66 sales of book two, worth $2 each, so $132,
- 44 sales of book three, so $88,
- 30 sales of book four, so $60,
- 20 sales of book five, so $40.

In sum, the total lifetime revenue for 100 sales of book one is $520, so the LTV of a sale of book one is $5.20. In other words, you can expect each sale of book one to generate $5.20 of revenue in total down the line.

If this seems daunting, at least know that this part is, by far, the most difficult one in the process, but sadly also the most important.

One of the issues is that it's impossible to figure out an exact, unmovable figure for that lifetime value. Amazon doesn't offer authors any data around read through, leaving us to guesstimate it based on the volume of sales of our different books.

But naturally, that sales volume can be impacted by, well, anything. A BookBub Featured Deal[8] on one of your books in the series can throw off the numbers completely. A TikTok video that goes viral will do the same. A free promo on book one will impact read through negatively for several weeks, as many freebie seekers will not actually read the book, let alone buy the following books in the series.

That's why it's important to estimate your read through over a period of time when you ran no strong promotions, didn't change pricing, and didn't have any unexpected surges in sales. If that sounds too complicated, you can always look at your overall lifetime sales. If your books have been out for long enough, and have had a reasonable number of sales, looking at lifetime numbers should statistically smooth any discrepancies caused by one-time

---

[8] Reedsy blog post on BookBub Featured Deals: https://blog.reedsy.com/guide/bookbub/bookbub-featured-deals/

promos.

Once you have that read through estimate, don't hesitate to lower it a bit. It's better to work with a conservative estimate for read through than with an optimistic one.

For example, if you find that your read through from book one to two is 80%, go with 75% or even 70% for your LTV calculations. That way, you'll be on the safe side if that read through suffers once you start advertising the series (which can happen).

Once you've figured out a valid conservative estimate for the LTV of a book one sale, it's time for the easy part: comparing it to your campaigns' cost per order. If it costs you more than the LTV to produce a sale of book one, then you know you're losing money. Inversely, if a campaign's cost per order is lower than the LTV, that campaign is profitable.

As you'll remember, the cost per order is a metric that is not displayed in the dashboard, so you'll need to calculate it mentally, or through a spreadsheet.

Let's go back to our example of the five-book series with a book one LTV of $5.20 and consider the following screenshot (cost/order metric added manually by me):

Keyword	Suggested bid		Keyword bid	Impressions	Clicks	CTR	Spend	CPC	Orders	Sales	Cost/order
Total: 475				914,571	4,138	0.45%	$1,100.87	$0.27	402	$6,569.80	
keyword 1	$1.59	Apply	$ 0.19	78,292	177	0.23%	$37.39	$0.21	13	$203.01	$2.88
keyword 2	$0.13	Apply	$ 0.55	3,599	138	3.83%	$40.41	$0.29	35	$494.01	$1.15
keyword 3	$0.97	Apply	$ 0.20	49,069	126	0.26%	$24.65	$0.20	3	$31.47	$8.22
keyword 4	$0.64	Apply	$ 0.22	16,610	122	0.73%	$26.34	$0.22	10	$124.27	$2.63
keyword 5	$1.59	Apply	$ 0.13	3,582	89	2.48%	$18.53	$0.21	3	$36.37	$6.18

We can deduce that

- Keywords 1, 2, and 4 are profitable (cost per order below the LTV)
- Keywords 3 and 5 are loss-making (cost per order above the LTV)

Of course, this would be for a series that is not in Kindle Unlimited, and therefore only earns the author money through book sales. For series enrolled in KDP Select, you need to take the KENP reads into account as well, which complicates things a bit.

Lifetime value of a KU borrow

The same logic that applies to sales applies to Kindle Unlimited borrows as well: there is a probability that a reader who borrows and reads book one through KU will borrow and read the following books in the series. That probability is what I call the KU read through and can be estimated in a similar way to the read through on sales.

The only hiccup is that, contrarily to sales, KDP does not give you a figure for borrows (despite countless high-hitting authors requesting this metric since the very start of KU). Instead, the only metrics Amazon gives us are KENP reads and KENP royalties.

If all your books in the series are of similar length, then that is fine. You can calculate your KU read through by simply comparing the total number of reads of book one to that of the other books in the series.

But if the books are of varying length, then a higher/lower number of reads on a given book might be caused not by a difference in read through, but simply because one book is longer or shorter. In that case, you need to weigh your read through calculations by the length of each book and effectively work out an estimated number of borrows for each book.

Going back to our five-book series, let's say that they're all in KU and present the following metrics:

- Book one is 300 KENP pages long and has had 3m lifetime page reads.
- Books two and three are 400 KENP pages long and have had 3m lifetime page reads each.
- Books four and five are 375 KENP pages long and have 2.5m lifetime page reads.

To work out an estimated number of borrows for each, we just divide the lifetime page reads by the length of each book, which gives us

- Book one: 3m/300 = 10,000 borrows
- Books two and three: 3m/400 = 7,500 borrows
- Books four and five: 2.5m/375 = 6,667 borrows

With that, we can work out the KU read through for the series:

- From book one to book two: 75%
- From book one to book three: 75%
- From book one to book four: 67%
- From book one to book five: 67%

> Note: Since KU borrows and reads are unaffected by price changes and there is no friction for a KU reader to borrow and read the next book, they can be a much better measure of reader satisfaction throughout your series than Sales read through.

Once you've worked out your series' KU read through, you can use it to estimate the LTV of a borrow of book one. The formula is similar to that of the LTV of a sale—we just have to replace the sales royalties by KENP read royalties (which are a factor of the length of the book and the KU payout rate per page).

For the purposes of Kindle Unlimited royalty calculations in this book, we'll use a figure for KU payouts of $0.005 per page, which is higher than the usual payout rate ($0.004713915 in September 2022), but will help round off calculations.

Going back to our example, 100 borrows of book one would generate, over the lifetime of the readers

- 100 book one borrows, each worth 300 pages x $0.005 = $1.50, so $150

in total
- 75 book two borrows, each worth 400 x $0.005 = $2, so $200 in total
- 75 book three borrows, also worth $200 in total
- 67 book four borrows, each worth 375 x $0.005 = $1.88, so $188 in total
- 67 book five borrows, also worth $188 in total

In total, the LTV of 100 borrows of book one is the sum of all the above—$826. So the LTV of a borrow of book one is $8.26.

Now that we have both the LTV of a sale and LTV of a borrow, we can go back to the advertising dashboard and judge the performance of the campaigns, ad groups, and targets by comparing, on one hand, the cost and, on the other hand, the LTV of all the orders and borrows generated.

Let's look at these four ad groups:

Ad group	Status	Total targets	Spend	Orders	KENP read
Total: 3			$237.30	24	6,797
Christmas keywords	Delivering	8	$126.90	17	2,372
Similar ASINs	Delivering	13	$22.18	2	778
Similar authors	Delivering	25	$88.22	5	3,647
Similar authors #2	Delivering	25	$123.35	8	1,287

As you can see, Amazon Advertising doesn't give us a figure for borrows, so we calculate it based on the KENP reads. Since we're only advertising book one in this campaign, and we know it's 300 pages long, we can work out that:

- The *Christmas keywords* ad group generated 2,372/300 = 8 borrows (rounded up)
- The *Similar ASINs* ad group generated 778/300 = 3 borrows (rounded up)
- The *Similar authors* ad group generated 3,647/300 = 12 borrows (rounded down)
- The *Similar authors #2* ad group generated 1,287/300 = 4 borrows (rounded down)

Since we know exactly how much an order and a borrow are worth ($5.20 and $8.26, respectively), we can now calculate whether each ad group is profitable or not.

- *Christmas keywords* generated 17 orders, worth 17 x $5.20 = $88.40 and 8 borrows, worth 8 x $8.26 = $66.08, for a cost of $126.90. This leaves a **profit** of $88.40 + $66.08 – $126.90 (Spend of the campaign) = $27.58.
- *Similar ASINs* generated 2 orders, worth 2 x $5.20 = $10.40 and 3 borrows, worth 3 x $8.26 = $24.78, for a cost of $22.18. This leaves a **profit** of $10.40 + $24.78 – $22.18 (Spend of the campaign) = $13.
- *Similar authors* generated 5 orders, worth 5 x $5.20 = $26 and 12 borrows, worth 12 x $8.26 = $99.12, for a cost of $88.22. This leaves a **profit** of $26 + $99.12 – $88.22 = $36.90.
- *Similar authors* #2 generated 6 orders, worth 6 x $5.20 = $31.20 and 4 borrows, worth 4 x $8.26 = $33.04, for a cost of $123.35. This leaves a **loss** of $31.20 + $33.04 –$123.35 = $59.11.

I now know that I should focus my efforts on optimizing the last ad group, and probably reduce bids or pause targets in it—while I can afford to raise bids on the first four ad groups since they're clearly making me money (in the long term).

The prerequisite: advertising book one only, and only in one format

As mentioned earlier, using the LTV method for calculating profitability has one important prerequisite: you can only advertise the first book in your series, and only its Kindle edition.

If you advertise several books in the series within the same ad group (in a Standard campaign), then Amazon will report the sales of all these books—not just the figures for book one. So you will not be able to apply the calculations above to the numbers of your dashboard, because the figure for Orders and for KENP reads will be a mix of orders and reads of book one, as well as other books advertised in the ad group.

It's also recommended that you only advertise the Kindle edition, or else the figure for orders might include paperback sales as well. And as we saw in the last chapter, paperback sales are generally not worth the same to an author as ebook sales.

You could get around this by calculating the lifetime value of a print sale (based on your read through and the net royalties you earn on print) and then figuring out what percentage of your sales comes from ebook versus print, to work out an average lifetime value per sale, but this is a lot of extra hassle, which I don't believe is worth the effort.

My recommendation would be to stick with the one format that accounts for the majority of your earnings (usually, that will be the ebook) and advertise the first-in-series in that format only. Your ads might generate some print sales that will not get tracked in the dashboard, but you can treat those as a bonus (same as audiobook sales).

The fact that this method only works if you advertise the first-in-series presents several advantages: first, you make sure that Amazon doesn't show ads for books two or three to readers who haven't yet purchased book one. More importantly, though, this means you can use Custom text campaigns, which a lot of authors still swear by. So while it's not my favorite of the two methods, it certainly is a valid one to use.

Method #2: Advertising all the books in the series

This second method is in many ways the opposite of the first one.

First, instead of advertising only the first book in the series, you advertise all the books in the series. This means you can't use Custom text campaigns, and instead rely on Standard ones (with ad groups).

Second, this method involves next to no mathematical calculations, because, instead of seeing just book one sales and borrows, Amazon will report on the sales and borrows generated by ads for all the books in your series.

Incidentally, this will make your numbers look a lot better in the dashboard, as the Orders, Sales, and KENP Reads will include all sales and reads for any of your books within the fourteen-day attribution window. It might just be psychological, but it makes it a lot more enjoyable to look at an Amazon Advertising dashboard when those sales metrics look healthy.

Let's look at the following automatic campaign. I'm advertising all the books in a series, in ebook format only. All the books are at $3.99, except for the first-in-series, which is permanently discounted to $0.99.

Automatic targeting groupe	Status	Bid	Impressions	Clicks	CTR	Spend	CPC	Orders	Sales	ACOS	KENP read	Estimated KENP royaltie
Total: 4			51,352	284	0.55%	$91.55	$0.32	36	$95.64	95.72%	35,010	$140.90
Loose match	Delivering	$ 0.41	36,092	183	0.51%	$54.54	$0.30	29	$85.71	63.63%	22,869	$186.06
Complements	Delivering	$ 0.25	13,966	59	0.42%	$24.22	$0.41	4	$3.96	611.62%	4,771	$21.38
Close match	Delivering	$ 0.51	1,294	42	3.25%	$12.79	$0.30	3	$5.97	214.24%	7,370	$33.46

An automatic targeting campaign advertising all the books in a series.

By including all the books in the series, Amazon reports all the reads and KENP royalties generated by the ads, and just with a quick glance I can see that loose match and close match are both profitable thanks to page reads (without even taking sales into account).

For complements, the four orders generated $3.96 in sales, meaning they were all on the first ebook (at $0.99). I can therefore deduce that these four orders generated $0.35 x 4 = $1.40, and that they did not generate any read through within the first fourteen days; otherwise, I would have seen sales of the following books reported. Still, this extra dollar and a half, added to the page reads, puts the complements target at more or less break even.

As you can see, with this method, you can quickly judge whether a target is profitable or loss-making, without the need for any read through calculations. Of course, your estimates won't be exact with this method either, as we are limited by Amazon's attribution window.

The limits of the fourteen-day attribution window

I mentioned the fourteen-day limit a couple of times, but I think it's important to stress it again and understand its implications. Any sales and reads resulting from an ad click, but happening more than fourteen days after that ad click, will not be reported in the dashboard.

For many readers, and "whale readers" in particular (whale readers of commercial fiction read a book a day, or more), fourteen days is enough to go through several books in a series. But this is only the case for a small minority of readers. Most might only read a handful of books a month.

A 2021 survey by Written Word Media revealed that over 40% of their non–Kindle Unlimited audience read five books or fewer a month.

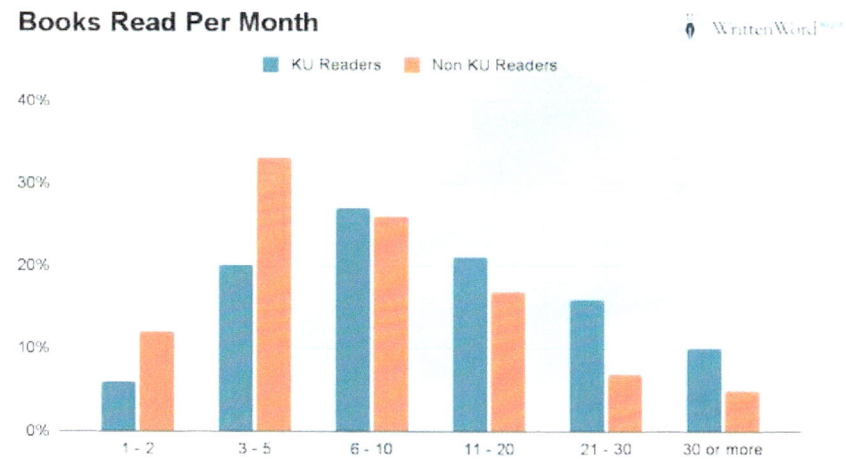

Written Word Media 2021 survey[9]

For Kindle Unlimited readers, the numbers were much higher, with 45% reading 11 books or more. But let's bear in mind that these figures are

---

[9] Survey of readers by Written Word Media in 2021: https://www.writtenwordmedia.com/kindle-unlimited-subscribers/

probably a bit optimistic, since they come from Written Word Media's audience—an audience that loves reading enough to sign up for newsletters alerting them about book deals.

More importantly, most readers won't start reading a book right after they purchase it or borrow it in Kindle Unlimited. In many cases, they will already be reading something, or have something else in their to-be-read pile.

But even if we ignore both these facts, and consider that readers immediately start reading a book after purchasing/borrowing it, these figures would mean that

- The average non-KU reader reads around 2 to 3 books in a 14-day period, and
- The average KU reader reads around 5 books in a 14-day period.

This shows how limiting the fourteen-day attribution window is for authors writing long series. If you're advertising a ten-book series, more than half of the data would be missing from the dashboard on average because the majority of sales and reads would happen outside of the window.

This is not necessarily a bad thing, though. It simply means that the data for sales and reads reported in the dashboard is conservative; your actual sales and KU royalties resulting from your ads will be higher, and in some cases much higher. It gives you a healthy margin, or safety net, to play with.

If you can get your campaigns to break even—according to the limited data in the dashboard—you can be 100 percent confident that you are actually making a positive return on investment in your ads. Which is why my objective, when advertising series with this second method, is to get all campaigns to a break-even point. If a campaign is hugely profitable, but isn't spending much, then I'll raise bids significantly to scale the result, even at the expense of hurting the ROI, since I know I have that safety net.

In the case of very long series, you can even do a mix of the two methods and include a margin directly within your ROI calculations. For example, if I'm advertising a fifteen-book series with a strong read through, I could potentially multiply the reported sales and reads by 1.5, or even 2, to account for the read through happening outside of the fourteen-day period. But in my experience, if you have a good commercial fiction series of four books or more, with strong covers and helpful blurbs, you should be able to make your campaigns profitable with method #2 relatively easily—and keep that extra read through as pure extra profit.

Once you know how to judge whether a particular campaign, ad group, or individual target is profitable or loss-making, the only thing left to do is tweak your bids accordingly: lower them in case of loss, keep them stable in case of break even, and raise them in case of profit.

18

Optimizing for the break-even bid

Now you know how to evaluate the profitability of a campaign, it's time to consider the optimization part. Optimizing a campaign is generally all about tweaking the bids of the targets included in the campaign.

Since the bid represents the maximum amount you're ready to pay per click, the goal here is to figure out what bid would make each target break even. This is what I like to call the break-even bid.

For example, if a campaign generated 500 clicks and returned $100 in net earnings, your break-even bid is $0.20 — because if you had paid $0.20 for each click, then that campaign would have cost you $100 and would have therefore broken even.

Calculating the break-even bid for each target in a campaign is the first and most important step in the campaign optimization process. Once you know which bid makes a target break even, you can tweak your actual bid to get your CPC closer to that break-even bid.

Calculating your break-even bid

In essence, the calculation for the break-even bid is a simple ratio, that of net revenue divided by clicks.

```
break-even bid = net revenue / clicks
```

That said, while the formula looks simple, it does have a trick: you need to be able to calculate your net revenue, using the methods from Chapter 16. Let's go through these methods again with the break-even bid in mind.

Break-even bid with the average net royalty rate

Once you know your average net royalty rate, calculating your net revenue is easy: you just multiply your Sales figure by that royalty rate.

```
break even bid = sales x net royalty rate / clicks
```

Example: Let's say we're advertising a mix of wide ebooks and paperbacks, with an average net royalty rate of 45%.

Keyword	Match type	Status	Bid	Impressions	▼ Clicks	CTR	Spend	CPC	Sales	ACOS	ROAS
Total: 79				72,809	394	0.54%	$622.42	$1.58	$362.88	171.52%	0.58
inspirational books	Phrase	Paused Details ▾	$ 0.40	22,744	131	0.58%	$206.49	$1.58	$143.43	143.97%	0.69
happiness	Phrase	Paused Details ▾	$ 0.40	27,378	101	0.37%	$163.68	$1.62	$93.85	174.41%	0.57
kindness	Phrase	Paused Details ▾	$ 0.40	5,292	50	0.94%	$79.25	$1.59	$63.53	124.74%	0.80

Using the break-even bid formula, we can deduce that the break-even bid for each keyword is as follows:

- *Inspirational books*: $143.43 x 45% / 131 = $0.49
- *Happiness*: $93.85 x 45% / 101 = $0.42
- *Kindness*: $63.53 x 45% / 50 = $0.57

These are slightly higher than the current bids I have set for each keyword, so in most cases (see exceptions below), I would raise these bids to match the break-even bid.

Break-even bid with the average revenue per order

If you're using the revenue per order method, you can simply deduce your net revenue by multiplying your total Orders by your net revenue per order. For example, if you're advertising both an ebook and paperback in your campaign, and you know that you earn around $2 for each copy sold (whether of the ebook or paperback), you can simply multiply your total orders by 2 to get your net revenue.

Which gives us the following formula for the break-even bid:

```
break-even bid = orders x net revenue per order / clicks
```

Consider the following example:

Keyword	id	Keyword bid	Impressions	▼ Clicks	CTR	Spend	CPC	Orders	Sales	ACOS
Total: 500			2,479,766	11,281	0.45%	$2,872.26	$0.25	1,238	$16,447.18	17.46%
keyword 1	Apply	$ 0.20	570,505	1,379	0.24%	$244.66	$0.18	59	$749.26	32.65%
keyword 2	Apply	$ 0.28	119,471	681	0.57%	$186.92	$0.27	102	$1,290.35	14.49%
keyword 3	Apply	$ 0.27	75,509	670	0.89%	$178.43	$0.27	70	$906.95	19.67%

The average revenue per order is $2, so we would have the following break-even bids:

- *keyword 1*: 59 x $2 / 1,379 = $0.09
- *keyword 2*: 102 x $2 / 681 = $0.30
- *keyword 3*: 70 x $2 / 670 = $0.21

Our current costs per click for keywords 1 and 3 are above the break-even bid, so these targets are not currently profitable. I would therefore lower their bids to their respective break-even bid.

Inversely, keyword 2's CPC is below the break-even bid, so I would raise the current bid to $0.30.

Break-even bid with KENP reads

If some (or all) of your advertised products are in Kindle Unlimited, then you will need to factor in your KENP royalties into your break-even bid calculations. This is fairly easy to do, as you just need to add them to your net revenue on Sales.

Depending on the method you're using:

```
break even bid = (sales * net royalty rate + KENP royalties) /
clicks
```

Or:

```
break even bid = (orders * net revenue per order + KENP
royalties) / clicks
```

Take the following example:

Automatic targeting groups	Bid	Impressions	Clicks	CTR	Spend	CPC	Orders	Sales	ACOS	KENP read	Estimated KENP royalties
Total: 4		440,810	404	0.09%	$268.65	$0.66	29	$195.71	137.27%	20,002	$85.88
Complements	$ 0.67	279,486	247	0.09%	$156.57	$0.63	15	$94.85	165.07%	11,023	$47.33
Loose match	$ 0.64	78,759	94	0.12%	$60.00	$0.64	6	$47.94	125.16%	2,978	$12.79
Close match	$ 0.85	82,565	63	0.08%	$52.08	$0.83	8	$52.92	98.41%	6,001	$25.76

Assuming that the author's average net royalty rate is 50%, we would have the following break-even bids:

- *Complements*: ($94.85 x 50% + $47.33) / 247 = $0.38
- *Loose match*: ($47.94 x 50% + $12.79) / 94 = $0.39
- *Close match*: ($52.92 x 50% + $25.76) / 63 = $0.83

My current bids and CPC for complements and loose match targets are well above the break-even point, so I should both lower them to $0.39. Inversely, the close match targets are breaking even, as their CPC is equal to the break-even bid—so I won't touch the bid.

As you can see, once you've figured out what your break-even bid is for each target, you simply need to compare it to your historical cost per click and then adjust your bid accordingly.

Adjusting your bids

After you've set up your first wave of campaigns, 90 percent of the time you'll spend on Amazon Advertising will be dedicated to adjusting your bids. This is what campaign optimization is all about, and it can certainly get tiring/repetitive after a certain point, but as long as you know how to figure out your break-even bid, it's a very simple process.

There are a few exceptions, which I'll explore, but, in general, you should simply set your bid for each target to the break-even bid—because that bid represents exactly how much you're ready to pay per click for the target to not lose money.

"But shouldn't I optimize my targets so that they make me money, not just break even?"

Ideally, yes. But there are several reasons why I generally recommend optimizing for break even, rather than for profit.

First, as discussed in the last chapter, the limits of the fourteen-day attribution window mean that a target that is supposedly breaking even—according to the data reported in the Amazon dashboard—is actually likely to be turning a profit.

Second, your ads can drive collateral sales that Amazon doesn't track in the dashboard, as is the case with audiobook sales. Or if your ads manage to push your book high enough in the ranks, you might earn some additional sales as a result of the increased organic visibility.

Finally, there are sales driven by word of mouth. A reader who discovers your book through an Amazon ad might enjoy it enough to recommend it to their friends. Naturally, if such friends then buy it, their purchases won't appear in your Amazon Advertising dashboard, but they can be (indirectly) attributed to the ads.

All that is to say, in many cases, your ads will actually generate a lot more income than what you'll see in the Amazon Advertising dashboard. So much so, that some Amazon Ads experts out there actually recommend that authors ignore the metrics in the dashboard and instead only look at their KDP reports to judge the effectiveness of the ads.

I definitely wouldn't go that far. While it can't hurt to keep an eye on your KDP reports while you run your ads, you should very much base your decisions on the Amazon Advertising data—if you know how to interpret it well and calculate your net revenue.

But this is the reason why I generally optimize all campaigns and targets for break even: I know that breaking even according to the dashboard's data means that the author is actually earning quite a bit of money (through those additional collateral, untraceable sales).

Naturally, you don't necessarily need to follow my lead on this. Instead, you can set bids that are a bit below your break-even bid, to make sure you have a margin of profit. You should just be aware that this will limit the deliverability of that target and the number of auctions you will win against other advertisers.

Sometimes, lowering your profit on the ads to gain more visibility (while still breaking even) can be the best bet for your career, but that naturally depends on how flexible you are in terms of budget. You can always start optimizing for profitability, and once you've made a bit of money and want to scale things, lower your bids to break even.

"If I want to optimize for break even, should I just set all my bids to the break-even bid for each target?"

Yes and no. As I mentioned, there are a few exceptions to that rule.

Exception #1: When you don't have enough data

This first exception will actually apply to the majority of your targets—at least within the first few months of your campaigns.

Calculating your break-even bid and tweaking your actual bid only make sense once your target has generated enough clicks for the data to be meaningful. In other words, if a target has generated two clicks but no sales or page reads, you shouldn't lower its bid just yet.

Making bid optimization decisions based on incomplete or statistically insignificant data is one of the most common mistakes I see authors make with Amazon Ads, so I'll dedicate the next chapter to that.

Exception #2: When bid and CPC don't align

While the bid you set on a target indicates to Amazon how much you're willing to spend per click, this doesn't mean that each click will cost you that much. In many cases, Amazon will only make you pay a fraction of your actual bid.

Let's take an example from an automatic campaign, whose bid hasn't been modified in the period we're looking at:

Automatic targeting groups	▾ Bid	Impressions	Clicks	CTR	Spend	CPC	Orders	Sales	ACOS	KENP read	EstimatedKENP
Total: 4		519,895	1,337	0.26%	$193.56	$0.14	21	$291.79	66.34%	12,777	$68.71
Close match	$ 0.61	12,070	87	0.72%	$23.42	$0.27	5	$57.95	40.41%	4,777	$25.70

As you can see, the CPC of the close match target is under half of the bid I set. In other words, despite my signaling that I was ready to spend more per click on this target (in order to scale its delivery), Amazon keeps charging me a lot less than what I bid.

What could the reasons be for this?

1. The target (or group of targets) has little competition, meaning there

aren't many advertisers competing against me to win the auctions, and/or their bids are much lower than mine.

2. My ad quality score for the target is much higher than that of competitors (meaning my book is more relevant), so it takes a lower bid for me to win the auction. In this case, even if my bid is similar to that of other advertisers, Amazon will still charge me less per click.

So where can this usually happen? On targets that are either noncompetitive (for example, small, obscure comp titles or authors) or for which you have an unfair relevance advantage (brand/defense keywords). It can also happen on automatic campaigns for the close match targeting group, as exemplified above, since that group often targets defense keywords.

Now, you might be wondering why such targets should be treated differently in terms of bid optimization. After all, you can simply use your break-even bid for those as well, and if Amazon decides to only make you spend a fraction of that per click, then that's all the better!

That is certainly a way to go. But on the other hand, you might be thinking: "Is there any way I can get Amazon to have me win all the auctions for that target, even at the cost of paying a bit more per click?" And there certainly is: just increase your bid to above your break-even bid. You know that Amazon won't make you pay that much per click (unless the competitor landscape for the target suddenly changes), and by setting a higher bid, you might win a few extra auctions.

In the example, since the close match targeting group is working so well (breaking even just in KENP royalties), what I would do is actually further raise the bid, in order to encourage Amazon to scale the delivery of that targeting group.

Exception #3: When your main goal is not profitability

Of course, this book focuses on optimizing your ads for profit (well, for breaking even, but we discussed this already), because that tends to be an author's most common goal when running Amazon Ads.

However, there are some cases where it can make sense to run ads without caring much about ROI.

A common reason is if you run ads on a preorder with the sole objective to build its Also Boughts. This kind of campaign will generally never return a profit, since advertising a preorder is much harder than advertising a book that is instantly available. But it is still worth running them at a loss because your objective here is not ROI, it's to build the Also Boughts.

Another example is if you're running a price promotion and are looking to boost your rank during a limited time. You might not care as much about the profitability of the ads and instead focus on getting as many orders during that limited time period.

Exception #4: When you're using up and down bidding optimization

In most cases, Amazon will respect the bid you set for each target, so you won't ever pay more per click than you bid—except if you're using up and down dynamic bids. When using this type of bidding optimization, there is a strong possibility that Amazon will bid higher for certain targets than the bid you set, meaning your actual CPC may be higher than your bid.

This can make it hard to optimize your campaigns and may require that you lower the bid by a lot, as Amazon can still increase it by up to 100 percent. Overall, it's not a bidding optimization type that lends itself well to ROI optimization, though this strategy can be useful in other cases. But more on this in the next chapter.

19

Up, down or fixed?

When you create a Sponsored Products campaign on Amazon, you have three choices for bidding optimization:

- Fixed bids
- Dynamic bids—down only
- Dynamic bids—up and down

Your bidding optimization strategy will determine how Amazon treats your bids in regard to the various auctions for placements.

In the case of fixed bids, it's simple: Amazon will use the exact bid you set for each target.

In the case of dynamic bids, Amazon may modify your bids in real time based on—in their words—whether your ad is more or less "likely to convert to a sale."

For down only dynamic bids, Amazon may only lower the bid you set, if they estimate that the particular ad is less likely to convert to a sale.

When using up and down dynamic bids, Amazon may both lower the bid as well as raise it (by a maximum of 100%) if they think the ad is more likely to convert to a sale.

To give you a practical example, if I set a bid of $0.50 for a particular target:

- When using **fixed bids**, Amazon will use my exact bid, so I will always bid exactly $0.50 per click. This doesn't mean that all my clicks will cost me $0.50, though, as the actual CPC will depend on the competition as well, but I definitely won't pay over $0.50 per click.
- When using **down only dynamic bids** (or down bids), Amazon may lower my bid on searches or products that they deem less likely to lead to a sale. When compared to fixed bids, down only dynamic bids usually translate into a cheaper cost per click on certain targets (those where Amazon lowers my bid), but also a lower number of impressions (lower bids win fewer auctions than the $0.50 one).
- When using **up and down dynamic bids** (or up and down bids), Amazon may either lower or raise my bid by up to 100 percent for top-of-search placements, and up to 50 percent for all other placements. Each click can cost me anywhere from $0 to $1, depending on the competition, and on how likely that click is to lead to a sale (according to Amazon).

As you can see, the more flexibility you give Amazon to play with your bids, the higher the uncertainty of what you'll end up paying per click—which can interfere with your optimization efforts, but can also potentially work in your favor if Amazon actually knows what they're doing.

Dynamic Bidding "Up and Down" Max. and Min. Bid Range

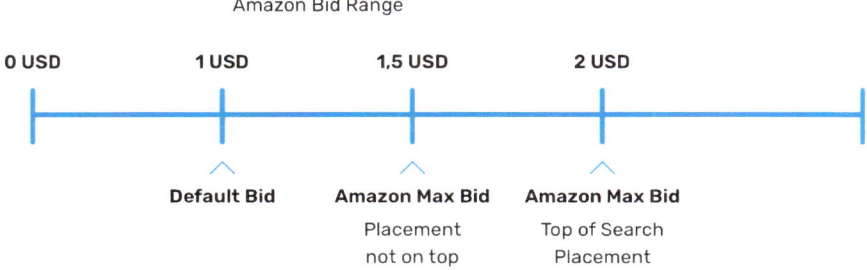

The risks of up and down bids

For a long time, up and down bids were my preferred bidding optimization. As you might have inferred from this book, I'm of the mindset that we authors are less knowledgeable than Amazon—because we don't have access to their truckloads of data—and are therefore less capable of customizing our ads to each customer.

This is why I prefer Standard campaigns over Custom, and that is also why I immediately adopted up and down bids as soon as they became available to authors. After all, if Amazon offers to tweak my bid, in real time, based on their data-driven knowledge of how likely each customer is to buy my book, who am I to say no to that?

And yet, at the same time, you'll have probably noticed that I'm a bit of an optimization freak when it comes to bids. I found myself in an uncomfortable situation, time and again, when using up and down bids.

First, I would start with relatively high bids to get the ads to deliver and quickly test the targets. Once a target had enough clicks, I would calculate its break-even bid and generally reduce its bid to that, or below.

After a few weeks, I would check the campaign again and, to my dismay, find out that my CPC actually hadn't varied all that much on a bunch of my targets—because Amazon decided to raise my real-time bids on these targets. And since Amazon can raise the bids by up to 100 percent, it often didn't matter if I further reduced the bids, as Amazon could just keep doubling them.

Now, this doesn't usually happen on all targets, but even if it happens on just one or two, it can become extremely frustrating, especially to an optimization freak like me. Here's a typical example of a campaign with up and down bids where you can see what I mean:

Keyword	suggested bid		Bid	Impressions	Clicks	CTR	Spend	CPC	Orders	Sales	ACOS	KENP read	Estimated KENP royalties
Total:	apply all			183,174	508	0.28%	$413.51	$0.81	124	$802.76	51.51%	86,034	$334.63
witch	$0.63	Apply	$ 1.21	61,103	61	0.10%	$58.97	$0.97	24	$217.76	27.08%	3,315	$24.71
blai...	$1.89	Apply	$ 0.91	3,732	52	1.39%	$26.91	$0.52	30	$216.70	12.42%	14,159	$52.62
wit...	$4.17	Apply	$ 1.11	2,054	51	2.48%	$27.22	$0.53	16	$80.84	33.67%	10,421	$45.89
wit...	$0.91	Apply	$ 0.81	12,994	44	0.34%	$55.70	$1.27	14	$65.86	84.57%	666	$3.08
wit...	$0.43	Apply	$ 1.31	4,725	39	0.83%	$18.27	$0.47	15	$72.85	25.08%	24,167	$109.18

For all the targets here, except one, my cost per click is lower than my default bid—probably because it didn't need to be quite as high to win the auctions.

However, in the case of the fourth one, Amazon is raising my bid by over 50 percent, despite my gradually lowering this target's bid as I saw it not performing as well as the other ones. As a result, the target with the worst performance (by far), and the lowest bid, actually ends up having the highest CPC.

But why would Amazon keep raising the bid for the one target that performs the worst?

That is a question we can't know the answer to for sure—as we don't know exactly how Amazon's up and down dynamic bids work. However, we can make some educated guesses.

First, it's likely that this particular target is much more competitive than the others—and while you can't read the whole keyword for confidentiality purposes, I can confirm that's the case. So one hypothesis is that Amazon raises our bid for it to remain competitive and still deliver impressions and clicks.

A second hypothesis would be that Amazon raises the bid because it doesn't identify this target as performing badly. If we go back to how Amazon defines up and down bidding:

When you select dynamic bids—up and down, we will raise or lower your bid based on the likelihood of the potential click converting to a sale. That means we will increase your bids in real time to help win impressions that may be more likely to convert to a sale, such as when your ad appears for a highly relevant shopping query.

As you can see, up and down bids—and dynamic bidding in general—are focused solely on "the likelihood of the potential click converting to a sale." There is no mention of ACOS, RoAS (Return on Advertising Spend), ROI, or any profit-related metric. If Amazon believes that a potential click is likely to convert to a sale, they will raise your bid, regardless of whether your ad earns or loses you money with the new, real-time bid.

In our example, the low-performing target in question still generated 14 orders out of 44 clicks—a conversion of 32%, which is very high for a nonbranded, competitive keyword. As a result, Amazon understands that clicks on this target are highly likely to convert to a sale, and thus increases the bid substantially.

The fact that this bid increase means that the target becomes loss-making is irrelevant to the bidding optimization, and if I were to further lower the bid, Amazon would probably keep increasing it to a similar level because, for them, that is a high-performing keyword.

Therefore, should you completely disregard and stay away from using up and down bids? Not necessarily. While I now favor down and fixed bidding, there are some cases in which I think up and down bidding is still more than relevant.

Here are the case scenarios for which Amazon recommends the use of up and down bids:

> *A dynamic bids – up and down strategy is best to use when:*
> *– Your key objective is sales*
> *– You want to win the ad placements at the top of the page for keywords within your selected campaign*
> *– You have a high-performing campaign and want to help maximize results*
> *– You have a campaign that features ASINs with excess inventory*
> *– You have a campaign that features deal ASINs*

Again, Amazon makes no reference to profit here, it's all about maximizing sales, no matter what these sales end up costing you. That said, there can definitely be cases in which maximizing sales actually is your number-one objective.

For example: When you run a price promotion or discount deal. Usually, the main goal of a price promotion is to get the book to rise as high as possible in the Amazon rankings during the time period of the deal, and then reap the rewards when the book goes back to full price (or in the form of read through sales or page reads). In such cases, orders become more valuable to you than profit, at least during the time of the promotion—and getting additional orders is exactly what up and down bids are good at. That's a good time to switch your campaign to up and down bids or, even better, to start a brand new campaign (so as not to pollute the data in your existing one).

The same goes for launches, or any other time when you might want to favor sales volume over profitability.

Finally, a last good case for using up and down bids is when you're not overly worried about budget and you want to scale the results of a fixed or down bids campaign that is working well already. This is what Amazon means as maximizing results in the excerpt just cited, and I'll discuss it more in depth in the next part of this book.

Down bids versus fixed bids

In theory, down only bids offer the best of two worlds: it allows you to take advantage of Amazon's data-driven auto-optimization on bids, while making sure that Amazon will never bid above your default bid.

If Amazon detects that a particular search term or product is less likely to drive a sale, then you have nothing to lose from Amazon lowering your bid in real time—to the contrary, it will reduce your loss if the reader does click on the ad and ends up not purchasing.

And if Amazon detects that a particular target is likely to lead to a sale, they'll still respect your maximum bid, ensuring that you can accurately optimize your campaigns for profit.

This does mean that you'll earn fewer impressions, and therefore clicks, on certain search terms/products, but these should in theory only be queries and products that Amazon has already identified as unlikely to convert to a sale.

There is one drawback, however: down bidding optimization needs data in order to work well. If you're just starting out, Amazon will have no data to accurately predict the likelihood that a particular target is to lead to a sale. So it might lower bids on queries or products that could actually be a perfect fit and lead you to lose valuable auctions—at least until you accumulate enough clicks to prove Amazon wrong.

Let me give an example. Say that you create your very first Amazon Advertising campaign, with just one ad group containing fifty targets, down only dynamic bidding, and relatively high bids for all the keywords. If one keyword in particular gets a few clicks and generates no sales, Amazon will automatically start lowering your bid for that keyword—because its limited, early data indicate that it is not converting well. As a result, you could get into a situation where delivery pretty much stops for that keyword after just a few clicks, just because none of those early clicks delivered a sale.

This is why I generally always start with fixed bids when creating new campaigns and only switch them to down only dynamic bids once they're mature enough to be able to benefit from Amazon's bidding optimization. This way, I ensure that Amazon respects my bid on all my targets, which allows me to progressively gather data, and optimize my bids, before poten-tially switching to down only bidding if I want to remain conservative—or to up and down bidding if I want to scale.

> Fun fact: You might think that fixed bids were the default bidding optimization before Amazon introduced dynamic bid optimization, but it's not the case. The default that all advertisers used before being able to choose was down bids, so fixed bidding is somewhat of a new feature on the platform.

The future: target ACOS bidding optimization?

As I mentioned, I'm a big believer in advertising automation and in giving more control to the players that have more data and computing power than I have: the advertising platforms themselves.

If you've followed the evolution of mature advertising platforms such as Facebook or Google in the past few years, you'll have seen that they've gone from a manual model to an automated one.

Ten years ago, the Google Adwords platform was very similar to the Amazon Advertising platform today: you entered keywords that you wanted to target, specified a match type (exact, phrase, broad), and manually set a bid for each one based on how much you were ready to pay per click.

Progressively though, Google Adwords (now Google Ads) introduced machine learning into the bidding process. First, advertisers were able to let Google raise or lower the bids (dynamic bidding) based on their goals (brand awareness, sales, profit, for example). And now, Google Ads' recommended bidding for advertisers is the target RoAS, which doesn't even require you to set a bid in the first place. Instead, you simply tell Google what your target Return on Advertising Spend (target RoAS) is and let Google automatically optimize each bid for you.

Facebook has followed a similar path, moving from CPM bidding (cost per thousand impressions) in the beginning to optimized CPM, and finally purchase value optimization.

I expect Amazon Advertising to follow in their footsteps. Dynamic bidding is already there, and its only flaw is that the type of dynamic bidding that could really be helpful to advertisers (up and down) currently only allows to optimize for sales (not profit).

I have little doubt that, in the next few years, Amazon will release a form of bidding optimization focused on profit instead—such as a target ACOS setting through which you'd tell Amazon what you want your ideal ACOS to be for a campaign, and let them tweak each bid accordingly. It could very well be that, in a few years, we won't even have to touch bids anymore (crossing fingers).

In the meantime, you'll have to optimize your bids manually, which is, after all, what this book is all about! As I realize the past few chapters may still feel very much conceptual to you, I'll soon get into some practical examples of how to go through a campaign and reoptimize it with break-even bids in a few chapters. But first, you need to learn the virtue of patience.

20

The importance of patience

What's the number-one cause of Amazon Advertising mistakes? Making decisions based on incomplete data.

It's an understandable mistake. After all, you're pouring your own hard-earned money into these ads, so you're naturally eager to see some sort of result. If that result doesn't happen quickly enough, you may be tempted to shut down the ads altogether. Or, in a much less frequent but still possible scenario, if your sales start rocketing after starting the ads, you may be tempted to double the budget and bids to further scale these results.

While these are natural, instinctive reactions, you should be careful not to make them too early or else they could have the opposite effect to what you hoped. Instead, you want to make sure that every time you optimize a target, you're meeting the following conditions:

1. The reporting period you're looking at is not affected by potential Amazon attribution delays, and
2. The target has generated enough data (clicks) for the sales/reads results to be statistically meaningful.

I'll explore both these points more in depth in this chapter.

Selecting the right reporting period

As we already know, it can take up to fourteen days after a click for Amazon Advertising to show the full picture of what that click generated in terms of sales and page reads—or rather, the full incomplete picture, since it's limited by the fourteen-day attribution window.

Because of this, I always avoid looking at the results of any campaign, ad group, or target within the last seven or even fourteen days. If I look at a longer recent period (such as thirty days), I'll generally exclude the last week, to make sure I only look at a period for which I have all the data I'm able to get from Amazon.

Of course, excluding recent days can be more or less important depending on your campaign setup. If you're advertising one wide ebook only, then results (ebook sales) will pretty much instantaneously appear in your dashboard. But if you're advertising a KU book, or a whole series, the past seven days data will often be incomplete—as reads and read through sales will take time to trickle in.

One alternative, if your campaign has been running for long enough, is to look at lifetime data. While lifetime also includes the past two weeks—for which the data might be incomplete—it sort of buries it under a much vaster amount of complete data, on the condition that you launched the campaign at least a few months back. In other words, you might not get 100 percent of the picture with lifetime view (because some sales/reads might be missing for the last few days), but you'll have a good 99 percent or more of it.

There are, however, times when lifetime is not the best reporting period to select—and that's when you've made substantial changes to your campaign over its lifetime, which may have modified your optimization objective.

For example, let's say you're running a simple campaign promoting one ebook, priced at $3.99. In this case, you're optimizing for a royalty-adjusted ACOS of 70 percent. But what if suddenly, you run a $0.99 price promotion on that ebook (not through KDP Select)? During the price promotion period, your ACOS objective will drop to 35 percent. One month later, you check the campaign and decide to optimize it based on its lifetime data. The problem you'll run into here is that the lifetime data will contain Orders and Sales both at the $3.99 and $0.99 price points—so you won't know what ACOS to optimize for.

The same goes if you add a product to your campaign that earns you a different royalty percentage (such as adding a paperback to a campaign advertising ebooks), or any other price or product change that might affect your optimization objective.

What should you do instead if you want to run that $0.99 price promotion?

My recommendation would be to create a separate, duplicate campaign for that price point and pause the main campaign for the duration of the price promo. This way, you keep all $0.99 sales within a separate campaign and don't pollute the data of the $3.99 price point campaign, which you can simply restart once the price promotion is over. If you run another similar promo in the future, you can simply reuse that $0.99 campaign. It's a little bit of extra work, but in my opinion it's worth it to keep clean lifetime data in each campaign.

You might be wondering why I put so much emphasis on keeping clean lifetime data, when one can simply select any time period to look at in the last sixty-five days (and therefore look at the days/weeks/months since the last price promotion or major campaign change). I like to have as much data as possible for each target—and sixty-five days are sometimes not enough to get a statistically significant number of clicks. Which leads us to the next topic.

Excluding statistically insignificant results

Optimizing your campaigns for profitability is similar to optimizing them for click-through-rate, in that the first step is to exclude any targets that haven't accrued enough data for their results to be statistically significant.

In the case of CTR optimization, those data are the number of impressions: if a target hasn't had many impressions, it's impossible to judge its click-through-rate. I placed the barrier of statistical significance at 1,000 impressions—which is 100 percent arbitrary, I'll admit, but is a good guideline to follow.

When optimizing for profitability, the conversion you're effectively look-ing at is that from clicks (which cost you money) to Orders and KENP reads. So the data point that needs to be statistically significant is the number of clicks.

Think about it this way: if a target has gotten two clicks and generated nothing in sales or reads, are you going to pause it? Or reduce its bid? Probably not, because it is too soon to tell whether it can be a good target or not—it only had two clicks.

But what about a target that's had ten clicks and no sales/reads? Or one that's had twenty clicks? How many clicks does a target need to gather before it becomes statistically significant?

Well, this will depend on how much value a click can generate for you. If you're advertising a single $2.99 ebook, the maximum value you can get from a click is 70% x $2.99 = $2.10.

If you're advertising a series of ten ebooks, all at $2.99, a click could lead to a sale of all ten books in the series, for a total net value of $21.

This is what I like to call the revenue potential per click—that is, the maximum amount of money that a click can generate for you in a given campaign. It is a factor of the number of products you advertise, their prices, and their royalty rates.

As you can imagine, the revenue potential makes a huge difference when it comes to statistical significance.

In the first scenario, 10 clicks on a target may already make the results statistically significant:

Categories & products	Suggested bid	Bid	Impressions	▼ Clicks	CTR	Spend	CPC	Orders	Sales	ACOS
Total: 10			199,071	1,241	0.62%	$492.96	$0.40	105	$1,879.64	26.23%
category="Writing Skill Reference"	$0.55 — Apply — < 0.41		2,425	10	0.41%	$3.30	$0.33	-	-	-

A target with 10 clicks (at $0.33 per click), but no sales.

Even if the next click generated by this target led to a sale, the target would still be loss-making because that sale is worth a maximum of $2.10 to you. So you can go ahead and either pause the target, or significantly reduce its bid.

In the second scenario, however, 10 clicks would be way too early to make any decision on the campaign: if the 11th click led to a sale, that sale would potentially be worth $21 to you—which would make the target hugely profitable.

The higher your revenue potential per click, the lower you can afford your conversion to be from click to sale. In our second scenario, even if just one out of 60 clicks led to a sale, that target could still be profitable—as long as the click fulfills its maximum revenue potential.

In theory, you'd have to wait until you have over 60 clicks on a target before you make a decision on it.

In practice, however, you'll rarely want to wait for a target to gather a huge number of clicks before you start modifying its bid. After all, you're paying for every one of these clicks, and if a target generated 60 clicks and no sales, you might not want to keep the same bid in the hopes that a 61st click will lead a superfan reading through all your books!

Instead, you'll want to work out some guidelines to quickly go through your targets and optimize them. In my case, I tend to use the following logic for targets that are not profitable:

- If an unprofitable target has 30 clicks or more, I just set its bid to the break-even bid.
- If an unprofitable target has 20 to 30 clicks, I set its bid to slightly above (for example, 10 to 20%) the break-even bid.
- If an unprofitable target has 15 to 20 clicks, I set its bid to well above (50%) the break-even bid.
- If an unprofitable target has 10 to 15 clicks, I just reduce its bid a bit (by 20% to 30%) to get it closer to the break-even bid.
- If an unprofitable target has fewer than 10 clicks, I just ignore it.

Now, what about profitable targets, you may ask? Well, I apply more or less the same logic to them, but instead of being optimistic in my projections (that is, considering what would happen if the next click generated its maximum value), I'm cautious.

For example, if a target has generated one click and led to $5 in total earnings, I'm naturally not going to set its bid to $5—which would technically be its break-even bid at this point. If I did that and the next 10 clicks (costing me $5 each) led to $0 in sales, I'd be in for a major disappointment.

Instead, what I do is gradually increase the bid based on the statistical significance level:

- If a profitable target has fewer than 10 clicks, I slightly increase its bid (by 20% to 30%).
- If a profitable target has 10 to 20 clicks, I set its bid to a bit below (10% to 20%) the break-even bid.
- If a profitable target has 20 clicks or more, I just set its bid to the break-even bid.

Naturally, I'll always adapt this based on the actual break-even bid of each target—and will never go above $1.50 for a bid except in extremely rare circumstances.

Profitable?	Number of Clicks	Action on the bid
No	>30	Set bid to break-even bid
No	20-30	Set bid to 10%-20% above the break-even bid
No	15-20	Set bid to 50% above the break-even bid
No	10-15	Reduce bid by 20%-30%
No	<10	Nothing
Yes	<10	Increase bid by 20%-30%
Yes	10-20	Set bid to 10%-20% below the break-even bid
Yes	>20	Set bid to break-even bid

Recap table on bid optimization.

Now, I want to stress that these are variable guidelines, which I slightly change and adapt based on the campaign's revenue potential per click and how aggressive I want to be with the bids. You might not want to apply these exact optimization rules when going through your campaigns, but instead use them to come up with your own guidelines.

Feeling overwhelmed? That's understandable, but the good thing is that we're now ready to put theory into actual practice with examples, which I promise are going to be much more fun.

21

Practical examples

In this chapter, we're going to apply everything you've learned so far to some actual campaigns and give you an idea of how to practically go through your own campaigns and optimize your targets' bids.

Example #1: Ebook + paperback

This campaign advertises the ebook (not in KU) and paperback formats of the same book. Since both formats net the author a similar amount of money (around $3 per sale), we're applying the revenue per order method.

Categories & products	Status	Bid	Impressions	Clicks	CTR	Spend	CPC	Orders	Sales	ACOS
Total: 9			4,353,642	3,116	0.07%	$1,776.67	$0.57	371	$1,852.56	95.90%
category="Motivational Self-Help"	Delivering	$ 0.70	2,452,158	2,029	0.08%	$1,372.14	$0.68	262	$1,404.08	97.73%
category="Social Activist Biographies"	Delivering	$ 0.41	1,331,277	797	0.06%	$300.91	$0.38	86	$290.03	103.75%
category="Philanthropy & Charity"	Delivering	$ 0.51	352,873	198	0.06%	$88.82	$0.45	16	$96.62	91.93%
category="Spiritual Self-Help"	Delivering	$ 0.21	30,912	32	0.10%	$4.59	$0.14	3	$43.47	10.56%
category="Social Work"	Delivering	$ 0.21	94,973	31	0.03%	$5.53	$0.18	1	$5.39	102.66%
category="Biographies of Social Activists"	Delivering	$ 0.21	47,289	16	0.03%	$2.57	$0.16	2	$6.98	36.82%
category="Motivational Self-Help"	Delivering	$ 0.21	4,595	6	0.13%	$0.83	$0.14	-	-	-
category="Social Work"	Delivering	$ 0.21	37,429	6	0.02%	$1.21	$0.20	1	$5.99	20.20%
category="Motivational Growth & Spirituality"	Delivering	$ 0.21	2,136	1	0.05%	$0.07	$0.07	-	-	-

Sponsored Products campaign targeting Categories.

Let's go through all these targets together. First, we need to discard all those that don't have statistically significant results:

- The second *category="Motivational Self-Help"* and *category="Motivational Growth & Spirituality"* both haven't generated any orders, but they also haven't gotten enough clicks for us to make a decision on the bid. If the next click generated an order, they would instantly become profitable. So we won't touch them.
- The second *category="Social Work"* also hasn't gotten many clicks, but still managed to generate an order, and is currently turning a profit of $3 - $1.21 (the Spend of the category) = $1.79. So even if it's still early, I'll raise its bid a bit to encourage Amazon to prioritize it.

Now that we've dealt with these, let's turn our attention to the highest-spending targets. As a reminder, the formula we're using to calculate the break-even bid is

```
break-even bid = net revenue / clicks
```

- *Category="Motivational Self-Help"* has generated 262 orders, worth $3 x 262 = $786 in total, while spending $1,372.14—so it's far from breaking even. If we apply the formula, the break-even bid should be: $786 / 2,029 clicks = $0.39. That's what I'll set the bid to.
- *Category="Social Activist Biographies"* generated 86 orders out of 797 clicks, which gives us a break-even bid of $0.33.
- *Category="Philanthropy & Charity"* generated 16 orders out of 198 clicks, which gives us a break-even bid of $0.24.
- *Category="Spiritual Self-Help"* generated 3 orders out of 32 clicks, which gives us a break-even bid of $0.28.
- *Category="Social Work"* generated 1 order out of 31 clicks, which gives us a break-even bid of $0.10. Since that's a very low bid (even for a category), and considering that 31 clicks is not entirely statistically significant—if the next click generated an order, the break-even bid would double—I'll actually set the bid a bit higher, at $0.12, instead.
- *Category="Biographies of Social Activists"* is also in a statistical gray zone with its 16 clicks—so while it's very much profitable so far ($6 generated out of a $2.57 spend), I don't want to set its bid quite as high as the current break-even bid would be ($0.38). Instead, I'll set it to $0.31.

Pro tip (or not?): You might have come across a common recommendation in the Amazon Advertising world to always bid one cent above round numbers—which is why I bid $0.31 above, instead of $0.30. The reason is that most advertisers will favor round numbers (more intuitive)—so by increasing your bid by just one cent, you can theoretically outbid them.

In practice, we've seen that the behind-the-scenes calculation for awarding the auction is more complicated, and involves a quality score, but still, using that extra cent bidding tactic can't hurt, and more importantly, makes me feel clever.

To recap, here are the new bids for this campaign, after this round of bid optimization:

Categories & products	Status	Bid	Impressions	▾ Clicks	CTR	Spend	CPC	Orders	Sales	ACOS
Total: 9			4,353,642	3,116	0.07%	$1,776.67	$0.57	371	$1,852.56	95.90%
category="Motivational Self-Help"	Delivering New bid: $0.39	$ 0.70	2,452,158	2,029	0.08%	$1,372.14	$0.68	262	$1,404.08	97.73%
category="Social Activist Biographies"	Delivering New bid: $0.33	$ 0.41	1,331,277	797	0.06%	$300.91	$0.38	86	$290.03	105.75%
category="Philanthropy & Charity"	Delivering New bid: $0.24	$ 0.51	352,873	198	0.06%	$88.82	$0.45	16	$96.62	91.93%
category="Spiritual Self-Help"	Delivering New bid: $0.28	$ 0.21	30,912	32	0.10%	$4.59	$0.14	3	$43.47	10.56%
category="Social Work"	Delivering New bid: $0.12	$ 0.21	94,973	31	0.03%	$5.53	$0.18	1	$5.39	102.60%
category="Biographies of Social Activists"	Delivering New bid: $0.31	$ 0.21	47,289	16	0.03%	$2.57	$0.16	2	$6.98	36.82%
category="Motivational Self-Help"	Delivering Don't change the bid	$ 0.21	4,595	6	0.13%	$0.83	$0.14	-	-	-
			Statistically unsignificant							
category="Social Work"	Delivering New bid: $0.25	$ 0.21	37,429	6	0.02%	$1.21	$0.20	1	$5.99	20.20%
			Statistically unsignificant							
category="Motivational Growth & Spirituality"	Delivering Don't change the bid	$ 0.21	2,136	1	0.05%	$0.07	$0.07	-	-	-
			Statistically unsignificant							

Example #2: Ebook + paperback series (not in KU)

This particular author has a series of nonfiction books, all wide, and advertises both their digital and print editions. They earn 70% royalties on ebook sales, and around 10% on print. They've found that a majority of their sales (75%) come from print, so they've worked out that their average net royalty rate is 70% x 25% + 10% x 75% = 25%.

Keyword	Status	Suggested bid		Keyword bid	Impressions	▼ Clicks	CTR	Spend	CPC	Orders	Sales	ACOS
Total: 47					196,338	1,922	0.98%	$949.44	$0.49	374	$4,498.19	21.11%
writing book	Delivering	$0.77	Apply	$ 0.49	57,770	361	0.62%	$146.99	$0.41	55	$730.94	20.11%
how write	Delivering	$0.53	Apply	$ 0.67	39,238	351	0.89%	$184.68	$0.53	58	$689.69	26.78%
how to write a book	Delivering	$0.64	Apply	$ 0.67	15,265	260	1.70%	$136.31	$0.52	65	$731.27	18.64%
how write nonfiction b ...	Delivering	$0.72	Apply	$ 0.75	1,026	35	3.41%	$17.27	$0.49	10	$90.22	19.14%
public speaking books	Delivering	$0.79	Apply	$ 1.00	2,934	15	0.51%	$10.60	$0.71	1	$8.99	117.91%
publish book	Delivering	$0.66	Apply	$ 0.65	1,221	13	1.06%	$5.59	$0.43	3	$39.98	13.98%
writing memoir	Delivering	$0.57	Apply	$ 0.65	1,222	9	0.74%	$4.66	$0.52	4	$40.19	11.59%
writing books for adults	Delivering	$0.65	Apply	$ 0.50	1,827	9	0.49%	$4.15	$0.46	-	-	-
start writing your book ...	Delivering	$0.23	Apply	$ 0.65	802	8	1.00%	$3.30	$0.41	-	-	-

Sponsored Brands campaign targeting broad match keywords.

Again, let's start with the targets with the lowest statistical significance:

- Keyword *writing books for adults* and *start writing your book...* both have under 10 clicks, so even though they generated zero sales so far, I won't touch their bids for now. The alternative would be to slightly reduce them, but considering we're advertising a series, the revenue potential is quite high, and I wouldn't want to hamper their delivery too early.
- Keyword *writing memoir* also has a low number of clicks, but it's incredibly profitable already—so much so that its current break-even bid would be 25% x $40.19 / 9 = $1.11. While I don't want to raise the bid quite that high, I will set it to $0.91 to encourage delivery.

Now, let's look at the high spenders. The first thing to notice is that for all of them, the actual cost per click is much lower than the last bid we set. This could be due to one of two factors:

1. Either we only recently raised the bid, and since we're looking at lifetime data here, we're seeing an average that is naturally lower, or
2. Since we're using down bidding optimization, Amazon is simply bidding quite lower on average than the upper bid we set (more about

that in the next chapter).

To find out which of these two options are causing this, we can simply check the data for a recent period (let's say the last thirty days). If in that period, the CPC is higher, then I'll know that reason #1 is the likely culprit. If it's at the same level, then I can put it down to the down bidding optimization.

For the purpose of this example, we'll go with option #2: the down bidding optimization is causing much lower CPCs.

- Keyword *writing book* generated $730.94 in sales, therefore $183 in net earnings (25% of the sales), for a spend of $146.99, so it's quite profitable. If we calculate it, the break-even bid would be: $183/361 = $0.51. This is only marginally more than the current bid ($0.49), and since we know that Amazon tends to bid much below that, I can safely raise it higher to $0.61.
- Keyword *how write* brought in $172 in net earnings for 351 clicks, which gives us a break-even bid of $0.49. This is lower than our current bid, but more or less at the same level as our current CPC—so I'll only slightly lower the bid, to $0.56.
- Keyword *how to write a book* generated $183 for 260 clicks, which gives us a break-even bid of $0.70. With the down bidding optimization in mind, I'll raise that to $0.81.
- Keyword *how write nonfiction b...* generated $22.50 for 35 clicks, giving us a break-even bid of $0.64. Again, that's lower than our current bid, but much higher than the current CPC. It seems that with a $0.75 upper bid, Amazon only bids at $0.49 on average for this target—and since I want to increase the delivery, I need to further increase the bid. I'll set it to $0.81 as well.

Finally, we have two targets that are in a gray zone of statistical significance:

- Keyword *public speaking books* has generated just one order, with $8.99 in sales. Because of the price point, I know that this is actually a paperback, so I can apply the actual royalty rate (10%) instead of my calculated average, which gives us a net earnings figure of $0.90, and a break-even bid of $0.06. Setting the bid that low would effectively kill the target, and 15 clicks is far from enough to properly test it. Instead, I'll just decrease the current bid by two-thirds and set it to $0.33.

· Keyword *publish book* had fewer clicks (13), but brought in close to $40 in sales, or $10 in net earnings, which gives us a break-even bid of $0.77. This is a reasonable enough figure to use as my actual bid, even at this early stage.

Pro tip: You might be wondering why some of the keyword targets don't sound natural (for example, *how write*). This is because we're using broad match targeting, so by including fewer words and excluding articles such as *a, an*, and *the* and infinitives such as *to*, we can get the ads delivered on a maximum of search terms. This might not be the best tactic if you're starting out, but it's a smart way to scale the delivery of your keyword campaigns.

To recap, here are the new bids for this campaign, after this round of bid optimization:

Keyword	Status	Suggested bid		Keyword bid	Impressions	Clicks	CTR	Spend	CPC	Orders	Sales	ACOS
Total: 47					196,338	1,922	0.98%	$949.44	$0.49	374	$4,498.19	21.11%
writing book	Delivering	$0.77	Apply	$ 0.49 New bid: $0.61	57,770	361	0.62%	$146.99	$0.41	55	$730.94	20.11%
how write	Delivering	$0.53	Apply	$ 0.67 New bid: $0.56	39,238	351	0.89%	$184.68	$0.53	58	$689.69	26.78%
how to write a book	Delivering	$0.64	Apply	$ 0.67 New bid: $0.81	15,263	260	1.70%	$136.31	$0.52	65	$731.27	18.64%
how write nonfiction b...	Delivering	$0.72	Apply	$ 0.75 New bid: $0.81	1,026	35	3.41%	$17.27	$0.49	10	$90.22	19.14%
public speaking books	Delivering	$0.79	Apply	$ 1.00 New bid: $0.33	2,934	15	0.51%	$10.60	$0.71	1	$8.99	117.91%
publish book	Delivering	$0.66	Apply	$ 0.65 New bid: $0.77	1,221	13	1.06%	$5.59	$0.43	3	$39.98	13.98%
writing memoir	Delivering	$0.57	Apply	$ 0.65 New bid: $0.91	1,222	9	0.74%	$4.66	$0.52	4	$40.19	11.59%
writing books for adults	Delivering	$0.65	Apply	$ 0.50 Don't change the bid	1,827	9	0.49%	$4.15	$0.46	-	-	-
start writing your book...	Delivering	$0.23	Apply	$ 0.65 Don't change the bid	802	8	1.00%	$3.30	$0.41	-	-	-

Example #3: Ebook + paperback series (Kindle Unlimited)

This third author has a seven-book series out, with all books enrolled in KDP Select. She advertises both the ebook and paperback formats of each book within the following ASIN targeting ad group. She has worked out that her average net royalty per copy sold is around 40%.

For confidentiality reasons, I've blurred the targeted ASINs and have named them "ASIN X" instead for our purposes.

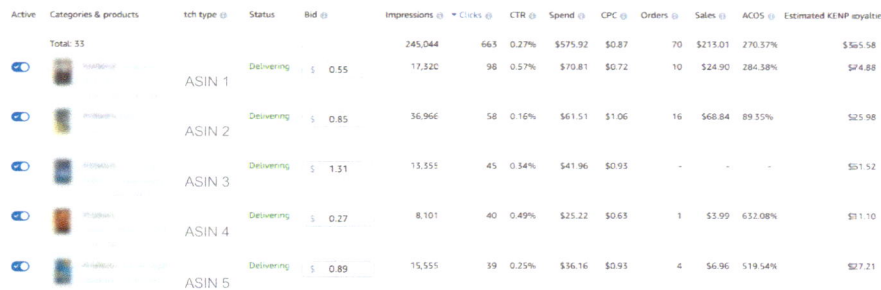

Active	Categories & products	tch type	Status	Bid	Impressions	Clicks	CTR	Spend	CPC	Orders	Sales	ACOS	Estimated KENP royalties
	Total: 33				245,044	663	0.27%	$575.92	$0.87	70	$213.01	270.37%	$565.58
⬤	ASIN 1		Delivering	$ 0.55	17,320	98	0.57%	$70.81	$0.72	10	$24.90	284.38%	$74.88
⬤	ASIN 2		Delivering	$ 0.85	36,966	58	0.16%	$61.51	$1.06	16	$68.84	89.35%	$25.98
⬤	ASIN 3		Delivering	$ 1.31	13,355	45	0.34%	$41.96	$0.93	-	-	-	$51.52
⬤	ASIN 4		Delivering	$ 0.27	8,101	40	0.49%	$25.22	$0.63	1	$3.99	632.08%	$11.10
⬤	ASIN 5		Delivering	$ 0.89	15,555	39	0.25%	$36.16	$0.93	4	$6.96	519.54%	$27.21

Sponsored Products campaign targeting comp title ASINs.

Here, all the targets are more or less statistically significant, so we'll start with those that have gathered the most clicks, and work our way down.

- ASIN 1 generated $24.90 in sales, worth $24.90 x 40% = $9.96 to the author, and $74.88 in page reads, for a total revenue of $74.88 + $9.96 = $84.84. Since ASIN 1 only spent $70.81 to achieve this, it is a profitable target. Its break-even bid is $84.84/98 = $0.87.
- ASIN 2 generated $68.84 x 40% = $27.54 in net royalties, and $25.98 in reads, so $53.52 in total, through 58 clicks. Its break-even bid is $53.52/58 = $0.92.
- ASIN 3 generated 45 clicks, no orders, but $61.52 in reads. Its break-even

bid is $61.52/45 = $1.37.

- ASIN 4 generated one sale, at $3.99. Given the price point, we know it's an ebook, so we can apply the 70% royalty (rather than the 40% average). This gives us $3.99 x 70% + $11.10 = $13.89 in total earnings, and a break-even bid of $0.35.
- ASIN 5 generated $6.96 x 40% + $27.21 = $29.99 in total earnings, with a break-even bid of $0.77.

Target	Bid	Clicks	Spend	CPC	Sales	Net royalties on Sales	KENP royalties	Total revenue	Profit/loss	Break-even bid
ASIN 1	$0.55	98	$70.81	$0.72	$24.90	$9.96	$74.88	$84.84	$14.03	$0.87
ASIN 2	$0.85	58	$61.51	$1.06	$68.84	$27.54	$25.98	$53.52	-$7.99	$0.92
ASIN 3	$1.31	45	$41.96	$0.93	$0	$0	$61.52	$62	$20	$1
ASIN 4	$0.27	40	$25.22	$0.63	$3.99	$2.79	$11.10	$13.89	-$11.33	$0.35
ASIN 5	$0.89	39	$36.16	$0.93	$6.96	$2.78	$27.21	$29.99	-$6.17	$0.77

As you may have noticed, the break-even bids for all five ASIN targets are higher than the current bids. But if you look at the dashboard, you'll see that the current CPCs for each target are also much higher than the bids.

How is this possible? This campaign is using up and down dynamic bids, which allow Amazon to automatically increase the bid if they believe the click is likely to result in a sale. In cases like this, you don't want to set your bids to the break-even bid, but instead modify them based on the profitability of each target.

Here's how I would reason it:

- For ASIN 1, I'm bidding $0.55 per click, which leads to clicks costing me $0.72 instead. Yet, even with this higher bid, my target is still profitable, so I can afford to increase my bid a bit more (to $0.66). This will signal to Amazon that I am ready to pay a bit more per click to get more impressions.
- ASIN 2 spent $61.51 to generate $53.52 in total revenue, so it's not profitable at the current CPC of $1.06. Therefore, I need to decrease my

current bid in order to get my CPC closer to my break-even bid ($0.92). I'll lower it to $0.71.

- ASIN 3, inversely, is spending less per click ($0.93) than my bid ($1.31), yet is my most profitable target. So I can afford to further increase the bid to encourage Amazon to spend more. I'll raise it to $1.51.
- ASIN 4 and ASIN 5 are similar to ASIN 2: they're all loss-making, and their respective CPCs are higher than their bids. Therefore, I need to reduce the bid to get the CPC closer to the break-even point.

Here's a table recapping the new suggested bids, so that you can better visualize the relationship between the CPC, break-even bid, and the new bids I'm setting:

Target	Bid	CPC	Break-even bid	New suggested bid
ASIN 1	$0.55	$0.72	$0.87	$0.66
ASIN 2	$0.85	$1.06	$0.92	$0.71
ASIN 3	$1.31	$0.93	$1	$1.51
ASIN 4	$0.27	$0.63	$0.35	$0.21
ASIN 5	$0.89	$0.93	$0.77	$0.71

Now, while lowering (or raising) your bid generally has an immediate effect on CPC, this is not always the case with up and down dynamic bids. For example, even though I lower my bid from $0.92 to $0.71 in this example, Amazon might still keep bidding at $1.06 or above, as it can effectively increase my bid by 100% if it believes the click can lead to a sale.

So you might end up in a situation where you lower your bid time and time again, but Amazon keeps artificially raising it through the up and down bidding optimization. In cases like this, there's one simple solution: switch your campaign to fixed bids or down dynamic bids.

Pro tip: You can change the bidding optimization of a campaign at any point, with immediate effect. If a campaign is too hard to manage on up and down, just switch it to down or fixed. Similarly, if a campaign is doing particularly well on fixed or down bids, switching it to up and down is a good way to immediately boost its delivery.

If you use different types of bidding optimization across your campaigns, make sure to include Down, Up and Down, or Fixed in the name of each campaign and ad group, so you can immediately identify the current bidding optimization each campaign is on.

Hopefully, this gives you a taste of how I personally go through my campaigns and optimize their bids to get them to break even in the first place. As you can see, it can be a long and painful process if you go through each target one by one, which is why I've created four spreadsheets (The four Break-even Bid Calculators) you can use to automatically calculate the break-even bid of each target in a campaign.

You will find those in the Bonus Resources section at the end of the book, with instructions on how to make the most of them.

22

Placement optimization

We haven't touched yet on this final topic: placement optimization. The good news is it's something you won't need to look at or touch often—in fact, I tend to ignore it on most campaigns until they've gathered hundreds of clicks. But in some cases, doing some light placement optimization can make a difference.

First, let's take a look at what these placements are.

What are placements?

A placement is essentially a type of place where your ad is displayed. In the case of Facebook Ads, for example, you have different types of placements where your ads can appear such as these:

- Facebook feed
- Facebook stories
- Instagram feed
- Instagram stories

In the case of Amazon Ads, we've seen that ads can appear in a bunch of different places, but Amazon groups these into three different placement types:

- Top-of-search (first page): These placements are reserved for ads that show up at the very top of the first page of search results for any particular query.
- Product pages: These include all the ad placements on Amazon product pages, most of which can be found in the "Sponsored products related to this item" section.
- Rest of search: This is for any other placements in search results that are not at the top of the first page of search results. For example, if your ad shows up at the bottom of the first page, or the top of the second page, it would be considered Rest of search.

The reason why Amazon has created these three placement categories is to allow advertisers to get a sense of where their ads are getting impressions. Because let's face it, not all placements are equal.

The fight for top-of-search

If you're advertising on Amazon for the first time, you might intuitively think that a manual campaign targeting specific keywords will mostly yield you impressions on search results for these keywords. And yet, even a manual keyword campaign targeting popular searches like *psychological thriller* or *female detective series* will often get you more impressions on product pages than top-of-search placements.

Why? Because top-of-search placements are a lot scarcer: Amazon only displays up to two Sponsored Product ads at the top of a search result page; whereas, you can find hundreds of ads in the "Sponsored products related to this item" section of a product page.

What search result placements lack in number, though, they make up for in quality. On a product page, you have to scroll down past the Also Boughts (or Similar Books or Related Items) to find the Sponsored Products, but on a search result page, these are right there among the search results.

So search result placements are both scarcer and (generally) more valuable to advertisers. This, in turn, means the auctions for these placements are more competitive and require higher bids. If you bid low in your manual keyword targeting campaigns, then you will get few search result placements, and your ads will show predominantly on product pages instead.

Inversely, if you bid high, you'll get a higher proportion of search result placements. The exception to that is keywords for which you have a natural competitive advantage—such as brand/defense keywords—where you should be able to win the Top-of-search auctions even with low-ish bids.

You can see the proportion of top-of-search auctions each keyword is winning directly in your dashboard, through the Top-of-search IS column (you might have to customize your columns to see it).

Keyword	Bid	Impressions	Top-of-search IS NEW
Total: 57		49,485	
amazon ads	$ 1.01	15,278	10.05%
book marketing	$ 1.01	6,849	9.49%
how market book	$ 1.01	544	24.75%
book promotion	$ 1.01	1,888	34.62%
reedsy	$ 1.01	46	64.71%

Top-of-search Impression Share shows how often your ad is seen at the top of search pages.

As you can see, I'm winning a fair number of auctions for terms related to book marketing, and the vast majority of them for a brand keyword like *reedsy*.

While the Top-of-search IS metric is helpful, it's not a very actionable one: you're not going to raise/lower a bid just because the keyword's Top-of-search Impression Share is low/high, as that is usually not correlated to performance. A keyword might have a low Top-of-search IS (and serve most of its impressions on product pages instead), but a high conversion and profit margin—and inversely, a keyword with a high Top-of-search IS might not be profitable at all.

There is one place, however, where it does make sense to make bidding decisions based on placement performance: that is the Placements tab.

Placement optimization

The first thing you need to know about placement optimization is that it happens on the campaign level, not on the ad group or targets. The only place where you can access that Placements tab is when looking at a campaign (see the screenshot), and any changes you effect there will affect all the ad groups within the campaign.

In other words, you cannot customize your placement optimization for each ad group; you can only control it for the whole campaign.

The Placements tab on a campaign is where you customize your placement optimization.

As you can see, this tab offers you the opportunity to create bid adjustment rules for two of the three placement types: Top of search and Product pages.

Bid adjustments allow you to increment all your bids on such placements by a chosen percentage. For example, if you set a bid adjustment of 10% for

Product pages, Amazon will increase your bid, in real time, by 10%, when competing for an auction to win a placement on a product page. This 10% increase will be effective across all the ad groups and all the targets in your campaign.

It's worth noting that while you can increment your bids by up to 900%, you cannot use bid adjustments to decrease your bids. In other words, you cannot set a negative percentage for the bid adjustment.

So how do you actually use feature this to optimize your campaigns and make them more profitable? It's simple, you just apply the same logic as when optimizing individual targets' bids. If a particular placement type is profitable, and performing much better than another, you can increase its bid by a small percentage (or a big one, in case it's doing much better than the other placement types).

Let's take an example, from a campaign advertising an ebook and paper-back, with a cost per order objective of $7.

Placement ⊖	Bid adjustment ⊖		Impressions ⊖	Clicks ⊖	CTR ⊖	Spend ⊖	CPC ⊖	Orders ⊖	Sales ⊖	ROAS ⊖
Total: 3			841,005	857	0.10%	$561.42	$0.66	76	$786.61	1.40
Top of search (first page)	0	%	40,647	268	0.66%	$220.68	$0.82	25	$266.25	1.21
Product pages	10	%	670,386	450	0.07%	$257.48	$0.57	40	$350.58	1.36
Rest of search	-		129,972	139	0.11%	$83.26	$0.60	11	$169.78	2.04

Example of placement optimization.

As you can see, this campaign is generating four times more product page than search result impressions. But the number of clicks coming from each type of placement is similar (450 vs. 407), because Top of search and Rest of search placements naturally have a much higher click-through-rate.

You can also see that Top of search placements cost more per click than Product pages for the reasons I just explained.

But what really matters to us, from a profit optimization perspective, is the cost per order of each placement type.

- Cost/order of Top of search: $220.68/25 = $8.83
- Cost/order of Product pages: $257.48/40 = $6.44
- Cost/order of Rest of search: $83.26/11 = $7.57

Considering that this campaign's cost per order objective is $7, only the Product pages placement is being profitable—though barely—so it's worth raising its bid adjustment by 10% to give it preference over the others.

Why not increase it by 20%, or more, you might ask, considering it's doing much better than the others? Let's think about it this way: what if the 450 clicks the campaign had generated on Product pages had cost 10% more than they did? This would have effectively increased the cost, and therefore the cost per order, by 10%, bringing it to $6.44 x 1.10 = $7.08. This would have meant that even this placement would have barely broken even.

So if I increase bids across this placement type by more than 10%, it's likely, based on the data so far, that the placement will go from profitable to loss-making.

In which cases should you adjust the bids of a placement type, and by how much? You can simply follow these simple guidelines.

1. First, make sure that the data you have on the placements is statistically significant. In general, I'd say that any placement type with fewer than 100 clicks is not worth looking at, much less adjusting.
2. Second, check if the placement type is profitable. If it isn't, there is no sense in incrementing the bids—you should reduce them instead, and you can't do that through the Placements tab.
3. If a placement type is profitable, you need to compare it to the other placements, and only adjust the bid of the one placement type that is clearly overperforming. If no placement is doing significantly better than the others, then you shouldn't touch the bid adjustments here, as there is no reason to give preference to one placement over another.

If all three conditions are met, the maximum percentage by which you should increase the bid of a placement is the difference (in percentage) between its break-even objective and its current performance.

For example, in this case, the break-even objective is a cost per order of $7, and the current performance is $6.44, so the difference is (7 - 6.44) / 6.44 = 8.7%.

This represents, based on the data so far, the maximum percentage by which I can raise my cost per click before the placement stops being profitable.

Isn't this almost as much fun as optimizing bids for targets? Since you're enjoying it, let's do another example. In this campaign, the author is advertising Kindle Unlimited books, with an average royalty percentage of 40%:

							Columns ∨	Date range - Lifetime		Export	
Placement ⓘ	Bid adjustment ⓘ		Impressions ⓘ	Clicks ⓘ	CTR ⓘ	Spend ⓘ	CPC ⓘ	Orders ⓘ	Sales ⓘ	ACOS ⓘ	KENP read ⓘ	Estimated KENP royal
Total: 3			414,421	528	0.13%	$359.18	$0.68	68	$402.32	89.28%	37,925	$16₉.97
Top of search (first page)	0	%	5,893	175	2.97%	$82.99	$0.47	37	$168.63	49.21%	17,339	$75.86
Product pages	0	%	384,094	253	0.07%	$190.40	$0.75	23	$176.77	107.71%	13,140	$5₉.61
Rest of search	-		24,434	100	0.41%	$85.79	$0.86	8	$56.92	150.72%	7,446	$3₉.50

Before we get into profit optimization, let's take a moment to analyze the placement breakdown here. You might be surprised to see that Top of search has by far the lowest CPC, while Rest of search has the highest. How can that be explained?

It's simple: this particular campaign is targeting a mix of brand and nonbrand keywords. The brand keywords are a lot less competitive and naturally have much higher click through and conversion rates, so Amazon is more keen to show your ad at the Top of result pages for these searches.

But this campaign also targets other nonbrand, highly competitive key-words. Getting Top of search ad placements for these keywords would take much higher bids than the ones we're using, so here we're only getting Product pages and Rest of search placements.

Because our brand targets trigger Top of search while our other keywords trigger the other placements, Top of search ends up being the cheapest placement in this campaign, and obviously the most effective.

Now, let's calculate the true ACOS for each of these placement types:

- True ACOS for Top of search: $82.99 / ($168.63 x 40% + $76.86) = 57.5%
- True ACOS for Product pages: $190.40 / ($176.77 x 40% + $59.61) = 146.1%
- True ACOS for Rest of search: $85.79 / ($56.92 x 40% + $33.50) = 152.5%

As I anticipated, the Top of search placement is vastly outperforming the others, so it is the one where we can adjust the bid.

By how much? The true ACOS right now is 57.5%, so we can theoretically afford to raise the bids by up to (100 - 57.5)/57.5 = 99%. However, as I discussed, it's likely that most of the ads related to this placement are for brand search queries, and the CPC is already at close to $0.50 (which is relatively high for defense keywords). So I definitely wouldn't adjust the bid by +99%, but rather by +20% or +30%.

Overall, and as a rule of thumb, I rarely adjust bids for placements by more than 30%. You'll see that small percentage changes can quickly have a big impact, so I'd encourage you to start small, and if after a few weeks/months the placement in question continues to vastly outperform the others, keep raising the percentage.

> **Pro tip**: Another, more elegant long-term solution for this last example would be to separate the brand keywords and move them to a different campaign so that they don't pollute the overall data on the placements level. As we've seen, defense targets often require a different bidding and placements optimization strategy, so it's generally better for them to have their own campaign.

When to optimize placements

As I hinted at in the opening of this chapter, placement optimization is something I spend very little time on—and you shouldn't spend much time on it either.

First, you need a whole lot of data on a campaign (at least 100 clicks on each placement) before it makes sense to tweak bids at the placement level. Moreover, there are many campaigns for which the vast majority of the budget, if not all, will go to the Product pages placement type—for example, if you're running a product targeting campaign with ASINs—so there won't be anything for you to optimize there.

Finally, if you adjust bids reasonably (without going overboard on the percentages) the first time on a campaign, it's rare that you'll have to tweak them much after that.

For all these reasons, I only tend to look at placements every couple of months, and rarely make big changes. However, there were definitely cases in which placement optimization played a big role in getting a campaign to scale or increase its profit margin—so it's not something you should discard altogether.

It's also something you should do in conjunction with bid optimization. In our second campaign in this chapter, we saw that the two placements that were getting the most spend were highly unprofitable (with true ACOSs in the 150% range). This should be a clear signal that you need to go into the ad groups and look at bids on the target level, as it's likely that the majority of them (especially for nondefense targets) need to be reduced.

You also need to keep in mind that changes on the placement level can potentially affect all the targets in a campaign. If you raise the bids by 30% for Top of search in that campaign, all your nondefense targets' bids will be raised by 30% for that placement as well. So you probably need to reduce your bids for these targets even more than you usually would and aim for an 80% or so true target ACOS, rather than a 100% one.

This is the reason why I don't like putting crazy percentages for placement optimization: they can completely undermine your target-level bid optimization—in the same way that up and down dynamic bids can. In that sense, I think placement optimization works better when it comes time to scale a campaign that is doing really well, rather than during the profit optimization phase.

VI

Scaling your ads

Scaling is often the million-dollar word in the world of Amazon Advertising. If you follow the advice and methodical bid optimization approach from the previous chapters, you should be able to have a few profit-making campaigns relatively quickly. That's just the start, though. The next step is to get Amazon to take more of your money and get those sales and profits growing.

23

Scaling a successful campaign

I already mentioned a few ideas for scaling a successful campaign in the previous chapters, such as using broad match types, switching to up and down bids, or increasing the bid percentages for your high-performing placements.

All these share one common denominator: they build on your preexisting strengths. In other words, you take something that is working already, and you pour more money into it to get it to work even better.

Now, pouring more money would be the simplest thing to do on any other advertising platform. But with Amazon Advertising, it's actually not that easy to get the platform to take more of your money when something is working well. In many cases, it can be even harder than getting something to work well in the first place.

In this chapter, we're going to look at simple tactics to achieve just that and get your successful campaigns to eat more of your money—so they deliver even more Orders and Sales.

Tactic #1: Increasing bids

If you wish to scale a campaign, you should first go over its targets with a fine-toothed comb and identify any where you can afford to raise the bid a bit.

Increasing bids is, by far, the most effective method to get Amazon to serve your ads more. Impressions are delivered based on auctions, so the higher you bid, the more impressions you'll win—and the more prominent placements you'll be able to capture (I'm looking at you, Top of search).

Naturally, this is a double-edged sword, because each click is going to cost you more money, and a campaign that was previously profitable might become loss-making if you keep increasing the bids to scale it.

This is why the bulk of this book focuses on break-even bid optimization, where you bid as high as possible—therefore winning as many impressions as possible—while still breaking even. That's the kind of balance between profit and scale that you should aim for.

One possibility, if you're not too worried about budget, is to significantly raise the bids of those targets that still haven't gotten a statistically significant number of clicks. This will get them to deliver and kill two birds with one stone: your campaign will scale (more impressions and clicks), and you'll get the necessary data to be able to optimize their bids properly.

You can even do this across all the campaigns in your account through the Targeting tab of the Amazon Advertising dashboard. As we've seen before, this tag aggregates all the keywords, products, and ASINs you target across all your campaigns, and handy filters immediately identify all the targets that match certain conditions.

For example, I could look for all the targets that are yet to receive an impression:

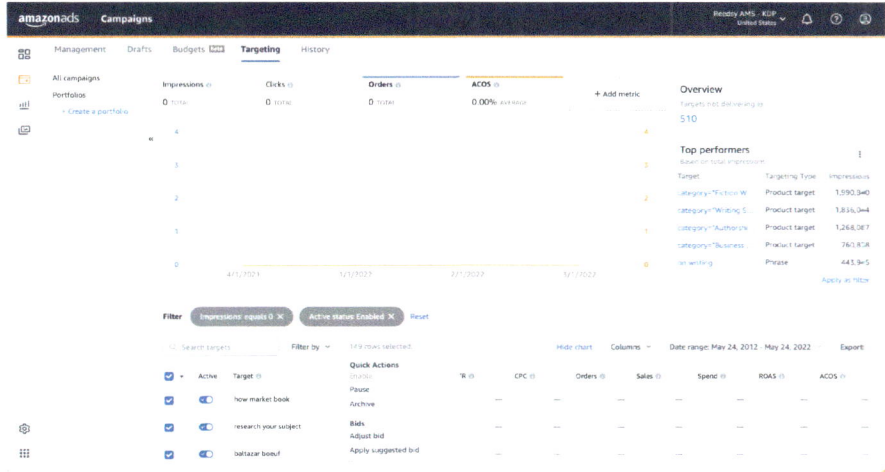

That's quite a few targets where I'm not winning any auctions, most likely because I'm not bidding high enough, so I can afford to raise their bids by a bit. The great thing about the Targeting tab is that it also allows me to perform bulk actions to update all these targets at the same time. For example, I could select Bulk actions > Adjust bid > Increase bid by 10%.

A 10% increase will likely not be enough to get all those targets to start delivering, but it'll move the needle for a few of them, and you can always go back and repeat the same operation one month later to keep raising the bids of those targets that still refuse to serve.

Tactic #2: Increasing budget

Increasing budgets is sort of the opposite to raising bids when it comes to scaling a campaign: it's not usually effective, but it has zero downsides, so you lose nothing by trying it.

It's a tactic that has been preached by Amazon Advertising experts since the first days of the platform: if you want a campaign to spend more, signal it to Amazon by raising its budget.

Now, to this day, I haven't been able to prove or even get a sense of whether that truly works or not. I've heard that it does from many Amazon advertisers and am keen to trust them on it. In any case, here's the important point: increasing your budget can't hurt. Amazon will never spend the entirety of your budget on a campaign (unless you use low $5 or $10 daily budgets), and raising the budget does not impact bids or CTR, so it doesn't affect the profitability of the campaign.

As a result, I run most of the campaigns on a multi-hundred-dollar budget. And as you can see in the screenshot here (taken from a thirty-day period), even the highest-spending ones only spent less than 3% of their daily budget:

Campaigns ⓘ	Budget ⓘ	Impressions ⓘ	▾ Clicks ⓘ	CTR ⓘ	Spend ⓘ	CPC ⓘ
Total: 14		1,373,225	1,444	0.11%	$1,006.10	$0.70
HMB SP - Auto - Cohe...	$ 500.00 Daily	442,070	504	0.11%	$354.26	$0.70
HMB SP - Auto - Ad C...	$ 500.00 Daily	508,548	495	0.10%	$339.47	$0.69
HMB SP - Categories -...	$ 200.00 Daily	351,802	288	0.08%	$204.32	$0.71
HMB SP - Auto - Disco...	$ 500.00 Daily	30,074	63	0.21%	$45.80	$0.73

"But what if I'm using high budgets already?" Well, you can always raise them. The idea here is to signal to Amazon that you want to spend more, in the hopes that Amazon offers you more impressions as a result—at the same cost per click. It doesn't really matter how high your current budget is, if you want a particular campaign to spend more, you can try to further raise its budget. For example, if I wanted the top campaign in this example to spend more, I'd double its budget to $1,000 a day.

Now, while I'm not 100% sure that high budgets have an impact on delivery, what I do know is that low budgets can definitely have a negative impact on it, which is why I recommend against running campaigns on a $5 or $10 daily budget.

If a campaign is not profitable, lower the bids, not the budget. Reducing a campaign's budget is never going to make that campaign more profitable, it'll only serve to hinder its deliverability, and potentially take you out of the race for important placements and impressions.

> **Note**: You might have read or heard advice recommending authors create hundreds of different campaigns, all with small $5 daily budgets. That advice is, in my opinion, very much outdated, and most Amazon Advertising experts I know today are recommending against it (so do I).

Tactic #3: Using up and down dynamic bids

Up and down dynamic bids are not ideal when you're starting out and focusing on profit optimization. However, they can be a good option when you've achieved profitability with a campaign and want to scale it.

Inherently, using up and down bids carries the same risk as raising bids manually, in that Amazon could decide to spend more per click than ends up being worth it for you. But it presents the advantage that, in theory, Amazon will only raise the bid when they're confident that the click is likely to lead to a purchase.

In other words, rather than manually raising the bids on the targets that you think could perform even better with a higher bid, you let Amazon decide which bids to raise, in real time, based on their internal historical data. Naturally, the older the campaign, and the more clicks, orders, and revenue it has generated, the better Amazon's dynamic bidding optimization will be, as the algorithm will have more complete and accurate data to base its bidding decisions on.

If you do switch a campaign from down to up and down bids with the objective to scale its delivery, you should closely monitor it in the weeks and months following the change. Remember: With up and down bids, Amazon can raise bids by up to 100% in real time, so the change can sometimes lead to a flood of expensive clicks. If that happens, you want to catch that early and reduce the bids on the relevant targets before you lose too much money.

Tactic #4: Leveraging match types

If we move away from bids and budget, there is one last way to scale a campaign without adding more targets to it—and that is to modify the targeting scope of the existing keywords.

As you may remember, there are three potential match types for each keyword target you add to a campaign:

- Exact match: Ads are only eligible to show up on searches/products matching your exact keyword.
- Phrase match: Ads are eligible to show up on searches/products including your exact keyword phrase in the same order.
- Broad match: Ads are eligible to show up on searches/products including all the words in your keyword phrase, in any given order.

If a particular target is working well on exact or phrase match and you're looking to scale these results, a simple option is to switch it to broad match. In most cases, this will significantly increase the number and variety of searches that your ads can reach.

For example, let's say you're targeting *dragon shifter romance* in phrase match. Switching that keyword to broad match would get you access to a bunch of new search placements like these:

- *shifter dragon romance*
- *dragon shifter paranormal romance*
- *shifter romance with dragons*
- *shifter romance with smoking hot dragon*

Most of the additional searches that you access through broad match targeting are long tail, so have a lower search volume than *dragon shifter romance*. As a result, you might not see a huge increase in impressions and clicks, but these extra clicks would probably come at a lower cost since fewer advertisers are competing for these long-tail searches.

In other words, switching to broad match would not only increase the reach of the target, but may also decrease its average cost per click.

Naturally, you need to mentally make sure that the additional searches that broad match gives you access to are all still relevant to your book—otherwise, you might gain more impressions and clicks, and at a cheaper cost, but these won't convert into sales.

Let's say that you're advertising an alien abduction book with no romance, and that the *alien abduction* exact match keyword is working well (granted, it's not a likely scenario, but it'll serve our purpose). Switching it to broad match, or even just phrase match, could trigger your ads on romance-related searches like these:

- *alien abduction romance*
- *alien abduction forced breeding*
- *alien abduction sex slave*
- *alien mate abduction*

In all likelihood, the impressions from these searches won't yield any clicks, so while it may not hurt your profit, it'll significantly hurt the click-through-rate of the target and lead to Amazon progressively halting the delivery of your ad, even on exact *alien abduction* searches.

In this particular scenario, the switch to broad match would eventually have the opposite effect to the desired one: not only will it not scale the campaign, it may hamper its deliverability.

Of course, the risk of broad match triggering irrelevant search and product placements can usually be mitigated with little effort through negative keywords. In the example, adding *romance, breeding, sex, mate, alpha, harem*, and other potential romance-related keywords, as negative phrase keywords to the campaign would effectively solve the relevancy issue, while still allowing the ad to serve on broad match.

There are many ways to scale a specific campaign, and get it to deliver even more impressions, clicks, and sales, without adding more targets to it. The scaling requires little work, and only small tweaks to your campaigns, which should only be applied to campaigns or ad groups that have proven to do well already.

That said, there is an even more effective way to grow your Amazon Ads: diversifying your targeting.

24

Diversifying your targeting

I covered the main tactics for finding your first targets in Chapter 10, but target hunting is not a one-time hunt—it's something you need to make a regular habit if you want your campaigns to grow and if you want to stay ahead of the competition.

For example, let's say that a well-known author in your niche is about to drop a new book. You can expect a lot of interest among your target readers for that book and consequently searches for it on Amazon, as well as visits to its product page. And yet, because it's just out (or still on preorder), it hasn't had enough visibility to be picked up by other advertisers. In other words, it has low competition and is about to receive a lot of volume, meaning it's an ideal target if you spot it in time and add it to one of your campaigns.

In this chapter, I cover simple tactics to make sure you don't miss any new targets that make it to your market and discuss a few ways to automate your target hunting. Because let's face it, we can't be keeping tabs on every new release in our niche, nor can we afford to spend hours trying to find new targets every week. That time is better spent, well, writing!

Tactic #1: Automated list monitoring

Remember how category Best Seller and Hot New Releases lists are a smart way to find some relevant targets for your first campaigns? These lists are not set in stone. They change regularly, which means you need to keep an eye on them regularly as well, as they can offer likely new targets to add to your campaigns.

Now, while the Best Seller lists generally have a slow turnover, the Hot New Releases change constantly, as books are only eligible to be on those for the first thirty days after launch (or while they're on preorder). Because of this, I like to set up some way of monitoring the Hot New Releases list in my most relevant category every thirty days, copy all the books on it, and add them to an existing campaign. Or if my Hot New Releases campaign is getting crowded (with some ad groups reaching the bar of 100+ active targets), then create a second one (an example might be HNR Epic Fantasy 2022).

"Wait, you want me to manually check the Hot New Releases list every month and copy-paste author names, book titles, and ASINs into the campaign? I thought my time was better spent writing!"

And it is. Unless you enjoy doing a lot of copy-pasting, my recommendation is that you automate this task. Now, I wish there were a software that could pull up clean author names, book titles, and ASINs clearly from a specific list page on Amazon, but I haven't found any so far, and I doubt that one will come out any time soon that can replicate the intricacies that a human being can offer.

Which is why my recommendation is to hire a human being. Check out several freelancer marketplaces where you can hire virtual assistants for a relatively cheap cost per hour (in the $5 to $15 range) who can do an excellent job at compiling this kind of information.

If you want some inspiration for your posting, I'm sharing the one I used on Upwork for an Amazon data entry analyst:

I'm an independent author looking for a talented VA to work from the comfort of their own home and help grow my business. This part-time position will require you to research products online on a daily basis and enter the results into a Google spreadsheet.

- *You must have substantial experience browsing and/or shopping within the Amazon website, strong command of verbal and written English, use of Google Sheets and Gmail.*
- *Knowledge of the Amazon Kindle Store, ASINs, sales ranking, and product categories is a plus.*
- *A reliable, high-speed internet connection is an absolute must.*

You will begin with one or two simple projects, which may lead to more part-time work. To apply, please respond with details of your Amazon product research and data entry experience, and as a small assignment, share a spreadsheet with the top 3 titles in the [insert your category here] category on the Kindle Store (including book title, author name, and ASIN).

Now, while you can wait for people to apply to your job posting, I recommend that you also do some quick scouting on your end and invite specific freelancers to apply. The skills to look out for are data entry, Amazon keyword research, and Amazon Advertising.

Once applications start to trickle in, review them individually and invite those who look like promising candidates (ideally, at least five to ten of them) to perform an initial assignment. The idea is to test them on a simple target research task to compare their turnaround times, final price, and cleanliness of the final data set.

While it may seem like a simple job, you're probably going to be working with that person repeatedly in the future, so it's worth making the extra effort to find that freelancer who'll present the spreadsheets exactly like you want them.

For example, here are two sample works I received from shortlisted freelancers (the assignment was to gather the top 100 of the Hot New

Releases across three Fantasy categories):

Arthurian Fantasy Hot New Releases Kindle categories

	Book title	Series name	Author	ASIN
1	Eve of Redemption	Books 1 to 6	Joe Jackson	B08QDSNZHL
2	Heretic Spellblade 2		K.D. Robertson	B08V8JQT8Y
3	United We Stand	The Pantheon Saga Book 6	C.C. Ekeke	B08L96ZW8F
4	Ascension	Dragons of Kendualdern Book 1	Sam Ferguson	B08NTSMHHP
5	An Emperor's Gamble	Legend of Tal Book 3	J.D.L. Rosell	B08KRL4DL1
6	Sands of Blood and Bone	Defying Divinity Book 2	Jamey Sultan	B08W1M9KF1
7	The Avalon Café	Books 1 to 6	Hermione Moon	B08VHPLVHZ
8	Things That Go Bump and the Knight	The Avalon Café Book 4.5	Hermione Moon	B08VHQHQR1
9	Legendary Dungeon Seed	The Mage's Academy Book 2	Marc Robert	B08V16C75R
10	Riddley Bundleforth & The Banshee Bell	A Dragon Mist Chronicle	Roulf Burrell	B08VD15XSF
11	The Book of Bastards		Ransom Stephens	B08LKKD5F3
12	The Divine Fist	The Ever Hero Saga Book 3	Jeff Pantanella	B08TLYGMZ3
13	Morgana		Tiegan Clyne	B08V4KWC8L
14	The Deceiver	Book Two of The Loro Chronicles	Christopher Crochet	B08W5G26ZS
15	The Death of a Dragon		Christopher Crochet	B08W5C554Y
16	Inferno	The Frozen Flame Book 4	Paul J Bennett	B08LP44C8K
17	Hunted		Nicole Leclercq	B08W5CBNLM
18	Curse Queen	Forbidden Forest Book 4	Amber Argyle	B08HJQ2Z9W
19	Town Lore	Hunters for Hire Book 2	Jonathan Yanez	B08NTPX99T
20	Sword Stone Table		Swapna Krishna and Jenn Northington	B08PJKFTP4
21	The Thief	Mate Hunt Book 3	Riley Onyx	B08VHRMH1Z
22	The Rebel	Mate Hunt Book 2	Riley Onyx	B08VJMJJSL
23	Half Sick of Shadows		Laura Sebastian	B08LK4XBG8
24	Blighted Heart	Primordials of Shadowthorn Book 2	Jessaca Willis	B08KKDJG52

Sheet1 ⌄

Assignment from freelancer #1 (Hot New Releases).

Serial No.	Book Title	Series Title	Author Name	ASIN
1	Dragon Mage	Rivenworld	ML Spencer	B08PDQ5XT4
2	Ashes of the Sun	Burningblade & Silvereye	Django Wexler	B07ZZ25BCX
3	Eve of Redemption		Joe Jackson	B08QDSNZHL
4	Fatemarked	The Fatemarked Epic	David Estes	B01MTEK3NM
5	Heretic Spellblade 2		K.D. Robertson	B08V8JQT8Y
6	Village of Hawkshead	The Abduction Cycles	John Cressman	B08SJ3KRHD
7	The Magelands Epic		Christopher Mitchell	B086MPC6NF
8	Heretic Spellblade		K.D. Robertson	B08NCDQFXG
9	The Unseen Blade	The Serpent's Heir	Ambrose Zack Adams	B08KWMMBG7
10	Assassin's Apprentice	The Farseer Trilogy	Robin Hobb	B000FBFMG6
11	The Silent Shield	Kingfountain	Jeff Wheeler	B01N9E6MMM
12	Creation Mage 2	War Mage Academy	Dante King	B08HXZRKXP
13	Dragon Heart Sea of Sorrow		Kirill Klevanski	B082S3HBHV
14	Servant of the Crown	Heir to the Crown	Paul J Bennett	B076QLKDM5
15	Wasteland		Mike Ignatov	B08NXVTT13
16	A King's Bargain	Legend of Tal	J.D.L. Rosell	B088PZ2N5G
17	Soulmarked	The Fatemarked Epic	David Estes	B01N80K913
18	Pilgrim		Harmon Cooper	B08DH7WTNS
19	The Forsaken Throne	Kingfountain	Jeff Wheeler	B01MTXL14F
20	Royal Assassin	The Farseer Trilogy	Robin Hobb	B000FBFMFW
21	Lord of Shadows	Daughters of Avalon	Tanya Anne Crosby	B07XF8V1WH
22	Shadows and Shade		Amanda Cashure	B07TN65C73
23	Truthmarked	The Fatemarked Epic	David Estes	B01MUR5CM4
24	Dragon Heart Land of Magic		Kirill Klevanski	B085F2WSKO
25	Pilgrim 2		Harmon Cooper	B08PJ6LRN5
26	Warbringer	Descendants of the Fall	Aaron Hodges	B08653PM1_
27	Paternus Rise of Gods	The Paternus Trilogy	Dyrk Ashton	B01CXPD8T4
28	The White Tower	The Aldoran Chronicles	Michael Wisehart	B01MA3CMIM
29	Deathmarked	The Fatemarked Epic	David Estes	B071FNBJV5

+ ≡ Arthurian Fantasy ▾ Sword & Sorcery ▾ Nordic Myth & Legend Fantasy ▾

Assignment from freelancer #2 (top 100).

While the two may look similar at first glance, a close inspection reveals that the second spreadsheet is much more useful. First, it doesn't include any "Book X" in the series titles, and also doesn't list "author X and author Y" in author names—which would make it impossible to copy-paste the data straight into Amazon Advertising.

As a minor point, but important from an organization standpoint, free-lancer #1 also submitted each category data in a different spreadsheet, while freelancer #2 included them all in the same sheet, using three different tabs—which I personally find more helpful.

I still paid and left a good review to freelancer #1, of course, but ultimately settled on #2 for a long-term relationship.

When establishing that long-term relationship, it's important to be up front about the number of hours per week/month that you'll require from them. In my case, it wasn't much—and it's important for them to know that so they don't block time in their schedules for you when you're not actually going to need them.

To ensure that the data they collect are as clean as possible, and ready for you to just copy-paste into your campaigns, you can also request that they do the following:

- Ignore (not include) any books whose cover or title imply that they are not relevant to your book—the most common example being romance/erotica books that are miscategorized.
- Exclude from the book titles any punctuation, series information, or long subtitle. For example, if the title is: *Cockier Spaniel: Book One in the hilarious Cocky Shifter Series,* make sure they only record *Cockier Spaniel* as title, and *Cocky Shifter* as the series title.
- Ideally, don't record the same author name or series title twice. This won't hurt your targeting, because Amazon automatically removes duplicates when entering a set of targets at once—but it could save them time, and therefore save you money.

Once you're comfortable working with a chosen freelancer, you can get them to set up a monthly monitoring and recording of the relevant Hot New Releases lists in your genre, as well as regularly add any new Also Boughts, Also Reads, or any other relevant targets you can think of.

Tactic #2: Automated new release monitoring

While list monitoring is the best way to consistently gather a bunch of relevant targets to add to your campaigns, it does have one flaw: it only works to find targets that are already present on a Best Seller or HNR list.

If a big author in your niche just launched a new book, or put it on preorder, that book likely won't show up on any list until a few days or weeks later. And even if it does immediately make it onto a list, you'll have to wait until your monthly list scraping to collect it and add it to a campaign.

This means you might miss out on several weeks during which the book is trending—getting a bunch of searches and product page views—but you're not actively advertising against it. What can you do to make sure you never miss an important new release like this? Set up automated new release alerts.

Several platforms allow you to do that, the first one being Amazon. On every author page, you'll find a button to +Follow the author "to get new release updates and improved recommendations."

Now, the issue with the Amazon Follow button is that it doesn't work systematically for New Releases. Amazon only wants to send a certain number of emails per day/week to its users, so even if you follow an author, you might not get an email about each new release of theirs—as Amazon might prefer to email you about kitchen appliances instead (yes, they make more money if you buy a toaster than if you buy a book).

Fortunately, there are other platforms where you can follow authors to get automatic new release emails. The most popular one is probably BookBub:

As opposed to Amazon, BookBub will immediately email all followers of an author when they detect a new release from said author. The same goes for Reedsy Discovery, where you can also follow authors who have an account.

Since it's possible that BookBub or Reedsy Discovery won't pick up all new releases or preorders immediately, I encourage you to follow close comp authors in your niche on all three platforms and join their mailing lists and reader groups, and follow them on social media. You want to make sure that you're among the first to know about any new release or promo they're running, so that you can be the first to attempt piggybacking on it through Amazon Ads.

Tactic #3: Scheduled search term reports

Automatic targeting campaigns can provide a wealth of ideas for new targets, as Amazon lets you peek under the hood of their automatic targeting algorithms and see exactly which targets they went after, as well as how each target performed. And the same thing can be said of manual category targeting campaigns.

This is a savvy way to identify high-performing search terms or products you may not have thought of yourself and add them to your manual targeting campaigns.

"But if my automatic targeting campaigns are already targeting these search terms, wouldn't adding them to a manual campaign get the two campaigns to compete against each other?"

In a small way, yes. But the thing about automatic targeting campaigns is that they tend to target a very wide range of keywords/products, and you cannot control the bids for each individual target. By adding those high-performing keywords or products to a manual campaign, you ensure that you get as much reach as possible for them and, more importantly, that you can control and adjust the bid for each target, allowing you to optimize each of them for profitability.

How do you peek under the Amazon hood and get that search term performance? You simply need to head to the Reports section of your Amazon Advertising account and request a Sponsored Products Search term report.

After a few seconds, you'll receive an email with a link to a spreadsheet containing all the search terms and products that generated at least one click across all your campaigns in your selected time period. It'll look a little bit like this (though with a lot more columns):

Targeting	Match Ty	Customer Search Term	Impressio	Clic	Click-Thru Rate (CTF	Cost Per Click (CP:	Spend	14 Day Total Orders (i
*	-	free kindle books	26702	32	0.1198%	$0.66	$21.25	12
*	-	b01lvjc4zn	1874	26	1.3874%	$0.69	$17.86	11
*	-	b099qvg1h8	14920	26	0.1743%	$0.67	$17.38	4
*	-	b08kbxzmjn	1503	19	1.2641%	$0.62	$11.84	8
*	-	b07n5wykd2	8055	15	0.1862%	$0.77	$11.60	7
*	-	affiliate marketing	1490	14	0.9396%	$0.66	$9.25	0
*	-	b08vnmzdbn	5359	13	0.2426%	$0.49	$6.38	7
*	-	b019h38jl2	699	12	1.7167%	$0.69	$8.31	2
*	-	b07b66dhx1	2571	12	0.4667%	$0.66	$7.94	5
*	-	b07k7zqd82	7730	12	0.1552%	$0.61	$7.34	6
*	-	b08ctnyljb	5673	12	0.2115%	$0.74	$8.86	4
*	-	b08xzp5ppg	6164	12	0.1947%	$0.67	$7.98	6
category="Authorship Reference"	-	b09gfccc5h	2026	11	0.5429%	$0.56	$6.18	2
*	-	b07n416vpz	11359	11	0.0968%	$0.77	$8.42	3
*	-	b086n586s4	4100	11	0.2683%	$0.76	$8.31	1
*	-	b09fgzqv4d	1156	11	0.9516%	$0.67	$7.34	2
*	-	free ebooks english	122	11	9.0164%	$0.74	$8.15	4
*	-	b089dq4s34	268	10	3.7313%	$0.65	$6.51	3
*	-	b01b35m3sm	1947	9	0.4622%	$0.83	$7.49	2
*	-	free	604	9	1.4901%	$0.71	$6.37	1
*	-	free books on kindle	6547	9	0.1375%	$0.76	$6.83	3
*	-	marketing	1018	9	0.8841%	$0.98	$8.79	5
atomic habits	PHRASE	atomic habits	678	8	1.1799%	$0.61	$4.91	3
category="Authorship Reference"	-	b09fgzqv4d	1355	8	0.5904%	$0.61	$4.85	0
*	-	b007urvzj6	528	8	1.5152%	$0.60	$4.81	4
*	-	b084sdv2zw	764	8	1.0471%	$0.40	$3.19	1
category="Writing Skill Reference"	-	b007mw2gjm	579	7	1.2090%	$0.58	$4.07	2
*	-	b08ckyhnn9	163	7	4.2945%	$0.84	$5.86	1
*	-	b08hncy1sp	237	7	2.9536%	$0.42	$2.96	1

Sponsored Products Search term report.

First, order that spreadsheet by number of clicks, or orders, to get the targets with the most data at the top. Then, you can filter out the search terms from your manual keyword targeting campaigns by only selecting those rows whose Match Type is "-" (which is the symbol for automatic targeting campaigns).

Now comes the time to analyze the results and handpick those search terms or ASINs that have yielded good results—depending on your optimization objective, of course.

In this example, my objective is a $2 cost per order. So what I can do is add a column to the spreadsheet to calculate the cost/order of each search term, and use some conditional formatting to highlight those search terms whose cost/order is below the $2 threshold:

Targeting	Match Ty	Customer Search Term	Impressio	Clic	Click-Thru Rate (CTF	Cost Per Click (CP	Spend	14 Day Total Orders (	Cost/order
*	-	free kindle books	26702	32	0.1198%	$0.66	$21.25	12	$1.77
*	-	b01iyjc4zn	1874	26	1.3874%	$0.69	$17.86	11	$1.62
*	-	b099qvg1h8	14920	26	0.1743%	$0.67	$17.38	4	$4.35
*	-	b08kbxzmjn	1503	19	1.2641%	$0.62	$11.84	8	$1.48
*	-	b07n5wykd2	8055	15	0.1862%	$0.77	$11.60	7	$1.66
*	-	affiliate marketing	1490	14	0.9396%	$0.66	$9.25	0	#DIV/0!
*	-	b08vnmzdbn	5359	13	0.2426%	$0.49	$6.38	7	$0.91
*	-	b019h38jl2	699	12	1.7167%	$0.69	$8.31	2	$4.16
*	-	b07b66dnx1	2571	12	0.4667%	$0.66	$7.94	5	$1.59
*	-	b07k7zqd82	7730	12	0.1552%	$0.61	$7.34	6	$1.22
*	-	b08ctnyljb	5673	12	0.2115%	$0.74	$8.86	4	$2.22
*	-	b08xzp5ppg	6164	12	0.1947%	$0.67	$7.98	6	$1.33
category="Authorship Reference"	-	b09gfccc5h	2026	11	0.5429%	$0.56	$6.18	2	$3.09
*	-	b07n416vpz	11359	11	0.0968%	$0.77	$8.42	3	$2.81
*	-	b086n586s4	4100	11	0.2683%	$0.76	$8.31	1	$8.31
*	-	b09fgzqv4d	1156	11	0.9516%	$0.67	$7.34	2	$3.67
*	-	free ebooks english	122	11	9.0164%	$0.74	$8.15	4	$2.04
*	-	b089dq4s34	268	10	3.7313%	$0.65	$6.51	3	$2.17
*	-	b01b35m3sm	1947	9	0.4623%	$0.83	$7.49	2	$3.75
*	-	free	604	9	1.4901%	$0.71	$6.37	1	$6.37
*	-	free books on kindle	6547	9	0.1375%	$0.76	$6.83	3	$2.28
*	-	marketing	1018	9	0.8841%	$0.98	$8.79	5	$1.76
atomic habits	PHRASE	atomic habits	678	8	1.1799%	$0.61	$4.91	3	$1.64
category="Authorship Reference"	-	b09fgzqv4d	1355	8	0.5904%	$0.61	$4.85	0	#DIV/0!
*	-	b007urvzj6	528	8	1.5152%	$0.60	$4.81	4	$1.20
*	-	b084sdv2zw	764	8	1.0471%	$0.40	$3.19	1	$3.19
category="Writing Skill Reference"	-	b007mw2gjm	579	7	1.2090%	$0.58	$4.07	2	$2.04
*	-	b08ckyhnn9	163	7	4.2945%	$0.84	$5.86	1	$5.86
*	-	b08hncy1sp	237	7	2.9536%	$0.42	$2.96	1	$2.96

This allows me to instantly spot all the search terms that are likely candidates for moving to a manual targeting campaign.

Now, as you can see, only a handful of those have generated enough clicks for their results to be statistically significant. And this is the big problem with Search Term reports: Amazon limits the maximum timeline to the last sixty-five days. For most accounts, sixty-five days is not long enough to gather data on a significant number of search terms. You might find a handful of good ones, but that is probably not going to cut it if you really want to scale your campaigns.

What's the solution? Scheduling regular search reports and manually aggregating their data in a spreadsheet.

I know, I know, that sounds awfully complicated, which is why I built a simple Google Sheets spreadsheet — the Sponsored Products Search Term Aggregator — that will do that automatically for you. Well, you'll need to read the instructions, schedule the reports, and import them into the sheet when they're ready—but aside from that, everything else is automated, and you can read the aggregated lifetime data for all your search terms.

As with all other spreadsheets I promised throughout the book, you'll be able to download this one for free in the Bonus Resources section, at the end of the book.

25

The more campaigns, the merrier?

So far, I've talked about scaling campaigns by either playing with bids, budget, or match types or by adding more targets. But there is another option: creating new campaigns.

There are different schools of thought regarding how many campaigns you should have in your Amazon Advertising account, so in this chapter we're going to explore the pros and cons of creating new campaigns versus adding targets to existing campaigns.

Is it better to have more campaigns?

For a long time, there was this speculation in the Amazon Advertising community that the best way to scale an account's spend was to create as many different campaigns as possible. The rationale was that, since you cannot get Amazon to spend a $100 daily budget on a campaign, you should split or duplicate that campaign into ten, each with a $10 budget.

This led to many advertisers having accounts with hundreds of con-comitant campaigns, all overlapping with one another, and each spending a few dollars a day, which is often unmanageable from an optimization perspective.

Thankfully, this myth (which, for all I know, could have been true back then) has been debunked in recent years by authority figures such as Janet

Margot—and Amazon Advertising's team itself now warns against having multiple overlapping campaigns.

The issue with having hundreds of small-budget campaigns is not only that they create overlap, and therefore compete against each other from a bidding perspective, it also makes it a nightmare to manage the accounts and optimize them. Since a particular target might be present across dozens of different campaigns, all with different bids and bidding optimization, it makes it nearly impossible to optimize that particular target's bid—because the corresponding impressions, clicks, and sales data will be split among all these campaigns.

More importantly, this severely limits any auto-optimization on Amazon's end, like down or up and down dynamic bids. Amazon optimizes bids in real time based on the campaign's historical data, so if you split the data for a particular target across a bunch of campaigns, instead of aggregating it in a single one, you effectively reduce Amazon's ability to auto-optimize the bid.

The same goes for automatic campaigns: the more duplicated auto-targeting campaigns you create, the more you split the data and make it harder for Amazon's algorithms to figure out which search queries or products to go after.

As a general rule, I'd say it's always better to have one campaign with a high daily budget than ten or a hundred identical campaigns with a small daily budget. That's just my opinion, though, based on my personal experience. As I said, you'll find different schools of thought and are welcome to test other techniques if you wish.

Now, this doesn't mean that you should put all your targets into one campaign to avoid it overlapping with other campaigns. As we saw in Chapter 9, you rarely want to have more than fifty or so targets per ad group. The Amazon algorithms responsible for allocating impressions across targets in a campaign are not that sophisticated. What they do is test a few targets at a time, starting with those with the biggest search volume and most competitive bids. Once they find five or ten that perform well (for example, they attract clicks at a reasonable enough click-through-rate), the algorithms will focus almost exclusively on those. In other words, if you add

200 keywords to an ad group, it's likely that Amazon will flat out ignore over 90% of them.

"So I can't have more than fifty keywords per ad group, but I shouldn't have too many campaigns in my account? How am I supposed to do it?"

It's simple: you just need to have a bunch of ad groups.

Ad groups: the best of both worlds

Ad groups are the main reason why I keep recommending that authors use Standard campaigns rather than Custom text ones and are huge part of my Amazon Advertising strategy today.

By using ad groups, you get the best of both worlds. If you split your targets across ad groups, you can have an unlimited number of targets in a campaign—and therefore feed Amazon's algorithms a bunch of data on the campaign level for them to optimize delivery and bids—while never having more than fifty in any individual ad group.

You can also keep your targets nicely organized, with each ad group containing only a certain kind of target, or match type, which will be of great help when time comes to review the campaign to optimize each target.

I usually split a campaign targeting a list of books (whether that's a top 100/HNR list or a list of Also Boughts or a list of another kind) into four different ad groups:

1. One contains the book titles, usually in phrase or broad match, unless the title is a short, one-word title.
2. One contains the series titles, with slightly higher bids (especially if I'm advertising a series).
3. One contains the author names, with phrase or broad match, and competitive enough bids to make sure I'll get impressions for each of them.
4. One contains the competing ASINs.

Sometimes, if I'm advertising both ebooks and print books in the campaign,

I'll even split the fourth one into two: one with the ebook ASINs and the other with the print ones.

This way, a campaign targeting a Hot New Releases list could end up containing 200 to 300 different targets, but organized into ad groups, and with no more than fifty or so targets per ad group (I tend to exclude a lot of irrelevant titles).

Now, imagine that you want to refresh this HNR campaign after a few months, with a new list of titles that your virtual assistant compiled for you. You have three options for that:

1. Either you add the new targets to the existing campaign (separating book titles, series titles, author names, and ASINs as you did previously) or
2. You create a new campaign or
3. You create four new ad groups within the same campaign.

The option you choose should depend on how crowded the ad groups of the existing campaign are. If they only have a few active targets, then it's safe to just add the new ones to the existing campaign. If the existing ad groups already have more than 100 running targets, then you should definitely either create a new campaign, or new ad groups within the same campaign.

For example, with this method, we're separating author names, book titles, series titles and ASINs across different ad groups. But these ad groups won't contain the same number of targets. While each book title and ASIN in the list will be different, there could very much be overlap in terms of author names and series titles.

If I were to refresh this campaign with a new month's scrape of new releases in the category, I'll want to create new ad groups (or a new campaign) for the book title and ASIN targets, but not necessarily for the author names, as these will probably have a lot of overlap with the current ones.

One last item to beware of when creating new campaigns for HNR targets is that, while books can only stay on the HNR list for thirty days post release, they can technically be there for months while they're on preorder, so you could very well end up having several identical book titles as keywords in a bunch of different HNR campaigns.

Now, having a bit of overlap between campaigns is not a terrible thing, and doesn't tend to have a huge impact on performance (your clicks might be a tad more expensive as a result, but that's it). Still, if when collecting or copy-pasting targets into the new campaign, you spot a title that you've seen already, it's best not to include it.

Creating author-specific campaigns

While creating a bunch of new, duplicate campaigns just for the sake of scaling is rarely productive, this doesn't mean that new campaigns can't be effective to grow an account's spend. The only condition for that to happen is that the new campaigns should target keywords/products that you weren't already targeting in your existing ones.

This is the case for Hot New Release campaigns, as titles more or less refresh every month or so (except for preorders). And it is also the case for one of my favorite scaling tactics: author-specific campaigns.

The idea is simple: if you've been running ads for a few months, you'll have probably identified some author names that work particularly well—whether they're close comps from your Also Boughts, or authors you picked up on top 100 or Hot New Releases lists. Raising the bid on these keywords and switching them to broad match (if they weren't already) will increase their reach, but it won't necessarily get you impressions on all of their product pages.

"But wait a second, I thought that by targeting the author name, my ads were already eligible to show up on all of the author's product pages. So isn't adding their book titles and ASINs as targets redundant?"

Yes and no: the keyword here is eligible. While targeting an author name will make your ads eligible to show up on all of this author's product pages, it doesn't mean that Amazon will actually display your ads on all product pages. Instead, they might prioritize some and skip others altogether. Or they might focus on search placements instead.

To find out, try a little experiment: check out the product pages of a particular author you're targeting. You'll see that your ad only shows up on a fraction of those, no matter how many times you refresh the pages.

If you want your ads to show up on all of their product pages—or in other words, if you want to maximize your advertising exposure to this author—you'll want to make sure you target all their titles and ASINs individually through an author-specific campaign.

Let's take an example. I've been running a campaign targeting close comp author names for a few weeks, and I'm now checking the results:

Keyword	Suggested bid		Bid	Impressions	Clicks	CTR	Spend	CPC	Orders	Sales	ACOS	KENP read	Estimated KENP
Total: 7	apply all			122,473	296	0.24%	$136.76	$0.46	1	$16.99	804.94%	23,965	$108.40
Jenny Writes	$0.75	Apply	$ 0.17	85,595	196	0.23%	$93.45	$0.48	-	-	-	23,662	$107.03
Carl Books	$0.71	Apply	$ 0.23	10,587	24	0.23%	$11.14	$0.46	-	-	-	2	$0.01
Martin Types	$0.67	Apply	$ 0.23	5,131	21	0.41%	$6.29	$0.50	-	-	-	-	-

First, the good news: *Jenny Writes* is performing well as a target, as it's more than breaking even thanks to the KENP royalties.

However, it looks like Jenny is also monopolizing impressions and clicks in the campaign, as the *Carl Books* and *Martin Types* got 90% fewer clicks than she did.

This makes Jenny Writes a perfect candidate for an author-specific campaign, which will kill two birds with one stone. First, it'll maximize my advertising exposure to this high-performing author comp. And second, by creating a whole new campaign dedicated just to her, I'll be able to pause her keyword in this existing campaign, which will solve the monopolization issue.

Author-specific campaign structure

Now, what does this author-specific campaign look like? Well, it depends on the kind of author you're targeting. In most cases, the author targets who warrant having their specific campaign will be relatively well known in your niche and have written a good number of books—often across different series. In such cases, it makes sense to first research all the books and series they've written that could make for good targets (hint: you can hire a VA for that) and then split the targets into ad groups.

To make sure that none of your ad groups contain too many targets, one good strategy is to have two ad groups for each series, one containing all the book titles in the series as keywords, and another one for the ASINs.

"What about the author name, then?" Excellent question, considering it's this very target that was causing the cannibalization problem in the other campaign.

Here's the thing: author names are generally much higher-volume targets than book titles or ASINs. So if I were to put the author name into one of the series ad groups in this campaign, it'd swallow all of the impressions, leaving the other targets in the ad group to starve. To avoid this, you need to isolate the author name into its own ad group.

One type of target you shouldn't forget in these campaigns is the series titles. In most cases, I tend to add them as a phrase or broad match keyword to each corresponding series ad group. In some rare cases, however, these series titles might be famous enough that they risk cannibalizing the book titles themselves.

For example, let's say I want to create an author-specific campaign targeting Brandon Sanderson for an epic fantasy series. *Mistborn*, which is the name of the series, is almost as popular a keyword as *Brandon Sanderson* itself; whereas, the individual titles of the Mistborn series are not that well known (such as *The Final Empire* and *The Well of Ascension*). So if I grouped *Mistborn* together with the book titles into an ad group, I can expect 99 percent of that ad group's impressions to go to *Mistborn*, and consequently for the book title keywords to be ignored.

To avoid that, a simple solution is to group the famous series title together with the author name instead. That way, all your targets will compete for impressions against other similarly sized targets within the ad group.

> **Pro tip**: Remember that series on Amazon have their own ASIN (different from the ASINs of each individual book in the series). Make sure to include those series ASINs into the corresponding ASIN targeting ad groups in the campaign. They probably won't get a ton of impressions and clicks, but these series pages are prime real-estate placements to attract the attention of series readers, and they're also less competitive as few advertisers think of targeting them.

Once you've finished setting up this author-specific campaign, the last step is try to remove any targeting overlap that this new campaign might have created, at least for big, high-volume keywords.

For example, I'd want to make sure that I pause all instances of the keyword *Jenny Writes* across all my existing campaigns, so that they don't compete with the brand new, author-specific one. This is relatively easy and quick to do through the Targeting tab.

I'll do the same for any big keyword associated with the author (such as a famous title or series of theirs), but not necessarily for every single new keyword/ASIN I'm adding to the new campaign. A bit of overlap on long-tail keywords won't hurt you.

In terms of bids, since this group of targets has a reasonable chance of performing well—after all, it's all titles and series from one of your top-performing author comps—you can afford to bid relatively aggressively to make sure the campaign gets results quickly.

For example, you could take the break-even bid of the author name target from the initial campaign and use that as a bid for all the targets in the new author-specific campaign. It's rare for book titles, series titles, or ASINs to be more competitive targets than author names, so by using a proven break-even bid for the author name as bid for all the targets in the campaign, it's likely you'll win most of the auctions. And if some of the targets fail to garner impressions, you can always crank up the bids incrementally week after week until they do.

Naturally, this is a campaign you'll need to monitor regularly and optimize for both CTR and profit—just like any other one. You'll also want to regularly add new keywords to it, or ad groups, as the author releases new books or series. Remember the new release monitoring tactics I mentioned in the last chapter? You should definitely put those in place for authors you're running author-specific campaign for, to make sure you're the first to target any of their new releases.

Author-specific campaigns are a perfect illustration of what scaling should be all about: you take something that has proven to work and increase your advertising spend on it. On other advertising platforms, increasing the spend is easy: you just raise your budget. On Amazon Advertising, you need to be more creative and play with bids, targets, and campaign structure instead, but it's definitely not impossible.

The future of Amazon Advertising

Even if you implement all the scaling tactics I went through, you'll see that growth is rarely linear. You'll always have ups and downs, peaks and valleys. This roller coaster is not always related to your advertising prowess; they can be circumstantial (launch of a new book) or cyclical (book sales tend to increase around November and December every year). What matters is that the overall trend goes upward rather than downward.

Scaling an Amazon Advertising account.

Scaling also presents some dangers. If you try to scale too quickly, or too aggressively, you might end up hurting your ROI. Here, for example, the increase in spend over the last two months didn't translate into more orders:

Trying to scale an Amazon Advertising account.

When this happens, you need to switch your focus back to profit optimization, and rein in the bids or placements that are failing to convert. Once you manage to get the ROI back on track, you can try to scale again (more reasonably this time), and so on.

Finding the right balance between scaling and keeping the same profit level can be difficult, all the more so since Amazon Advertising's algorithms often change, as does the competitiveness of your niche. As more authors and traditional publishers enter the Amazon Advertising world, we can expect bids and costs per click to keep growing over the next few years, which will make profit more of a challenge. Not to mention traditional publishers, who tend to focus their budgets on their big releases, and use high bids around the launches to win most of the auctions, which can disrupt the visibility of the rest of advertisers during that period.

On the other hand, Amazon Advertising is still in its infancy in terms of technical sophistication. We can expect the platform to become a lot better at identifying the right customers to show ads to, as well as auto-optimizing targets and bids. Even in the past few years, I have seen huge improvements on automatic targeting campaigns and have no doubt that this trend will continue.

To close this book, I want to imagine what the future might hold for us Amazon advertisers. And for that, we need to look at the more advanced advertising platforms available.

Compared to Google and Facebook (the other two giant advertising platforms), Amazon Advertising is a very young platform. As such, we can expect it to keep evolving and adding new features.

One if the main areas where I believe Amazon Advertising has huge room for improvement, and will probably improve dramatically in the near future, is the use of machine learning and artificial intelligence.

To understand what that could look like, you'll first need a bit of history on Google and Facebook advertising.

The integration of machine learning in Facebook and Google's advertising platforms

If you were running search ads on Google five or ten years ago, you had to manually put in the keywords (the search terms) you wanted to target and write out each ad individually, specifying one headline and one description.

Progressively, though, Google started leveraging all the data it was collecting from users and introducing machine learning to automatically predict the best targeting and ad copy for each advertiser. In other words, instead of you manually creating the ads and deciding whom to target them to, you let Google's artificial intelligence make these decisions for you— and more often than not, it yields you better results, because Google has even more data on your prospective customers than even you do.

For example, Google introduced responsive ad formats, where advertisers put in several headlines and descriptions, and let Google mix and match to find and use the best ones. Now, Google is not only favoring Responsive Search Ads, but also actually retiring the legacy ones.

This is similar to Facebook's dynamic ads, which allow you to put in several options for the headline, for the text, the description, and so on. Then, Facebook mixes and matches, runs a few tests, and serves to each user the combination that their algorithms have determined is most likely to get them to click.

But Google even went a step further with their own dynamic ads, where instead of using keywords to tell Google which searches to target, you simply plug in your landing page, and Google automatically selects the search terms to target for you (based on your landing page copy). If you plug in several landing pages, then Google is going to automatically select the right landing page for each search.

For example, if you were a shop selling both blenders and food processors, then you could create a dynamic campaign and include both your landing page about blenders and the one for food processors. When a user would search for *best blenders*, Google would serve an ad promoting your blenders page, and similarly promote your food processors page to users searching for food processor-related keywords.

For these campaigns, you don't even have to create responsive ads—instead, Google has a dynamic ad format where Google's AI crafts the headlines for the ads on its own, based both on the searcher's search terms and cn your landing page copy, so that each ad can be as relevant to the search as possible—and therefore as likely to get a click.

Future Amazon Advertising feature #1: AI-generated ad copy

Now, let's go back to Amazon. The tests I ran on the platform seem to suggest that custom marketing copy on ads doesn't seem to make a big difference in terms of click-through-rate, or conversion. But I could be an isolated case! The only people who actually have enough data to know for sure whether ad copy truly moves the needle is, of course, Amazon. And we can certainly expect them to follow the data and steer advertisers toward what is performing best.

For example, if they find that Standard ads perform just the same (or better) than Custom text ads, they might remove the option altogether. I certainly wouldn't be surprised if this happened, considering Books and Kindle Store are the only two departments on Amazon where Sponsored Products ads are eligible to display custom text.

But let's say that Amazon finds out that book ads do perform better when they include marketing copy. What direction could they take to standardize Sponsored Products ads for advertisers? In a similar vein to how Google and Facebook evolved, I could very well imagine Amazon Advertising automatically crafting custom marketing copy on behalf of the advertisers.

Think about it: Amazon has a ton of copy about your book (your product description, the editorial reviews, the reader reviews, and much more). And Amazon has data on what kind of copy works best for each placement, search term, customer, and so on. Therefore, in theory, Amazon could develop an AI to customize the ad copy on each ad, based on the reader's search terms.

For example, let's say you're targeting *epic fantasy series kindle unlimited* as a broad match—Amazon could adapt your ad copy to each search term where the ad appears, like this:

Search term	Ad copy
epic fantasy series	*"Get started on the new epic fantasy series by New York Times bestselling author Jenny Writes."*
high fantasy series	*"Get started on the new high fantasy series by New York Times bestselling author Jenny Writes."*
epic fantasy kindle unlimited	*"Get started on the new epic fantasy series by New York Times bestselling author Jenny Writes. Available in Kindle Unlimited."*

This is exactly what Google Ads do when you use their dynamic ads: they craft the advertising copy for you, based both on the user's search and on the copy of your landing page.

Does Amazon Advertising have the capacity to do this right now? Definitely not. Could it build it in the future? Absolutely, if, and only if, they figure out that custom copy actually makes a difference in the first place.

Now, there is another AI-powered feature that I expect Amazon Advertising to build much, much sooner than that.

Future Amazon Advertising feature #2: AI-powered product-to-customer matching

One thing you might have wondered about Standard campaigns containing several products is how Amazon selects which book to advertise to which customer. Do they simply select one randomly among your advertised products every time? Do they favor certain books over others? Do they pick a different book based on the customer?

All these are important questions that you are absolutely right to ask. I have done so myself, and the answer I got was along the lines of "that's not something we can disclose."

What I do know is that, right now, Amazon does not take a customer's buying history into account when selecting which product to advertise to them.

In other words, if you're advertising all three books in your trilogy in a campaign, and a reader has already read book one, they could still very much get an ad for it.

This honestly doesn't make a lot of sense to me, considering it's detrimental to everyone:

- The reader gets an ad that's irrelevant to them. Since they're never going to click on it and they can't "re-buy" the product,
- Amazon is losing money, and
- The author also loses the opportunity of selling them book two instead.

Because of this, I am fairly confident that this practice will change. Similarly to how Google developed machine-learning algorithms to automatically pick the right landing page to show to each user depending on their search, I believe Amazon will develop the capacity to smartly auto-pick the right product to advertise to the right customer.

This could start with super simple pitches like these:

- If the customer buys mostly print books, Amazon shows your print edition rather than your ebook one.

- If the customer is a KU reader, Amazon picks an advertised product that's in KU over one that isn't.
- If the customer has read the first three books in your series, Amazon advertises the fourth one to them.

If and when that happens, running Standard campaigns with multiple advertised products will become all the more powerful. Not only will you get more accurate sales data, you'll also get much better results, since Amazon will be able to show the right products to the right readers, thus boosting both your click through and your conversion rates.

And I actually believe that this potential future is not only highly likely, it's also closer than one might think.

That's good news, right? Well, good news is what we like to end our books on. So as I like to say at the end of my Reedsy marketing newsletters:[10] happy writing and happy marketing!

---

[10] Sign up to receive my (somewhat) weekly marketing newsletter here: http://rdsy.me/newsletter.

Bonus Resources

I promised several magical spreadsheets throughout this book, and it's time for me to make good on that promise.

I grouped all of them into a single Google Drive folder, which you can access by simply signing up to my Reedsy marketing newsletter here: rdsy.me/amazon-ads-spreadsheets. Naturally, you're free to unsubscribe from the newsletter at any point after that, but if you don't, you'll receive some helpful marketing tidbits straight in your inbox every two or three weeks (I'm not known for my consistency in sending out newsletters).

Why a Google Drive folder? Because all these are Google Sheets, which I found work best for sharing and for keeping them updated. That way, if Amazon changes its dashboard exports in the future, I'll be able to update the spreadsheets accordingly to make sure they keep working.

Before you use any of these spreadsheets, copy them to your own Google Drive—otherwise, you won't be able to edit them. Sadly, you also can't download them to open with Excel or Numbers, as the formulas and pivot tables will break, rendering them unusable. So you'll have to use Google Sheets (which I personally prefer to Excel at this point).

Once you have the spreadsheet in your own drive, just open it and follow the instructions you'll find on the first tab.

Amazon Advertising Target Deduplicator

As its name indicates, this spreadsheet allows you to identify and remove any potential duplicate targets from a new list, before adding them to your account.

Its functioning is simple:

- In one tab, you copy-paste the data from the Targeting section of your Amazon Advertising dashboard, containing all the targets you're currently targeting.
- In the other tab, you paste the list of new targets you're considering to add to a campaign.

The spreadsheet will automatically flag the duplicates for you to remove from the list.

Sponsored Products Search Term Aggregator

Search term reports are one of the most helpful features of Amazon Advertising, but they're limited to reporting on the last sixty-five days, which is usually not enough to have a whole lot of data.

This is where this aggregator comes in: you schedule a monthly Search term report, paste it every month in a tab of this spreadsheet, and the other tab will return aggregated data for each search term you've ever targeted.

You will be able to spot relevant long-tail search terms that you might not have thought of targeting otherwise, as they would have only had a handful of clicks in the last sixty-five days of reports.

Break-even Bid Calculators

I offer four spreadsheets here. There are two main methods to determine the profitability of a campaign:

- The average net royalty rate and
- The average revenue per order.

Depending on the method that you opt for, you'll find two spreadsheets for each:

- One for keyword targeting campaigns (including automatic campaigns) and

- One for product targeting campaigns (including category targets).

So, for example, if you were using the average net royalty rate method to figure out the break-even bids of a campaign targeting search keywords, you would use the spreadsheet named Break-even Bid - Keyword - Net Royalty. Similarly, for a product targeting campaigns where you'd use the revenue per order method, you'd pick the Break-even Bid - Products - Revenue per Order spreadsheet.

The functioning is simple:

1. You import (or copy-paste) the data from the campaign/ad group you want to analyze into the second tab,
2. You enter your average net royalty rate—or your average revenue per order—for the campaign/ad group in the third tab, and
3. The total net revenue and break-even bid of each target will auto-populate in the third tab.

The spreadsheets are set to filter out any targets with fewer than ten clicks, but that is something you can change by editing the settings of the pivot table.

Even with these magical spreadsheets, going through your campaigns to optimize the bids will be a bit of a manual process, but at least you'll be spared all the mathematical work and ensure you don't make mistakes when calculating bids. If you use a virtual assistant, this is also something simple that you can teach them to do.

Other resources on Amazon Ads

As you probably know, this book is not the only resource on Amazon Advertising available. There are several other books on the topic, and while many of them are outdated, or contain advice that is more than questionable, there is one that I would highly recommend, even if you've learned everything in this book inside and out: *Amazon Ads for Indie Authors* by Janet Margot.[11]

Janet worked for more than eight years within the Amazon Advertising team, specializing on ads for KDP authors, and she shares some useful insider knowledge in her book. It'll help you further your knowledge of Amazon Ads and gain a different perspective on certain elements of the platform.

Books are among my favorite ways of learning new skills, but they are also limited in terms of the visual information, and step-by-step instructions, you can share. If, after reading this book, you still feel as if you need a proper walk-through of Amazon Advertising, then there is one course I recommend above all others: Mark Dawson's Ads for Authors course.[12] It is by far the most complete course you'll find on Amazon Advertising (as well as on Facebook, BookBub, TikTok, and more). It's not cheap, and it only opens up for new registrations every semester, but it's worth every penny.

---

[11] *Amazon Ads for Indie Authors: A How-to Guide from an Industry Expert* by Janet Margot: https://books2read.com/u/mlAYVq

[12] Mark Dawson's Ads for Authors course (affiliate link): http://rdsy.me/ads-for-authors

Glossary

ACOS: The Advertising Cost of Sale. It is calculated by dividing spend (cost) by the total retail value of products sold, and expressed as a percentage. If a campaign spends $100 and generates $50 in sales, the ACOS is $100/$50 = 200%.

True ACOS: The ratio of spend divided by your actual net revenue on the product sold. If a campaign spends $100 to generate $50 in sales, of which $40 ends up in your bank account, the true ACOS is $100/$40 = 250%.

Also Boughts: The books featured in the "Customers who purchased/read this item also bought/read" section of a product page. They represent the books that have the closest relation to yours based on historical consumer data and are used by Amazon to inform their in-store and email recommendations.

ASIN: The Amazon Standard Identification Number is a unique number assigned to each product sold on the Amazon marketplace. It is automatically and arbitrarily assigned by Amazon to each book upon publication. Each format of a book (for example: ebook, paperback, hardback, audiobook) will have its own, unique ASIN. In the case of print books, the ASIN is the same number as the 10-digit ISBN. As such, ASINs are used in Amazon Advertising to target single, specific products.

Break even: An advertising campaign is said to break even when it earns you the exact same amount of money you spent on it.

Break-even bid: The bid you need to set for a particular target in order for it to have broken even based on its historical data. It can be calculated by dividing the net revenue by the total clicks generated by the target. For example, if a keyword had 10 clicks and brought in $4 in net revenue, the break-even bid would be 4/10 = $0.40.

Click-through-rate (CTR): The ratio of clicks divided by impressions (number of times an ad is viewed). It is always expressed as a percentage. If an ad is viewed 15,000 times and has had 50 clicks, its CTR is 50/15,000 = 0.33%. The click-through-rate is an important indicator of the overall health of a campaign.

Cost per click (CPC): The ratio of cost divided by clicks. It represents the average money spent to generate one click. If a campaign spends $100 and generates 1,000 clicks, the CPC is $100/1000 = $0.10.

Cost per mille (CPM): The average spend of the campaign to generate 1,000 impressions. It is calculated by dividing the cost by the number of impressions (expressed in thousands). If a campaign spent $10 and led to 25,000 impressions, the CPM is $10/25= $0.40.

Cost per order: The total spend (cost) divided by the sum of individual products sold (reported in the dashboard as Orders). This is effectively an indicator of how much money you need to spend to generate a sale.

Defense (or brand) targets: Amazon Advertising targets (keywords or products) that are related to your brand, such as your book titles, your ASINs, your author name. You can target these yourself to "defend" your books from other advertisers.

KDP Select: This program requires that you distribute your ebook exclusively to Amazon for a period of ninety days (which automatically renews until you exit it). In exchange, it offers promotional advantages, the main one being the inclusion of your title in the Kindle Unlimited program.

KENP (Kindle Edition Normalized Pages): Since the size and number of ebook pages are ultimately controlled by the e-reader settings (a bigger font will increase the number of pages), Amazon has developed a normalized page standard based on word count. If you are enrolled in KDP Select, you can view the KENP length of your titles at the bottom of the Promotion tab of your KDP Bookshelf.

KENP royalties: The royalties earned by a book through KENP read in Kindle Unlimited. They are calculated by multiplying the number of KENP read by the current Kindle Unlimited payout rate per page. For example, in September 2022, the KU payout per page was around $0.0047. So a book that had 50,000 KENP read that month would have earned 50000 x $0.0047 = $235.

Kindle Unlimited (KU): A subscription service allowing readers to access a vast catalog of books for a set monthly fee. Only books enrolled in KDP Select are eligible to be part of Kindle Unlimited and earn royalties based on the number of pages read.

Long-tail vs short-tail keywords: Short-tail keywords are the keywords that receive the vast majority of searches (and therefore impressions) from users. They tend to be short, popular, and competitive to target. Long-tail keywords are the opposite: they are more niche, less competitive, and receive a small amount of searches each. For example, *cozy mystery* would be considered a short-tail keyword, whereas *cat cozy mystery, cozy mystery with female protagonist,* or *cozy mystery series* would be long-tails.

Net revenue per order: The actual net revenue you receive when selling one copy of the book. It is a factor of the price of the book, multiplied by the net royalty rate.

Net royalty rate: The royalty rate you earn on a product, after factoring in printing costs and Amazon's distribution cut. For example, the net royalty rate of an ebook priced between $2.99 and $9.99 is 70%.

Placements: In advertising jargon, placements are the places where ads are displayed. Placements on Amazon are grouped in different placement types, such as Top of search, Rest of search, or product pages.

Read through: This is used to estimate the percentage of readers who read through to a particular book in a series after having read the first book. For example, if 60% of readers who read book one end up reading book four, then the read through of book four is 60%.

RoAS: The Return on Advertising Spend. It is the inverse of the ACOS and is therefore calculated by dividing sales (total retail value of products sold) by spend. If a campaign spends $100 and generates $50 in sales, the RoAS is $50 / $100 = 50%.

ROI: The return on investment. This is a broad business term that is generally applied to investments rather than advertising, and that seeks to define how profitable or loss-making an investment is. In the case of advertising, the ROI of a campaign is the ratio between the profit (or loss) generated by the campaign, divided by the cost. It is expressed as a percentage. For example, if a campaign spends $10 and generates $15 in revenue—and therefore makes $5 in profit—the ROI of the campaign is $5 / $10: 50%. Note that the ROI might be a negative figure: if the same campaign generated only $5 in revenue, the ROI would be -$5 / $10 = -50%.

Wide: An ebook is said to be "wide" when it is available for purchase on multiple retailers, rather than exclusive to Amazon. Wide distribution is effectively the opposite of KDP Select (and Kindle Unlimited), and the debate between one option and the other is often referred to as "KU vs wide."

About the Author

Ricardo Fayet is one of the four founders of Reedsy, a marketplace connecting authors to the world's top publishing talent—from editors to cover designers, book marketers, or literary translators. He's the author of several Reedsy Learning courses on marketing and a regular presenter at several prestigious writers' conferences: NINC, RWA, 20BooksMadrid, and The Self Publishing Show Live, among others.

He oversees the marketing for all Reedsy products—Marketplace, Book Editor, Learning, Discovery—and is a big SEO and digital advertising enthusiast.

In his spare time, he enjoys watching football (or "soccer" as y'all call it over there), and carrying tactical analyses to explain why his favorite team won, as well as referee mistake analyses when his team loses.

If you have any questions about this book, you can reach out to him at ricardo@reedsy.com. He promises to answer you in (first) person.

You can also sign up to his (somewhat) weekly marketing newsletter here: http://rdsy.me/newsletter.

You can connect with me on:

🌐 https://reedsy.com/ricardo-fayet

🐦 https://twitter.com/RicardoFayet

📘 https://www.facebook.com/wearereedsy

Subscribe to my newsletter:

✉ http://rdsy.me/newsletter

Also by Ricardo Fayet

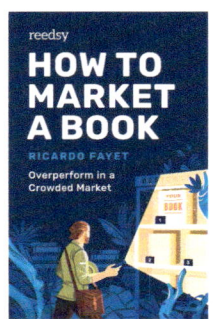

How to Market a Book: Overperform in a Crowded Market

https://blog.reedsy.com/books/how-to-market-a-book

Writing a book is hard. Marketing it can be even harder.

Marketing a book can seem like a full-time job, what with the crazy number of things authors seem to be expected to do: social media, blog tours, advertising, price promotions, mailing lists, giveaways, you name it.

But here's a little secret: you don't need to do all those things to successfully set your book on the path to success. What you need is a solid plan to find the one or two tactics that will work, and start to drive sales... in a minimum amount of time. And that's exactly what you'll find in this book.

Best of all, the ebook is 100% free on all retailers! Get your copy now and benefit from all the experience of a seasoned marketing professional.